T0305841

ASEAN Champions

With a population of about 620 million people, and a combined GNP of more than $2.4 trillion, the ASEAN Economic Community (AEC) is set to become the seventh largest economy in the world. Launched in December 2015, the AEC unveiled initiatives to create a single market and production zone, a competitive and equitable region, and integrated links to the global economy. *ASEAN Champions* seeks to address the role of the strong local firms in regional integration; how these "champions" succeeded and endured, despite facing adverse circumstances; and the factors that facilitated or impeded their participation in regional integration. The book provides insights for future firm- and government-led strategies to enhance the integration process. By complementing current narratives that focus on macroeconomic, sociopolitical, and trade considerations, Park, Ungson, and Francisco offer an enlightening and engaging read, ideally suited to academics and professionals alike.

Seung Ho Park is Parkland Chair Professor of Strategy at China Europe International Business School. He was the founding President of Samsung Economic Research Institute China. He coauthored the awarding-winning book *Rough Diamonds: The Four Traits of Successful Breakout Firms in BRIC Countries*, and his research has been published in leading journals, including the *Academy of Management Journal*, *Academy of Management Review*, and the *Journal of International Business Studies*.

Gerardo Rivera Ungson is the Y. F. Chang Endowed Chair and Professor of International Business in the College of Business, San Francisco State University. He was formerly a Senior Resident Scholar with IEMS in Beijing. With Seung Ho Park, he won the *Strategy + Business Award* for the 2013 Best Book on Globalization for *Rough Diamonds*.

Jamil Paolo S. Francisco is an Associate Professor of Economics at the Asian Institute of Management (AIM). He has published journal articles on financial markets, environmental economics, and household adaptions to climate change, and has led several research projects under the Economy and Environment Program for Southeast Asia of the IDRC, and under the East Asian Development Network.

ASEAN Champions

Emerging Stalwarts in Regional Integration

Seung Ho Park
Gerardo Rivera Ungson
Jamil Paolo S. Francisco

CAMBRIDGE
UNIVERSITY PRESS

CAMBRIDGE
UNIVERSITY PRESS

University Printing House, Cambridge CB2 8BS, United Kingdom

One Liberty Plaza, 20th Floor, New York, NY 10006, USA

477 Williamstown Road, Port Melbourne, VIC 3207, Australia

4843/24, 2nd Floor, Ansari Road, Daryaganj, Delhi - 110002, India

79 Anson Road, #06-04/06, Singapore 079906

Cambridge University Press is part of the University of Cambridge.

It furthers the University's mission by disseminating knowledge in the pursuit of education, learning and research at the highest international levels of excellence.

www.cambridge.org
Information on this title: www.cambridge.org/9781107129009

First published 2017

A catalogue record for this publication is available from the British Library

Library of Congress Cataloging in Publication data
Names: Park, Seung Ho, 1961. | Ungson, Gerardo Rivera, author. | Francisco, Jamil Paolo S., author.
Title: ASEAN champions: emerging stalwarts in regional integration / Seung Ho Park, Gerardo Rivera Ungson, Jamil Paolo S. Francisco.
Description: New York: Cambridge University Press, 2016. | Includes bibliographical references and index.
Identifiers: LCCN 2016026915| ISBN 9781107129009 (hardback) | ISBN 9781107569591 (paper back)
Subjects: LCSH: Southeast Asia – Economic integration. | Southeast Asia – Economic policy – 21st century. | Southeast Asia – Politics and government – 1945– | BISAC: BUSINESS & ECONOMICS / International / General.
Classification: LCC HC441.P347 2016 | DDC 337.1/59–dc23
LC record available at https://lccn.loc.gov/2016026915

ISBN 978-1-107-12900-9 Hardback
ISBN 978-1-107-56959-1 Paperback

To Our Beloved Family Members
Ja Young, Alexandra, and Amelia
Tegan Joann, Boden Kai, Ryan Makena,
and Charlotte Hazel
Baldwin and Josan

Contents

x   Contents

Exhibits, Table and Boxes

Exhibits

Table

Boxes

Notes on the Authors

Seung Ho Park is the Parkland Chair Professor of Strategy at China Europe International Business School. He was the founding president of Samsung Economic Research Institute China and Managing Director of Skolkovo-EY Institute for Emerging Market Studies. He is a Fellow of the Academy of International Business and 2015 winner of Outstanding Service to Global Community Award by the IM Division of Academy of Management. His current research focuses on firm growth, competitive dynamics, and corporate value in emerging markets.. His recent coauthored books on emerging markets include the award-winning book *Rough Diamonds: Four Traits of Successful Breakout Enterprises in BRIC Countries* (Jossey-Bass, 2013), *Scaling the Tail: Managing Profitable Growth in Emerging Markets* (Palgrave-Macmillan, 2015), and *Managing Emerging Multinationals: Solving International Challenges* (Cambridge University Press, 2016).

Gerardo Rivera Ungson is the Y.F. Chang Endowed Chair and Professor of International Business in the College of Business, San Francisco State University. He was formerly a Senior Resident Scholar with the Institute for Emerging Market Studies (IEMS) in Beijing. He has coauthored several books, including *Rough Diamonds: For Successful Traits of Breakout Firms in BRIC* (with Seung Ho Park and Nan Zhou) that was awarded the 2013 Best Book on Globalization by the *Strategy + Business Magazine*. His most recent book on emerging markets, *Scaling the Tail: Profitable Growth in Emerging Markets*, coauthored with Seung Ho Park and Andrew Cosgrove, was published by Palgrave-Macmillan in 2015.

Jamil Paolo S. Francisco is an associate professor of economics at the Asian Institute of Management (AIM). Prior to joining AIM, he was a lecturer at the School of Social Sciences of the Ateneo de Manila University. He has led several research projects under the Economy and Environment Program for Southeast Asia (EEPSEA) of the International Development Research Centre (IDRC) and under the

East Asian Development Network (EADN). He has published journal articles on financial markets, environmental economics, urban studies, and household adaptations to climate change. He is currently engaged in research on ASEAN economic integration and its implications on the socioeconomic development of its member states.

Foreword

When the Asian Institute of Management (AIM) was established in 1968, it was with the vision that AIM would develop the next generation of socially responsible leaders and managers who would make a difference in Asia's emerging markets. It is this core philosophy that has propelled AIM to constantly improve its curriculum and degree programs, and generate research and cases that our societies can learn and benefit from.

This 2015, we are presented with a multitude of opportunities, inasmuch as challenges, with the ASEAN economic integration. Our ten member states comprise an economic bloc that could easily become the fourth largest economy in the world by 2050. Our diverse population numbers over 620 million people.

With goals of a single market and production base, the need for talent has dramatically increased. We need leaders who can adeptly navigate the shifting ASEAN business landscapes. That is where AIM, as a pioneer in management education in Asia, can and has already contributed.

Professors Sam (Seung Ho) Park, Buddy Ungson of Rough Diamonds fame, and AIM's own Professor Paolo Francisco share invaluable insights into the economic integration through their stories on the fifty-eight ASEAN organizational champions. These champions represent industries ranging from power generation and distribution to air transportation and civil construction, from telecommunications and agriculture to health care, education, and real estate.

Learning from the experiences of these successful organizations, we get to understand what contributes to their resiliency, despite periods of financial crises, challenging macroeconomic conditions, cultural diversity, and inconsistent and/or inadequate government policies.

These analyses of the ASEAN champions included in this book are important to us because they are able to provide prescriptive frameworks on how to best take advantage of the regional economic integration and how we, as leaders, can best steer our respective organizations' strategies and take calculated risks to ensure that we can achieve sustained success.

But, most important, Sam, Buddy, and Paolo raise vital questions to remind us that the future of the region is in our able hands. How can we creatively bridge the gap between institutional voids and inclusive market growth? How do we compete with the large multinational companies? How do we grow with the economies? They see education through the enhancement of human skills as one way of addressing these questions, which I heartily endorse.

This book captures the energy of the bustling ASEAN economic community, and presents us with the exciting growth possibilities that lie ahead. I hope your reading experience is a most enriching one and you, too, will be able to capture the opportunities as they arise.

Steven J. Dekrey
President of The Asian Institute of
Management (2012–2015)

Foreword

ASEAN Champions is an excellent analysis on how a region is evolving toward the future. ASEAN is a complex region, composed of ten countries: Indonesia, Malaysia, the Philippines, Singapore, Thailand, Vietnam, Brunei, Cambodia, Laos, and Myanmar.

In today's world, many countries are connecting their economy with those of other countries of the same region. The impact of big economies, those of the United States, the European Union, India, China, and Brazil, is stimulating smaller and developing countries to better coordinate their economies. This is the case of ASEAN countries or the sub-Saharan countries in Africa.

The process presents challenges and opportunities for companies. Of course, for a big multinational company, a "mosaic" of different markets evolving toward a single one is an opportunity. For small local companies, however, it can be a difficulty because competition grows as markets open and they may not have the resources to quickly deploy internationally.

ASEAN Champions looks at these problems and opportunities from a wide perspective. There is no question that history helps in understanding a region and the authors get into this aspect in an attractive way. But their most important contribution is their direct access to many local companies that are playing a leading role in the region.

ASEAN Champions helps in understanding the relationship between global and local business in the ASEAN region, as well as the critical aspects of successful management in the area. The practical perspective of the research, well related to the conceptually proven theoretical frameworks of international business, makes this a useful contribution for academics and practitioners in international business, as well as a useful tool for decision makers of companies especially interested in the area.

Pedro Nueno
President
*China Europe International
Business School*

Preface

ASEAN Champions is a consortium project involving researchers in the region (Asian Institute of Management, Manila and China Europe International Business School, Shanghai), and the United States (San Francisco State University). In contrast to current narratives, we focus on the role of the private sector in economic integration. Because conventional macroeconomic and political theories typically use the country as the unit of analysis, the role of the private sector tends to be relegated to the background and inadvertently deemphasized in the analysis of regional integration.

The overarching argument of this book is that it is the firm that directly trades with others through export/import or indirectly through foreign direct investments. Moreover, production is determined by firms through their investments and decisions. Accordingly, a firm-level analysis of the AEC constitutes the focus of this book.

To be clear, this does not abrogate the role of governments or the impact of macroeconomic conditions on regional integration. National governments will continue to be pivotal in political and economic integration, particularly in matters relating to free trade agreements (FTAs), tariff reductions, security, ecological and climate change, and infrastructural development – all requisites for successful regional integration. While the role of a country or a government is limited regarding the actual exchange of goods and services, governments play a critical role in formulating guidelines that facilitate (or impede) trade, such as favorable trade agreements and fiscal and monetary policies. Moreover, trade is significantly affected by macroeconomic conditions such as in periods of growth and recessions, as well as by changes in account balances and currency fluctuations. Although these considerations underscore the important role of governments and the impact of economic circumstances, the role of firms has yet to assume center stage in AEC, and hence this book is intended to complement extant research.

As with any work of this undertaking, there are many persons and associations to acknowledge and thank for their involvement and participation. In particular, we benefitted from the earnest support of Steven DeKrey, the former President of the Asian Institute of Management, Jikyeong Kang, President and Dean of the Institute, Ricardo "Ricky" Lim, former Dean of the Institute, Francisco "Frankie" Roman, Associate Dean of Research and Publications, and Horacio "Junbo" M. Borromeo, former Dean and Professor. This project would not have been made feasible without their unwavering commitment. We thank our research associates, Shiela Grace Se, Katrina Gonzalez, and Jan Emil Langomez, for their excellent research and administrative support. They have been truly instrumental to the project. We thank members of AIM's Board of Governors, Pridiyathorn Devakula, Dato Timothy Ong, Tun Ahmad Sarji bin Abdul Hamid, and Boon Yoon Chiang, for helping us to connect with some of the companies interviewed. We thank Apple, Rugee, Debby, Imelda, and Richard of the AIM Representative Offices in Thailand, Indonesia, and Malaysia for their help in scheduling interviews. We also thank the staff of the AIM Office of Research and Publications and of the Office of the President for their support.

We thank Zirong Wang (an International Business undergraduate at San Francisco State) and Ji Hong (Senior Research Associate at CEIBS) for their assistance in collecting information and statistics about ASEAN. We likewise acknowledge the support provided by Linda Oubre, Dean of the College of Business, and Yim-Yu Wong, Department Head of International Business, both from San Francisco State University, and the CEIBS Research Grant, the Parkland Professorship, and the Research Center for Emerging Market Studies at China Europe International Business School. We are also greatly indebted to Paula Parish and the rest of the editorial team at Cambridge University Press, who offered invaluable assistance during the entire process of the project.

Finally, we thank Professors Anand Agrawal, Maria Veronica Caparas, and Frankie Roman for their immense contributions to the project. They were a huge help in conducting some of our best top-level executive interviews. We cannot thank them enough for their support.

The book is dedicated to various family members: Ja Young, Alexandra, Amelia, Tegan Joann, Boden Kai, Ryan Makena, Charlotte Hazel, Baldwin, and Josan.

Part I

The Antecedents of ASEAN Integration

What is the role of the private sector in the forthcoming ASEAN Economic Community (AEC)? What are the characteristics of local firms operating within the ASEAN member-community?

In the next three chapters, we provide an overview of our core arguments (Chapter 1), and abridged background on ASEAN (Chapter 2), and an appraisal of progress leading to the formal enactment of the AEC this year (Chapter 3).

In all, we argue that firms matter, but that participation will depend on their ability to leverage their competitive advantages into the broader ASEAN market. For this reason, we have selected the most successful firms, or our fifty-eight ASEAN champions, as they have exhibited a capacity to sustain and build advantage in highly adverse economic conditions.

1 Our Core Arguments

Introduction

A widely acclaimed mantra in strategy – in both military and business contexts – is the advantage derived from unity in numbers guided by a common purpose. Throughout history, such collectivity was forged by unions, agreements, alliances, collusion, partnerships, economic integration, and regional trading blocs. Not surprisingly, there are approximately forty economic regional blocs – bilateral and multilateral trade agreements – that comprise the global trading system today.

Beneath this scaffolding of events, obscured by the prominence of other headliners, is a quiet transformation that has been occurring in Southeast Asia: the evolution of an economic bloc called the Association of Southeast Asian Nations (ASEAN). Accordingly, the formal enactment of its next initiative – the ASEAN Economic Community (AEC) – in December 2015 has been much anticipated.[1] Against this backdrop, the AEC is the newcomer in this field of regional integration. Its eventual realization could be momentous.

Consider the region's economic data for 2015: a population of about 620 million, or close to 9% of humanity; a combined GNP of more than US$2.4 trillion, approximating the seventh-largest economy in the world; and a projection that it could easily become the fourth-largest economy by 2050 (Vinayak, Thompson, & Tonby, 2014; ASEAN Economic Community 2015a: Progress and Key Achievements; Forecast from International Monetary Fund, *World Economic Outlook*, 2014).

Motivations for purposeful collaboration can be numerous – political, cultural, and economic – but tend to converge on two basic objectives: the

---

[1] ASEAN was inaugurated in 1967 with Indonesia, Malaysia, Thailand, Singapore, and the Philippines as its founding members, and has since added Brunei, Vietnam, Laos, Cambodia, and Myanmar. In the Bali Concord II, which was held in 2003, three pillars were proposed: the ASEAN Economic Community (AEC), the ASEAN Security Community (ASC), and the ASEAN Socio-Cultural Community (ASCC). This book is primarily directed at the present and proposed activities of the AEC.

need for security and the economic benefits derived from formal cooperation (Roxas, 1970). These underlying objectives tend to be interrelated, if not tightly coupled. For example, it is difficult to comprehend the full consequences of economic integration without considering political/ security issues (and vice versa). Although it is generally acknowledged that these objectives cannot be separated in practice, it is not uncommon for scholars to parse them into specific categories to analyze their feasibility and tractability.

In this light, understanding the economic potential of the AEC is particularly challenging because of the diversity of the ASEAN community (Lim, 2004). Beyond its relatively recent initiatives toward a single market for trade and an investment base, the AEC is distinguished because of its mixed composition of advanced, emerging, and developing countries. Such diversity can be characterized in terms of cultural and institutional differences; uneven economic development; varying infrastructural levels; differing religions, languages, and cultures; and a history of political/ military confrontation (Lim, 2004; Acharya, 2012).

Because diversity can impede integration, a persistent question is whether the benefits derived from economic integration outweigh the differences and complexities of the participants. Unsurprisingly, current attention is focused on agreements to reduce political and economic barriers to integration.[2] These agreements cover trade, nontariff barriers, political and military security and cooperation, climate change and environmental degradation, and physical infrastructures (see Acharya, 2012).

Focus on Exemplary Firms-ASEAN Champions

The overarching theme of this book is the selection and description of the most successful firms operating in ASEAN for a period of time, or the ASEAN Champions.[3] Because of their sustained success, prominence, and visibility in their respective local markets, these firms cannot be ignored as potential players in regional integration.

But will these successful firms necessarily be the drivers of regional integration? Among the primary goals of the AEC include a single market and

[2] Although it is true that governments can trade by providing advice, outsourcing, and managing services, the extent to which such activities can favorably compare with interfirm trade across borders is hardly disputable. See http://www.economist.com/news/international/ 21595928-countries-have-started-outsource-public-services-each-other-unbundling-nation.

[3] Whereas most studies focus on governments as the unit of analysis, one notable exception is Sanchita Basu Das (ed.), *Achieving the ASEAN Economic Community 2015: Challenges for Member Countries & Businesses* (Singapore: ISEAS Publishing, 2012), which addresses firm-level analyses. This book is intended to complement her work, and her ideas are presented in detail in Chapter 11.

production base, a competitive region, balanced economic and equitable development for firms of varying sizes, and integration with the global community. Conceivably, some exemplary firms will not be as involved in these goals, but more focused on building capabilities that are aligned with their domestic objectives (i.e., real estate development, commercial banking, or specialized local services, such as utilities). Nevertheless, their propensity to become involved in the future, if propitious circumstances arise, has implications for the AEC, and this subject is addressed later in this book.

But will less successful firms necessarily be excluded from regional integration? Although these firms might not be as successful (profitable), or might have erratic performance, we submit that they could be key players in the integration process. Consider that these prospective integrators include up-and-coming firms that are relatively new or relatively small and that hence fall outside the radar of established financial databases and timelines for analysis. Arguably, they could be key players in the future of the AEC. Therefore, understanding the barriers and facilitators to regional integration that impact both current and prospective participants will affect the future of the AEC, and this subject is likewise included in our analysis.

What about the role of foreign multinational firms? Indubitably, these firms will play an important role in the AEC. Notable scholars have already touted the potential of well-established global icons, specifically Ben & Jerry's, Apple, Givaudan, H&M (Hennes & Mauritz), Samsung, Huawei, Kinokuniya, Procter & Gamble, Inditex, and Honda, among others, which are positioned to become involved in the "New ASEAN" (cited in Kotler, Kartajaya, and Huan, 2015).

Although we acknowledge their important role in the AEC, our focus on local firms within ASEAN underscores our intent to examine indigenous conditions underlying the success of these local firms. This focus includes their historical origins, their colonial past, and their fledgling institutions – conditions that generally do not apply to most foreign multinationals from highly advanced economies. As we will detail, the challenges and experiences confronting local firms differ markedly from successful foreign multinationals. Historically, these multinationals entered into emerging and developing markets not primarily to build markets and secure customers, although this strategy is currently changing; the main strategy of multinationals was to capitalize on lower labor costs, access key resources, or secure markets for their maturing products (see Jones, 2005).[4]

---

[4] Although there are historical accounts of multinationals selling their goods and services to emerging and developing economies, it is generally acknowledged that this was not done for the purposes of building a market and securing customers in the sense and context in which we selected our successful local companies (ASEAN champions).

Based on these considerations, the following key questions provide the format for this study: Which local firms will lead this charge? How might they be represented in each of the ten ASEAN countries? What are the characteristics of such firms? What sustained their competitive advantages? What enabled these firms to succeed in the context of highly difficult and largely unfavorable circumstances? What are the facilitators and obstacles to regional integration? What are the implications for regional integration?

A Brief Word on the Selection Process

Our selection process was particularly stringent, incorporating multiple screens and criteria of available financial information and consultations with industry experts. Although these are described in detail (see Box 1.1), our objective was to select firms that were resilient to changing political and economic challenges over time. We were occasionally prodded to include certain firms that had received fanfare from academic and populist sources. Even so, a closer assessment of these cases indicated that high performance was confined to a much shorter period of time when compared to the final list of successful firms. When appropriate, we cite these firms but do not select them as primary sources for the in-field interviews. Our premise is that ASEAN champions are able to sustain high performance amid highly adverse conditions over a comparable study period (see Table 1.1 for the list).

Box 1.1. Selecting ASEAN Champions

ASEAN champions represent high-performing local private enterprises in ASEAN member countries. The Rough Diamonds project by Park, Zhou, and Ungson (2013) developed a rigorous framework to identify sustained high-performing local companies in emerging markets. We follow a similar guideline to that of the Rough Diamonds project but had to loosen the selection criteria to secure enough companies for this study. The Rough Diamonds companies show higher annual growth rate, profitability, and efficiency ratio for at least seven of the ten years of their observation than the averages of the annual top five hundred companies in each BRIC country. ASEAN Champions generally satisfy higher revenue growth and profitability for at least four years during 2003–2012 than the averages of the annual top five hundred companies in each ASEAN country. The selection is country based to include all ten ASEAN countries in the study. The process involves the following three specific steps, which lead to a list of fifty-eight ASEAN champions.

First, according to operating revenues, we identify annual top five hundred companies for 2003–2012 in six ASEAN countries that have enough companies included in ORBIS. The six countries are Indonesia, Malaysia, the Philippines, Singapore, Thailand, and Vietnam. This was not possible for other countries (Brunei, Cambodia, Laos, and Myanmar) due to the small sample sizes in ORBIS. For these countries, as described below, we follow experts' recommendations to identify high-performing local private companies among the ASEAN champions for this study.

Second, we calculate the ten-year average revenue growth rate and profitability of the 2012 top five hundred companies and the averages of the annual top five hundred companies in each country. We select 202 companies from the 2012 top 500 list whose 10-year averages in both growth rate and profitability are higher than the averages of the annual top 500 companies. We further narrow down the list to forty-six companies that show higher annual growth rate and profitability than the averages of annual top five hundred companies in each country for at least four years during the study period. These forty-six companies are then carefully examined to assure the majority ownership belongs to local private investors. Among these, we replace seven companies with their shareholding companies that are better identified in each local market. For two companies we include the most representative subsidiaries since they are highly diversified holding companies.

Lastly, we consult with multiple local experts to confirm the validity of our selection and identify potential candidates of ASEAN champions for the remaining four countries. The forty-six companies are well supported by experts as leading companies in each of the six countries. Their recommendations lead to five more companies that are well respected and sector leaders in each country. Experts also identify seven companies as potential ASEAN champions from the remaining four countries. The final list of ASEAN champions includes fifty-eight companies, with two from Brunei, one from Cambodia, eleven from Indonesia, three from Laos, four from Malaysia, one from Myanmar, twelve from the Philippines, three from Singapore, fifteen from Thailand, and six from Vietnam. Table 1.1 includes the list of these fifty-eight ASEAN champions.

Table 1.1. *List of ASEAN Champions*

The ASEAN Champions	Country	Industry
Aboitiz Power Corporation	Philippines	power generation and distribution
Adinin Group of Companies	Brunei	civil construction
Advanced Info Service PCL	Thailand	telecommunications
Ayala Land, Inc.	Philippines	real estate
Bangkok Cable Co., Ltd.	Thailand	cable products
Bangkok Dusit Medical Services PCL	Thailand	healthcare
Bood Rawd Brewery	Thailand	brewery
Cebu Air, Inc.	Philippines	air transportation
Charoen Pokphand Foods PCL	Thailand	agro-industrial products
Dao-Heuang Group	Lao PDR	coffee and tea products
DIALOG Group Berhad	Malaysia	services for oil and gas
Dutch Mill Co., Ltd.	Thailand	dairy products
EDL-Generation Public Company	Lao PDR	electricity
EEI Corporation	Philippines	industrial construction
Energy Development Corporation	Philippines	renewable energy
Far Eastern University, Inc.	Philippines	education
FPT Corporation	Vietnam	information and communication
Hanoi Production Services Import-Export JSC	Vietnam	agriculture and handicraft
Holcim Philippines, Inc.	Philippines	cement and aggregates
Jollibee Foods Corporation	Philippines	fast food
Keppel FELS Limited	Singapore	rig building
Lafarge Republic, Inc.	Philippines	cement and aggregates
Lao Brewery Co., Ltd.	Lao PDR	Brewery
Manila Electric Company (Meralco)	Philippines	electricity and utilities
Masan Consumer Corporation	Vietnam	diversified consumer goods
Mudajaya Corporation Berhad	Malaysia	engineering and construction
PETRONAS Dagangan Berhad	Malaysia	petroleum production
PetroVietnam Gas JSC	Vietnam	oil and gas
Philippine Long Distance Telephone Company	Philippines	telecommunications
Phnom Penh Water Supply Authority	Cambodia	water supply and distribution
Pruksa Real Estate PCL	Thailand	real estate
PT FKS Multiagro Tbk.	Indonesia	agro-industrial products
PT Global Mediacom Tbk.	Indonesia	integrated media
PT Indofood Sukses Makmur Tbk.	Indonesia	packaged food
PT Lippo Karawaci Tbk.	Indonesia	real estate and property development
PT Malindo Feedmill Tbk.	Indonesia	animal feed
PT Mitra Adiperkasa Tbk.	Indonesia	lifestyle retail

Table 1.1 (*cont.*)

The ASEAN Champions	Country	Industry
PT Petrosea Tbk.	Indonesia	mining, oil, and gas
PT Solusi Tunas Pratama Tbk.	Indonesia	telecommunications
PT Sumber Alfaria Trijaya Tbk.	Indonesia	mini mart
PT Summarecon Agung Tbk.	Indonesia	property development
PT Ultrajaya Milk Industry & Trading Company Tbk.	Indonesia	liquid milk products
PTT Exploration and Production PCL	Thailand	oil exploration
QAF Brunei Sdn. Bhd.	Brunei	conglomerate
Sembcorp Marine Limited	Singapore	engineering solutions
Siam Cement Group	Thailand	cement products
Singapore Aero Engine Services Limited	Singapore	engine maintenance and repair
SM Prime Holdings, Inc.	Philippines	shopping centers
Summit Auto Body Industry Co., Ltd.	Thailand	automotive systems
TC Pharmaceutical Industries Co., Ltd.	Thailand	beverages
Thai Beverage PCL	Thailand	beverages
Thai Metal Trade PCL	Thailand	steel solutions
Thai Union Frozen Products PCL	Thailand	seafood products
Tien Phong Plastic JSC	Vietnam	civil plastics
TOA Paint (Thailand) Co., Ltd.	Thailand	paint products
Vietnam Dairy Products JSC (Vinamilk)	Vietnam	dairy products
WCT Land Sdn. Bhd.	Malaysia	property development
Yoma Strategic Holdings Limited	Myanmar	real estate

Throughout the study, we deliberated on the appropriate measures for deciding which firms to include and which to exclude. Although we initially settled on established financial measures along with stringent criteria, we acknowledge the importance of other nonfinancial factors. In this regard, we consulted with industry experts in several ASEAN countries and included other firms. After we analyzed our first selection of firms, however, it became evident that the meaning of success (high performance) principally defined in terms of financial measures was in itself a major consideration. The appropriateness of performance measures largely used to describe the experiences of firms in advanced/developed economic settings had to be contextualized in terms of ASEAN regional integration. We deliberated whether the experiences of successful firms from advanced economies might be totally suitable for comparing the relative success of ASEAN firms.

This issue is further addressed in our next sections. By way of an overview, we argue that narratives about successful firms, which have been extolled in bestsellers largely in the developed world (Collins & Porras, 1994; Collins, 2001), are nuanced toward what scholars call an "internalist view" (Adelman, 2015). This refers to explanations that attribute high performance to internal or "organic" characteristics of these firms, specifically their inane ability to build, nurture, and sustain core competencies. In contrast, a differing view – the "externalist view" (Adelman, 2015) – posits that such high performance could not have occurred without incorporating the full context of external events.

In a review of the origins of capitalism, specifically the transformation of the cotton industry (Beckert, 2014), Adelman (2015) cites external factors such as slavery, external trade, and the factory system as contributing factors. In our own analysis of ASEAN, these arguments resonate well with theories of modernization and dependency, which we develop as another theoretical prism through which to understand the success of local ASEAN firms and to differentiate them from erstwhile successful firms from advanced economies. Following these narratives, we propose a different explanation for the success of local firms based on an integration of theories about institutions and economic development, as well as strategic management.

Qualifying the Meaning of Success for ASEAN

Researchers generally acknowledge that successful multinationals originate from countries in which these firms are able to develop core competencies that they can transfer and sustain in other parts of the world. Conventional wisdom suggests that firms in this environment generally succeed because they employ low-cost labor or have access to important raw materials (see Cavusgil, Knight, & Riesenberger, 2014). In addition, as in the cases of Japan, South Korea, China, and other successful emerging countries, firms also have to develop capabilities to export their products and compete with others in the world market.

Undoubtedly, this argument is valid for a number of cases. In the case of ASEAN, however, except for some countries, most operate in highly underdeveloped institutional environments characterized as "institutional voids," defined broadly as the absence of market intermediaries that enable and facilitate efficient market transactions (Khanna & Palepu, 1997). It is precisely this condition of economic and institutional underdevelopment, coupled with the risk and uncertainty of political regimes that has made multinationals from other countries leery of entering into ASEAN and other developing countries for the purposes of building markets and securing customers. Yet, despite formidable challenges, some exemplary firms within ASEAN have been able to overcome these unattractive conditions.

Uneven economic development raises questions of whether the experiences of highly successful firms in developed countries might be appropriate in our selection of our ASEAN champions. There are at least two reasons for some redirection. First, the economies of developed countries are much further advanced in industrialization, as reflected in their institutional munificence. No economy is so perfect that no institutional voids exist, but few would argue that institutional development in advanced countries is better than that in emerging and developing economies. Second, unlike the established multinational firms that extend their dominance by expanding into export markets, many firms within the ASEAN region face daunting catch-up strategies with operations that are largely confined to a few international markets (Cuervo-Cazurra & Ramamurti, 2014).

For these reasons, defining successful firms within ASEAN is much less tractable than might be gleaned from the surface. Currently, there is interest in emerging multinationals (EMNCs), but most are from emerging nations (China, Brazil, Russia, and India) that do not generally include most ASEAN countries (Sauvant, 2008; Ramamurti & Singh, 2009; Chattopadhyay & Batra, 2012; Guillen & Garcia-Canal, 2013; Santiso, 2013; Cuervo-Cazurra & Ramamurti, 2014). Although the firms within ASEAN excel domestically, many are still in their infancy in terms of becoming effective global multinationals. In fact, few of them can be considered full-fledged multinationals (Cuervo-Cazurra & Ramamurti, 2014). Catch-up strategies and the industrialization process are still in progress for most of these firms (Cuervo-Cazurra & Ramamurti, 2014).

What distinguishes the ASEAN champions is their financial strength and resiliency over time, despite challenges arising from regime changes, inconsistent government policies, periods of financial crisis, and adverse macroeconomic conditions. In this regard, the meaning of development and high performance is embedded in a different context, one that takes into account other considerations, such as cultures, institutions, and stage of economic development. These differences in high-performance firms have to be precisely defined not only for purposes of measurement but also from their historical origins. In terms of background leading to this argument, we provide a brief review of studies that have defined winners in developed economies.

Lessons for ASEAN and Developing Countries

A widely acknowledged belief is that history does not necessarily correspond to the totality of real events but is parsed by the winners (or persons of influence) in specific historical periods. Phrased differently, it is rare for losers – be it in military battles or business failure – to define, select, and interpret events surrounding them. Much as military conquests lead to the absconding of the spoils of battle, the winners typically are in a position to interpret the pivotal events and decisions of their times.

It is therefore not so surprising that developing countries have been admonished to emulate, if not imitate, the successful traits and patterns of developed countries – a line of thought called modernization theory (see Isbister, 2006). The renowned statesman Walt Whitman Rostow (*Stages of Economic Growth: A Non-Communist Manifesto*, 1960) argued that development takes the form of systemic stages of growth that are underpinned by supportive institutions. Written primarily to combat the mounting threat of communism, this work proposed the infusion of capital and technology from developed to underdeveloped countries. The end result would be prosperity, capitalism, and democracy.

Variants of modernization theory have emerged over time, but an underlying logic of "imitation and emulation" constituted the common thread among them. Neoliberalism, an influential form of market liberalism that took root in the 1970s, touted the merits of the free market system backed by global financial institutions. The high-water mark (also a point of discomfiture) was the application of this theory propounded by Nobel laureate Milton Friedman and his free-market economists (Chicago Boys) to address the problems in Bolivia and Chile (Klein, 2007). The Washington Consensus, a ten-point economic policy primer forged in 1989 that was largely based on market fundamentalism, was adopted by the IMF, the World Bank, and other financial institutions, as the core reform package for developing countries that had succumbed to financial crisis.

Despite its paradigmatic influence, modernization has yielded a highly mixed scorecard. Although the United States and Great Britain remain the poster children of the free-market orthodoxy, their success has been aptly challenged by Cambridge economic historian Ha-Joon Chang (*Kicking Away the Ladder: Development Strategy in Historical Perspective*, 2003). Using historical records, Chang argued that both countries employed highly protectionist policies during their ascent to power, only to disavow these policies and to prescribe free-market policies for others to follow later. Moreover, the record of neoliberalist reform programs levied on some Asian countries during the wake of the 1999 Asian Financial Crisis reveals a sullen record. Finally, the three developing economies that were transformed into developed ones – Japan, China, and South Korea – achieved success but not in the manner prescribed by modernization theorists (Chang, 2002).

With the center of economic gravity shifting from developed to developing economies, there is a need to rethink the premises of modernization theory in a different context. The two key questions are: How do developing (emerging) countries succeed? And what are the characteristics of successful firms in these economies? Japan is widely acknowledged to be the postwar economic miracle, surpassing all projected rates of growth despite its utter destruction during World War II. Even so, its impressive economic success does not conform to mainstream economic doctrine; in fact, its growth is attributed to its purposeful industrial planning (Johnson, 1982), its industrial business groupings (Gerlach, 1982), or excellent management by Japanese firms (Ouchi, 1978).

Alice Amsden, a former MIT economic historian, examined this same issue of "catch-up" economics or the success of latecomers with particular attention to South Korea. In an authoritative thesis (*Asia's New Giant*, 1989), Amsden posits that late developers (South Korea) were able to transform themselves through *systemic learning*. In context, this refers to government policies that favored big and strong local conglomerates (*chaebols*), and the ability of these firms to develop competencies in production, reverse engineering, and shop-floor management that were oriented to export success. But this desire to learn to become world-class enterprises did not occur in a historical vacuum; it was also grounded in deep cultural values that reward education, scholastic achievement, filial piety and respect, peer support, and group cohesiveness (Amsden, 1989). In sum, success is a confluence of governmental support, strategies to capitalize on propitious opportunities, the advantages of size and large-scale production, and supportive management structures, culture, and processes.

The growing proliferation and prominence of multinationals from emerging and developing countries (EMNCs or emerging market multinational companies) has called into question the validity and appropriateness of orthodox international business theories, notably the Ownership-Location-Internationalization (OLI) theory, which has been influential in explaining the success of multinationals largely from developed economies (Dunning, 1990). Critics have argued for an earlier formulation of internalization to describe these new multinationals (Rugman, 1980; Buckley, 1983). Other perspectives emphasize latent firm advantages, government support, home country characteristics, learning trajectories, and local embeddedness. However, supporters of the OLI theory maintain that these new multinationals still employ strategies similar to those from developed countries; market power can still materialize from firm ownership advantages, location, and internationalization, although differing contexts might create nuances in application.

Taken collectively, the search for high performing firms in developing countries has resulted in a booming industry of sorts, with a continuous stream of bestsellers, each extolling one or more well-accepted tenets of good management. The application to emerging and developing countries is much more nuanced and is characterized by some researchers extolling the experience of successful firms in developed countries, a reflection of an unabashed adoption of modernization theory. Critics argue for a different perspective, and although prescriptions are far from universal, they generally incorporate aspects of firm competencies, locational advantages, government support, learning systems, and excellent management. One area of commonality across all these studies is the acknowledgment of the importance of institutions and the extent to which their development has an impact on economic success. It is to this area that we direct attention as we delineate our rationale for selecting ASEAN champions.

Institutions, Economic Development, and Firm Performance

Management theorists generally borrow from our sociological brethren in conceptualization of the term "institutions." The essence of institutions involves a relationship between an individual and his/her environment, or "patterned ways of mediating ourselves with the world." Sociologists Bellah, Madsen, Sullivan, Swidler, and Tipton, in their book *The Good Society* (1992: 10-11), modified this understanding to include norms for human behavior: "Expected action of individuals or groups enforced by social sanctions, both positive and negative." Nobel laureate Douglass North (1990:3) placed institutions as the central theme of his arguments by including exchange and transactions as components: "humanly devised constraints that shape human interaction...they structure incentives in human exchange" In this formulation, institutions range from formal (laws, education, finance, and so on) to informal (cultural norms and mores), but with the capacity to address uncertainty with the reduction of transaction costs. One branch of institutional theory – transactional cost analysis – is popularly attributed to economist Ronald Coase and Nobel laureate Oliver Williamson (1985), who situates the reduction of transaction costs as the primary explanation for the existence of organizations, as well as forms of contractual arrangements.

Over the past decades, the beliefs about institutions as an exploratory variable have shifted markedly – from earlier criticisms that they were not "amenable to measurement" to "important elements in explaining differences in economic attainment" (Acemoglu, Johnson & Robinson, 2005, quoted by Mokyr, 2010:183). Economic development and prosperity are deeply linked to the development of supportive institutions for growth and renewal. In their 1973 treatise, *The Rise of the Western World*, Douglass North and Robert Paul Thomas assert:

Efficient economic organization is the key to growth; the development of an efficient economic organization in Western Europe accounts for the rise of the West. … Efficient organization entails the establishment of institutional arrangements and property rights that create an incentive to channel individual economic effort into activities that bring the private rate of return close to the social rate of return. (1973:1)

The Peruvian economist Hernando de Soto (*Mystery of Capital*, 2000) defines institutions, specifically the provision of property rights, as the raison d'être for progressive capitalist organizations. Because property rights bestow the owner the rights to loans, capital, official residence and basic services, impoverished countries where property rights are nonexistent or are very difficult to bequeath have an abundance of "dead capital," or close to $9.3 trillion in de Soto's estimation. In subsequent talks, de Soto argues that the lack of property rights stifles the entrepreneurship that is so essential for economic growth and development.

Against this backdrop, it is hardly surprising that pundits, largely from developed countries, are skeptical that rising firms constitute true multinationals in developing economies, such as ASEAN (Cuervo-Cazurra & Ramamurti, 2014). With the exception of Singapore (and Brunei), which boasts a per capita income comparable to those of leading economies, and Indonesia and Thailand, which have had some years of prolonged impressive growth, other countries tend to be inconsistent. For example, the Philippines experienced middle-to-low growth over an extended period, at least until five years ago in which it has since demonstrated strong economic growth. Vietnam holds considerable promise but remains an uncertainty in terms of sustained success. Brunei owes much of its prosperity to a single industry, while Laos and Cambodia are still relatively underdeveloped.

In addition, the economic landscape in many of the above countries is replete with institutional voids, defined by Harvard strategists Tarun Khanna and Krishna Palepu (*Winning in Emerging Markets*, 2010) as the absence of institutions (intermediaries) that facilitate market transactions or that generally support markets. Examples include lack of property rights, law and order, broker information, intermediaries, power to enforce contracts, and deficient financial and educational systems. Firms in developing economies face all these challenges in addition to continuously streamlining their operations to achieve profitable outcomes over time.

How did our ASEAN champions succeed under the most trying circumstances? What common characteristics do they share, if any? Our next section bridges conceptions of institutions necessary to firm success.

Reassessing Success in ASEAN: Mobilizing Institutional Grassroots

Our initial analysis of the ASEAN champions disclosed that these firms appear to have succeeded because they adopted the right strategies in alignment with their economic circumstances. These firms forged strategies similar to those of high-performing firms in developed countries: sound strategic analysis, opportunistic risk taking, entrepreneurship, and excellent management. Consistent with mainstream narratives, such interpretation casts the leaders of these enterprises as prescient, bold, and entrepreneurial.

Nevertheless, we probed further into how these firms succeeded in adverse environments when their competitors and erstwhile peers did not. Indeed, some of these firms were well supported by governments, but this was not the case for all. Many were family run, but this was not the standard. Moreover, the ASEAN champions took risks – even unwarranted at the time – that their better-financed competitors avoided. But beyond this patina of generality, there appeared to be a common characteristic, one that enabled them to overcome challenges considered to be risky by their local competitors and multinational firms in other countries.[5] We further explored the connection between national economic development, sustained high firm performance, and the manner in which firms were impacted by institutional frailties.

In sum, a deeper penetration into the strategies and activities reveals that ASEAN champions nurtured capabilities that transformed institutional inadequacies into competitive advantages. Far from being deterred by underdevelopment, these firms capitalized on this condition

---

[5] As stated earlier, multinationals entered emerging/developing economies to secure raw materials and access lower labor costs, not primarily for purposes of building a market and securing customers in the sense and context in which we selected our ASEAN champions.

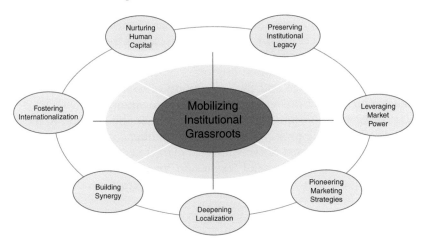

Exhibit 1.1 Mobilizing Institutional Grassroots

to build strengths that enabled them to compete with others, particularly to enter foreign multinationals, in due course. Based on continuing analysis of the data and ensuing consultations with industry experts, we stipulate that our firm champions enacted solutions to institutional voids in a variety of ways, such as by creating inclusive markets that hardly existed, by capitalizing on products and services that were aligned with the country's comparative advantage, by filling niches that were previously neglected, by proactively remedying deficient infrastructures, and by instituting administrative legacies through purposeful managerial successions.

In context, these firms conceived of entrepreneurial opportunities in still evolving fledgling institutions, whether these were political, economic, or social in character. In effect, these firms were able to *mobilize* human and financial resources that provided solutions to *institutional voids* that resembled fledgling states of economic and social development, and hence *grassroots* by their very nature. For brevity, we characterize these strategies and activities as "*mobilizing institutional grassroots*."

While we develop specific arguments in the course of this book, we introduce seven specific strategies used to transform erstwhile firms into ASEAN champions for perspective (Exhibit 1.1):

• *Preserving institutional legacy*: intergenerational transfer of norms, culture, and values in ways that align with industry evolution

- *Leveraging market power*: market power obtained through bequeathing the use of resources and/or access to critical assets during early stages of economic development
- *Pioneering marketing strategies*: innovative marketing strategies such as first-mover advantage and the recognition of nascent but propitious market niches that provide early advantages to entrants
- *Deepening localization*: ability of firms to identify and respond to local needs and provide products and invest in human capital in ways that meet the requirements of evolving local market needs
- *Building synergy*: purposeful expansion through acquisitions and diversification that create unifying strengths across product/market portfolios
- *Fostering internationalization*: systemic expansion to global markets that balances growth and profitability
- *Nurturing human capital*: harnessing the full power of human capital and resources to support overall strategies

Each of these characteristics is discussed at length as separate chapters of this book. The strategies are not mutually exclusive, nor are they necessarily sequential in order. *In fact, they are deeply interrelated. A successful firm will have attained several, if not most, of these strategies in the course of its development.* Nevertheless, in discussing each of the strategies in forthcoming chapters, we highlight the experiences of particular firms that excel in a specific strategy.

Collectively, this focus on mobilizing institutional grassroots yields some nuanced arguments that are introduced in this book:

- Institutions matter, although not nearly in accordance with the premises of mainstream management and international business theories. Voids provide ample opportunities to create firm-specific advantages;
- For latecomers and catch-up industrialization, governments can be pivotal not only through deliberate incentives or sanctions but also by enacting policies that change the competitive and institutional landscape;
- High-performing firms seek and find solutions to voids through creative use of resources, human capital, and administrative legacies that build on the country's comparative advantage;
- Deep localization constitutes the "new normal" for firms, multinationals or otherwise, that attempt to succeed in developing and emerging economies and markets;
- Nurturing human capital is a key correlate of success in that improved education and training provides a fast-moving target of continuous development;

• While successful over a period of time, ASEAN firms are hardly fully fledged multinationals, let alone regional champions. There are remaining obstacles that hinder the full potential of ASEAN.

The Book in Brief

The book is organized in four interrelated parts that correspond to the different phases of the project. The first part, *The Antecedents of ASEAN Integration*, covers the background of ASEAN. Chapter 1 provides an overview of the entire book and our core arguments. Chapters 2 and 3 present a history of ASEAN; its core objectives and operating platform; a timetable for achieving regional integration; a summary of accomplishments to the present time; a review of the relevant literature; and challenges leading to the bloc's formal declaration in December 2015. The second part, *ASEAN Champions – Strategies for Enduring Success*, describes the strategies of selected high-performing firms that build on the theme of mobilizing institutional grassroots. Specific strategies from case studies and field interviews are parsed in seven separate chapters: Preserving Institutional Legacy (Chapter 4), Leveraging Market Power (Chapter 5), Pioneering Marketing Strategies (Chapter 6), Deepening Localization (Chapter 7), Building Synergy (Chapter 8), Fostering Internationalization (Chapter 9), and Nurturing Human Capital (Chapter 10).

The third part, *Strategic Imperatives and Policy Recommendations*, synthesizes our findings and presents a prescriptive framework for enhancing regional integration. Chapter 11 presents implications for firms in regard to requirements for achieving the goals of the ASEAN Economic Community (AEC). Chapter 12 provides our epilogue, which covers impressions from prominent scholars and policy makers about future regional integration and AEC.

Accordingly, we envision three types of audiences for our book. The first audience would be academicians and policy makers in strategy, management, and public policy. Currently, there are questions relating to the appropriateness of mainstream theories developed largely from Western intellectual traditions in the context of developed economies for emerging and developing markets. Our book offers a particularistic perspective based on the institutional foundations of ASEAN firms. The second audience would be business practitioners who typically seek new templates for understanding the changes in emerging markets and strategies to respond to them. Firms that fail to fully recognize the changing context of underdevelopment are typically blindsided when extant and previously successful business models do not work. This book provides an alternative roadmap for entry and ongoing activities based on the experiences of high-performing firms within ASEAN. Relatedly, the third audience would be government officials who are interested in new insights about ASEAN. The current focus has been on the political and social aspects of regional integration with governments as the key actors. This book offers possible new templates at the microeconomic level that could extend their current initiatives to more fully realize the benefits of this new economic bloc.

2 Mapping ASEAN Integration

Introduction

Every decade can be defined and distinguished by epochal events. The fall of the Berlin Wall in 1989, the dissolution of the Soviet Union in 1991, the 1994 Mexican crisis, the 1997 Asian financial crisis, the 1998 Russian crisis, the 2001 Internet bubble, and the 2008 Great Recession are arguably the pivotal events that have characterized the political and economic landscape of their respective periods (Reinhart & Rogoff, 2009; Guillen & Esteban Garcia-Canal, 2013; Booth, 2014). Moreover, during these past twenty years, the rise of emerging markets, notably the BRIC countries (Brazil, Russia, China, and India) has significantly shifted the epicenter of global commerce from developed markets to emerging and developing countries, providing new imperatives for strategy, business, and practice. Even so, narratives about emerging markets in Asia tend to highlight the market potential of China and India and deemphasize the resurgence of Southeast Asia.

This lack of attention to Southeast Asia is no accident but is rooted in its history. Specifically, the concept of a Southeast Asia region is a contested one among scholars (Lieberman, 1995; Acharya & Rajah, 1999; Evers, 1999; Acharya, 2012). Apart from their geographical proximity, spatial concentration, uneven economic development, varying sociocultural characteristics, and identity as colonies of Western powers, there was little to bind the countries together as a region (Acharya, 2012; Roberts, 2012). In fact, if there is any uniting characteristic, it is the diversity of the countries in the region (Acharya, 2012). Even so, it is questionable whether sheer diversity, as exemplified in differences in geography, sociocultural elements, and economic development, is a coalescing factor of consequence for regional identity (Acharya, 2012:10). After all, it is argued that if regional identity is marked by diversity and differences, how can this advance any momentum toward integration?

Accordingly, a contemporary thread proposes a definition based on social constructivism that goes beyond geographic/sociocultural/

economic attributes of a region. Constructivism includes mental and ideological constructs that evoke unity ("imagined communities" or "regions created by simply imagining them in existence") (see Acharya, 2012: 22-23) and political commitment, or outright declarations of integration (Katzenstein, 2005; Chachavalpongpun, 2006), as the new defining elements. An even more recent proposal by Roberts (2012) raises the standard in situating cooperation and institutionalization as the binding elements of a security community. In this case, collective security against external factors is regarded as the defining factor in any regional integration.

In this context, ASEAN is a formal enactment of a proposed regional bloc underpinned by shared and binding economic, sociocultural, and institutional activities. ASEAN seeks to obviate differences and diversity in favor of purposeful interaction and engagement. The extent to which ASEAN becomes a truly regional bloc will depend largely on the successful accomplishment of these binding activities. In this chapter, we discuss historical events leading to the formation of ASEAN. But to what extent might these proclamations be supported by previous historical decisions? In response, the core argument of this chapter is that the histories of economic, political, and institutional development are tightly coupled and intertwined. One cannot be completely understood without the others. Moreover, their effects are systemic and consequential. As such, historical events earmark precipitating decisions that have some bearing on both the current and the future shape of ASEAN. Even so, this chapter should be read principally as a background to ensuing chapters, *not* as a comprehensive discourse on what regionalism is or might be. This latter issue is discussed in authoritative works on this subject cited in this chapter (Acharya, 2012; Das, 2012; Roberts, 2012).

ASEAN: The Legacy of Colonial Past

With the exception of Thailand, all other members of ASEAN were subjected to colonial rule.[1] Without question, the territorial boundaries and competitive landscape of present-day Southeast Asia bear testimony to decades of colonial or imperialistic rule. Colonialization was famously enacted when the Treaty of Tordesillas in 1494 formally divided the world outside Europe to be explored by Portugal and Spain.[2] Earlier, Christopher Columbus had sailed forth and laid claim to the Americas.

[1] For a comprehensive account of the histories of each ASEAN country, refer to Lim (2004) and Osborne (2013).
[2] https://en.wikipedia.org/wiki/Treaty_of_Tordesillas.

Following this treaty, a series of seafaring expeditions intensified, ushering in the Age of Exploration, which was punctuated by the voyages of Vasco de Gama, who discovered a direct sea route to India, Ferdinand Magellan, who was first to circumnavigate the world, and Hernando Cortez, who encountered and successfully occupied the Aztec world. Eventually, the Dutch, British, French, and a host of European countries joined the fray. In storied narratives, the objectives of such exploration was to open up new trade routes, secure much-needed spices and supplies that were unavailable in Europe, and evangelize the Christian faith (Chanda, 2007). But, in actual events, there was a dark side to exploration when initial motivations for trade and exchange gave way to plunder and conquests (Isbister, 2006). The age of colonial occupation and imperialism had set in.

John Isbister, in *Promises Not Kept: Poverty and the Betrayal of Third World Development*, argues outright:

Imperialism let loose the social forces that generated the poverty that is the current common denominator of third world countries. It created the national boundaries of most third world countries. It provided their national languages. It was the source of the ideologies that drive many of the political movements of the third world. It laid out the trade patterns and transportation networks that frame third world economies. It called forth the plantations, the mines, and the primary local crafts and manufactures. It pulled millions into urban slums and posed opportunities for new elites to accumulate wealth and power. The imperialists brought with them public health measures that lowered mortality and caused unprecedented population explosion in the third world. (2006: 66)

The extent to which this assertion applies to Southeast Asia and countries that comprise ASEAN is varied and complex, ranging from arms-length trading relations to oppressive subjugation, but there is no denial that colonialization was both disruptive and transformative. Its far-reaching ramifications extend to the volatility of ASEAN economies and the nuances of political commitment that can influence the future dynamics of ASEAN regional integration.

In the case of Brunei, the country experienced the full spectrum from simple trading relations with the Portuguese to military skirmishes with Spain and eventual occupation by the British from 1888 to 1984.[3] Cambodia started off as a protectorate of France that culminated in French Indochina, which gained independence during World War II. With the establishment of the Dutch East India Company in 1602, the Dutch occupied Indonesia up to the time of World War II, specifically in 1945,

---

[3] See Lim (2004: 8–11). This section also draws from various Wikipedia accounts on each of the ten countries.

when Indonesia formally declared independence. Long a protectorate of France, Laos became an independent country in 1953. Following the unification of various countries into the Pagan Empire, Myanmar (Burma) became a province of India under British rule in 1824, but became independent in 1948. The Portuguese, Dutch, and British took turns occupying Malaysia, but not before the passage of Muslims and the adoption of Islam had taken root. The Philippines traces its early colonial roots to Spain with the arrival of Ferdinand Magellan in 1521, and the country remained under Spanish rule up until 1898, when the Americans defeated Spain and occupied the country until 1945, when it declared formal independence as a sovereign nation. Singapore emerged as a trading outpost under the auspices of British Sir Stamford Raffles in 1818 and was a part of the Federation of Malaysia before racial tensions led to the country's expulsion in 1965. Vietnam was under the French up until 1954, when the country was demarcated into the North and the South, with North Vietnam effectively defeating the French and the United States in 1973. Thailand was the only country that did not experience colonial rule because European powers felt it necessary to keep the country neutral in colonial affinity in anticipation of future wars and disagreements (Lim, 2004).

As indicated earlier, colonialism has been both disruptive and transformational. The disruption and transformation of geographical and territorial boundaries, ethnicity and languages, indigenous cultural ethos, and economic landscape, as articulated by Isbister (2006) and other analysts, can be considered first-order effects. Even so, these effects have extended to eventual changes in Southeast Asia following colonial rule. On the political front, it is not difficult to ignore the influence of European legacies on the ensuing cultures of ASEAN nations. The warring factions of communists and noncommunist rules were a staple in the development of Cambodia, Malaysia, Laos, Vietnam, and Indonesia – all of which led to tensions, uncertainties, and temporary alliances. Indonesia's policy of *konfrontasi* cast suspicions and unrest in the development of the Federation of Malaysia. The Philippines' claim to Sabah stemmed from the country's refusal to recognize Britain's partition in 1962. Tensions were heightened with fears of a communist bloc led by Vietnam, with occasional intrusions by China. Vietnam's invasion of Cambodia and the concerns relating to Myanmar's membership exacerbated uncertainties about the future of ASEAN. In fact, the fear of communism was one of many driving forces that propelled the idea of ASEAN (Lim, 2004; Acharya, 2012).

From a cultural perspective, it is difficult to ignore the influence of Britain on Myanmar, Brunei, Malaysia, and Singapore; the Spanish legacy of Catholicism in the Philippines; the effects of French rule on Vietnam and Laos; language displacement in the Philippines and Vietnam; and the secular ideologies of the Dutch in Indonesia (Lim, 2004; Acharya, 2012). Even with the departure of the colonialists, and the upsurge of nationalism that led to the independence of several countries within ASEAN after World War II, the adverse consequences of prior colonialism were reflected in territorial disputes and intramural skirmishes. These events following colonial rule – actions and policies by Asia's local politicians and leaders – can be understood as second-order effects of colonialism.

Historical Assumptions and Premises Underlying Colonialism

In all, one pervasive legacy is economic, specifically decades of resource extraction that effectively transformed the system of agriculture in Southeast Asia. Consistent with similar patterns of colonialization in the rest of the world, the impact of colonialism was deeply etched in European ideologies, notably the doctrines of free trade and specialization (Lim, 2004; Isbister, 2006:87).

In the context of colonialism, specialization was understood in terms of resource extraction of spices and materials that were either imported by trade or expropriated by force from the native colonies (Isbister, 2006:87-88). Most colonizers had little or no regard for the well-being of local laborers who were drawn off their indigenous habitats in order to extract spices and materials for their colonizers (Bown, 2010). Nor were the colonizers particularly sensitive to the extent to which extraction marginalized the richness of agrarian fields. For most colonizers, the developing world was the source of important inputs to a fledgling manufacturing sector that was becoming prominent in Europe, particularly England, on the eve of the First Industrial Revolution (Acharya, 2012:118-119).

In a much acclaimed thesis titled "World Systems Theory" (1974, 1980, 2004), Marxist sociologist Immanuel Wallerstein approaches colonialism from the perspective of Dependency Theory. He argues that there is no such thing as the first, second, or third world, but one "world system" comprised of a systemic configuration of exchanges, dependency, and transactions. The organizing logic is based on the "dichotomy of capital and labor" and the endless "accumulation of capital" by capitalists. The capitalists, in this sense, refer to colonialists who extracted resources from peripheral countries (the third world) to bolster the manufacturing capability of the core countries (developed economies, primarily from

Europe). Extraction was by no means limited to the expropriation of natural resources but also constituted work arrangements, such as the *encomienda* and *hacendado*, that curtailed the basic sustenance (food) production for natives by decreeing that they had to spend a significant portion of their work attending to extraction of crops and minerals for export to the core countries (Isbister, 2006). Such far-reaching effects are manifested in the current state of agriculture and industrialization, as we will discuss in the next section.

Post–Colonial Era Secondary Effects

The modernist construction of the region of Southeast Asia can be traced to the appointment of Lord Louis Mountbatten as Supreme Commander of the South East Asia Military Command in 1943 as the Allies sought to reorganize their military operations in that part of the world (Deutch, Burrell, & Kann, 1957, cited by Roberts, 2012:34). At the time, the countries were regarded as a region but simply because of their geographic proximity and contiguity in an overall military context. Actually, these countries were exceedingly diverse not only in terms of culture, political regimes, religion, demography, institutions, and tradition but also in their affinity to the Allies or to Japan/Germany, partly as a consequence of their colonial past.

Over time, the Southeast Asia label morphed from a fledgling and nascent mosaic to a forged collectivity of common aspirations, ranging from an aspirant "security community" to an "economic union." Even so, scholars have disputed claims that ASEAN currently meets the requirements of a security community (Roberts, 2012), and it is agreed that even with impressive gains in regional economic integration, ASEAN will hardly be functionally equivalent to the European Union (Inama & Sim, 2015). As such, how might we appraise the potential of regional integration for ASEAN in light of its current state of economic development?

The aftermath of World War II ushered in the end of European, Japanese, and American colonialism and a surge of nationalism, a mix of deepening distrust of former colonizers along with security treatises with some of them, and polarizing elements resulting from the emerging Cold War period (Acharya, 2012). This subject is developed at length by Acharya (2012), and elements of his argument are presented herein for perspective. Released from the yoke of colonialism, the newly independent countries in the region unleashed fervent nationalistic ideals that reflected their country's needs and aspirations. Even so, such aspirations did not reach regionalist goals, as "Southeast Asian leaders (tended) to use regionalism as a tool of partisan ideology rather than of collective identity" (Acharya, 2012: 106). The decolonization process, in fact, created fissures among the countries on the appropriate alignment with former colonizers on security and economic issues. Thailand (although not colonized) and the Philippines secured security with the United States and proceeded to adopt free-market economic policies that contrasted with those of Vietnam, Cambodia, Laos, and Myanmar, which leaned more toward socialist/communist stances (Acharya, 2012).

In summary, while the topic of regionalism was occasionally invoked, if not used as a crucible of advocacy by some countries, its meaning was often obscured by partisan elements, self-serving nationalistic sentiments, and differing assumptions about economic development (Acharya, 2012). Eventually, such differences and notably the lessons borne by the Vietnam War led to a common realization that the key to a prosperous region, if not to the well-being of each country in the region, was economic growth and development. This was premised by a more widely acclaimed belief that the threat to the region was less a matter of external intervention, one that held steadily in the Cold War era, than one of internal strife instigated by extremism and separatists, regardless of ideology, that could only be rectified over time by economic transformation (Acharya, 2012).

The Founding of ASEAN

Earlier, we discussed the historical background that distinguished between primary effects, or the consequences of the colonial legacy, and secondary effects, or the aftermath of post-war independence that engendered a newfound wave of nationalism that was couched in the previous Japanese occupation and kindled by the emerging fissures between the U.S.-led pro-democracy free market and the Soviet-led socialist and communist blocs, now popularly referred to as the Cold War.

The Japanese occupation, as brutal as it was, stoked some sense of consciousness and unity for a previously disparate region in its proclamation of an East Asia Co-Prosperity Base (Beeson, 2009; Acharya, 2012). The intense rivalry between the United States and the Soviet Union had cast a dark shadow, notably with the outbreak of the 1950 Korean War and the Vietnam War (1955–1975), as well as the fear of China's intransigence toward its highly vulnerable neighbors. Moreover, the United States had eschewed a blanket security policy such as NATO had adopted in Europe, and instead opted for bilateral military agreements with military bases in selected countries, which had the consequence, intentionally or otherwise, of realigning the countries in terms of ideology (Beeson, 2009).

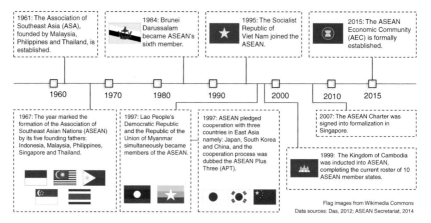

Exhibit 2.1 ASEAN: A Historical Brief

A fledgling movement toward some form of regional security against communist aggression took the form of the Southeast Asia Treaty Organization (SEATO) in 1954 that included the United States. Moreover, regional outbreaks, such as the territorial dispute between the Philippines and Malaysia regarding Sabah and the conflict between Indonesia and Malaysia on the formation of the Federation of Malaya, accentuated the urgency for some type of alliance based on security groupings. These groupings included the Association for Southeast Asia in 1961 (Malaysia, the Philippines, and Thailand) and MAPHILINDO (Malaysia, the Philippines, and Indonesia) in 1963. In all, while these "experiments" in regional security arrangements did not result in successes, they did pave the way for the establishment of ASEAN in 1967 (see Box 2.1 at the conclusion of this chapter).

While it is widely acknowledged that ASEAN was initially a product of security concerns, specifically the threat of communism, the union represented a confluence of several precipitating events described earlier. It is likewise noted that there was a period of inactivity lasting close to a decade following this inaugural meeting in 1967. The resuscitation of ASEAN was ignited by the Vietnam War, and its inclusive policy, oriented toward non-interference and consensus building (called the ASEAN Way), led to the membership of other countries in the region (see Exhibit 2.1). Even so, the full maturation of ASEAN from a loose coalition of countries with differing views of regionalism to a stronger collectivity committed to regional economic development did not occur until later, and this was shaped by some important events. Nowhere was this as particularly accentuated as in the aftermath of the 1997 Asian Crisis, a subject we turn to in the next section.

The 1997 Asian Financial Crisis – Aftermath

For most observers, the interlocutors in the region were blindsided by events that precipitated the Asian financial crisis. As with most crises, the events that led to it were inauspicious: the roots of the crisis can be traced to significantly large financial (capital) flows that had poured into the region, presumably for investment purposes (Goldstein, 1998). In this context, the success of Asian countries, specifically their reputation as manufacturing powerhouses, had also sowed the seeds of an imminent downfall. Specifically, the spectacular growth of Japan and South Korea had earned them accolades, prompting overzealous pundits to prematurely declare the twenty-first century to be an "Asian Century."

With enormous financial inflows, financial bubbles were being built underneath the thin veneer of prosperous real estate and other types of asset valuations. What had shifted was a flawed transformation of Asia from a production and manufacturing behemoth to a Western-type financial system bereft of supportive financial infrastructures (Delhaise, 1998).

The crisis started in the real estate sector with the fall of the Thai baht following an unsuccessful attempt by the government to issue its foreign currency reserves to support its fixed exchange rate. This failure raised alarm signals that had investors taking capital out of the region, activities that further weakened currencies and led to subsequent asset deflation (Delhaise, 1998; Goldstein, 1998). The paranoia that followed resembled a "contagion effect" that spread throughout the region and extended further to Russia and Brazil. It is estimated that Indonesia lost 80 percent of its value, followed by lesser but likewise consequential slumps in Malaysia, the Philippines, South Korea, Hong Kong, and Singapore (Lim, 2004). Similarly, Vietnam, Laos, and Cambodia lost opportunities in foreign direct investment (Lim, 2004; Acharya, 2012). Overall growth rates had dropped precipitously to –7.5 percent in 1998, accentuating what the World Bank called "the biggest setback for poverty reduction in East Asia for several decades" (Acharya, 2012: 243).

Even more notable were sharp differences among the countries in reaction to the crisis that afflicted them. South Korea reluctantly conceded to the World Bank's reform programs, as did Thailand and Indonesia, while Malaysia defiantly rejected what Prime Minister Mahatir Mohammed considered misdirected medicine, given his firm conviction that Western developed countries were primarily responsible for the crisis. The ensuing events led to the departure of Indonesian President Suharto in the wake of widespread riots.

Currently, it is acknowledged that the crisis undermined regional integration, the region's international stature, and most certainly the confidence of ASEAN countries in forging a stronger collective identity (Lim, 2004). Eventually, some of the countries in East Asia, notably China, would counter by building up foreign reserves as buffer to defend its currency against future crises. Even so, the paradox of learning is that while the crisis undermined the region's ability to protect itself from significant external globalizing forces, it also solidified a resolve to improve national economic performance through a greater urgency for inter-regional cooperation, such as was exemplified in ASEAN. Now thirty years removed from the financial crisis, we turn attention to the current economic development and performance of each ASEAN country.

ASEAN Economies

In this section, we discuss three aspects of economic development that apply to the ten ASEAN economies. Some of these aspects originate from colonialism, although they are certainly not determined by such legacy. Other aspects are constituted in the years following colonial rule, in which a wide variation in political regimes and economic development has taken place. The three aspects are (1) the economic divide in development between clusters of ASEAN countries, (2) the convergence and divergence of trade among ASEAN countries, and (3) the disparities in institutional development among ASEAN countries. Although the three aspects are intertwined in practice, they are discussed separately in order to underscore our core arguments.

The Economic Divide

Any casual stroll through the major capitals of ASEAN countries will invariably reveal a sharp disparity in development. In many cases, an observer will see cohabitation of richly adorned hotels, residences, and official buildings alongside clusters of shabby and makeshift habitats and impoverished surroundings. Such differences are not confined to any given country, but there is a clear demarcation of economic development across the ASEAN countries. An overview of national economies for Southeast Asia (2013) is provided in Exhibit 2.2.

Much like in the European Union, although not nearly as severe in terms of consequences, the uneven level of economic development

Country	Population	Surface area (in sq. km)	GDP (in million US$)[1]	GDP, PPP (in million international $)	GDP per capita (in US$)[2]	GDP per capita, PPP (in US$)[1]	Average annual GDP growth rates, 2009-2013	Export as percentage of GDP, 2009-2013	Foreign Direct Investment (in million US$)	Inflation rate (%, as of 2014)[3]
Brunei	417,784	5,770	16,117.5	29,987	39,679	73,775.0	3.0%	78.2%	895.00	−0.2
Cambodia	15,135,169	181,040	15,511.1	46,027	1,047	3,081.8	5.4%	57.2%	1,345.04	3.9
Indonesia	249,865,631	1,910,930	860,849.5	2,388,997	3,467	9,467.1	5.8%	24.6%	23,344.32	6.4
Laos	6,769,727	236,800	10,283.2	32,644	1,505	4,531.6	8.4%	36.0%	426.67	4.2
Malaysia	29,716,965	330,800	312,071.6	693,535	10,420	23,089.0	4.2%	88.6%	11,582.68	3.1
Myanmar	53,259,018	676,590	54,661.2	221,479[4]	916	3,464.4	5.9%*	n.a.	2,254.60	5.9
Philippines	98,393,574	300,000	269,024.0	643,088	2,707	6,403.8	5.4%	31.6%	3,663.92	4.1
Singapore	5,399,200	716	297,941.3	425,259	55,182	78,761.9	5.4%	195.4%	63,772.32	1.0
Thailand	67,010,502	513,120	387,573.8	964,518	5,678	14,131.6	3.2%	73.0%	12,649.75	1.9
Viet Nam	89,708,900	330,951	171,219.3	474,958	1,909	5,314.7	5.4%	75.6%	8,900.00	4.1
ASEAN	**615,676,470**	**4,486,717**	**2,395,252.5**	**5,920,492**	**3,837**	**9,389.8**				

Note: All figures are as of the year 2013 unless otherwise indicated.

Sources: World Bank
[1] ASEAN Statistics Publications (ASEAN Secretariat, 2014)   [4] International Monetary Fund (IMF) World Economic Outlook
[2] AEC Chartbook 2014 (ASEAN Secretariat, 2014)   Database April 2015
[3] Asian Development Bank (ADB) Basic Statistics 2015   * IMF estimate

Exhibit 2.2 Southeast Asia: Overall Picture

constitutes one principal challenge to ASEAN. Because ASEAN countries are diverse in terms of factor endowments, any type of regional integration is not likely to improve individual economies in the short run (Lim, 2004:41). The ASEAN economic charter appears to be cognizant of this condition in recognizing the evolving progression of each individual country without political interference from other members. This approach toward non-interference with a commitment to consultation is popularly known as the "ASEAN Way" – an issue that we revisit in Chapter 11. Moreover, there is a distinction between the ASEAN 6 (Singapore, Malaysia, Thailand, the Philippines, Indonesia, and Vietnam) and the CLMV (Cambodia, Laos, Myanmar, and formerly, Vietnam) blocs.

Economic development is closely related to rates of growth of GDP and related indicators for the region (Exhibit 2.3). In terms of countries, Singapore and Brunei have GDPs that compare favorably with advanced economies. Thailand, Indonesia, Malaysia, and the Philippines have shown impressive gains in recent years (see Exhibit 2.4).

ASEAN countries are noteworthy, in general, in terms of their large populations (see Exhibit 2.2). A popular belief is that economic growth

Recent economic indicators	2009	2010	2011	2012	2013
GDP at current prices (in billion US$)	1,538.2	1,898.1	2,204.6	2,333.7	2,395.3
GDP PPP (in billion international $)*	4,419.1	4,803.7	5,140.1	5,553.8	5,920.5
GDP per capita (in US$)	2,610.1	3,161.9	3,619.1	3,781.3	3,837.0
GDP per capita PPP(in international $)	4,901	5,221	5,520	5,869	9,616
Growth of GDP (% change yoy)	2.0	7.6	4.9	5.9	5.2
Current account balance (% GDP)	7.0	6.1	5.4	2.7	2.2
Inflation (% per year)	2.7	4.1	5.5	3.8	4.2

ASEAN's principal export destinations (2013)		ASEAN's principal import sources (2013)	
1. China	12.0%	1. China	16.0%
2. EU-28	9.8%	2. EU-28	9.8%
3. Japan	9.7%	3. Japan	9.5%
4. United States of America	9.0%	4. United States of America	7.4%
5. Hong Kong (SAR of China)	6.5%	5. Republic of Korea	6.6%

Sources: ASEAN Statistics Publications (ASEAN Secretariat, 2014)
             AEC Chartbook 2014 (ASEAN Secretariat, 2014)
             Asian Development Outlook 2014 (Asian Development Bank, 2014)

*Calculated using data from World Bank and IMF World Economic Outlook Database (April 2015)

Exhibit 2.3 A Promising Region

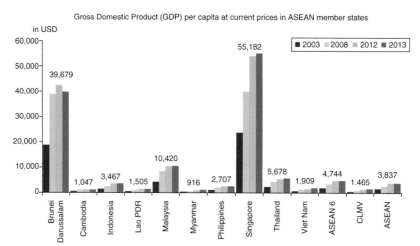

Gross Domestic Product (GDP) per capita at current prices in ASEAN member states

GDP per capita of the Member States varied extremely, ranging from US$55,000 to less than US$1,000 in 2013. Singapore and Brunei Darussalam posted a GDP per capita of above US$35,000 while Myanmar's GDP per capita stood at less than US$1,000. Meanwhile, GDP per capita in Indonesia, Malaysia, Philippines and Thailand ranged from US$2,700 to US$10,400.

Notes: Myanmar's data is based on the exchange rate in the IMF-WEO database of April 2014, which is US$1–965 kyats (for 2013).

Source of data: ASEAN Secretariat Database and IMF World Economic Outlook Database April 2014

Adapted from the AEC Chartbook 2014
© ASEAN Secretariat

Exhibit 2.4 A Mixed Bag

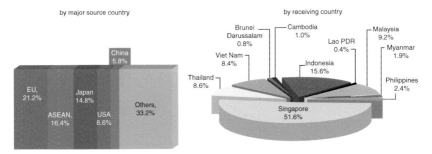

Net inflows of foreign direct investment (FDI) to ASEAN, 2009–2013

by major source country

by receiving country

FDI inflows from EU-28 and Japan accounted for about 36 percent of the total FDI inflows in ASEAN. Singapore received more than 50 percent of the FDI inflows in the regions, followed by Indonesia (with 15.6 percent), Malaysia (with 9.2 percent), Thailand (with 8.6 percent), and Viet Nam (with 8.4 percent).

Notes: Data for 2012–2013 are preliminary figures. Lao PDR's data on 'by source country' are not yet available; intra-/extra-ASEAN breakdowns for 2012 were estimated by the ASEAN Secretariat.

Source of data: ASEAN FDI Database

Adapted from the AEC Chartbook 2014

Exhibit 2.5 Cumulative FDI Net Inflow to ASEAN

is more likely spurred by a larger population because of its greater potential for marketing and development (Lim, 2004:3–4). However, although population growth might foreshadow development, this goal is not likely to occur without thoughtful measures to reduce poverty and income inequality (Lim, 2004:15–16). If poverty persists, then economic growth could be stunted with even more possibility of economic decline.

Foreign direct investment (FDI) is generally considered to improve a recipient's welfare to the extent that capital spurs domestic business, enhances local managerial skills and capabilities, increases labor productivity, and leaves a significant residue of financial resources to the recipient (Lim, 2004: 137–138). In the case of ASEAN, a good portion of FDI emanates from the EU and Japan, and Singapore is the favored recipient (Exhibit 2.5). This is not altogether surprising in light of Singapore's liberal policies on foreign investment that can be contrasted with more restrictive policies by other ASEAN member countries (Lim, 2004:137).

Convergence and Divergence of Trade

In classical and neoclassical economics, it is widely accepted that trade is beneficial for all participating countries, particularly if the basis of trade is rooted in specialization and comparative advantage. Because a common market is one of the cornerstones of the ASEAN Economic Community, trade is not simply discretionary but an imperative. In this

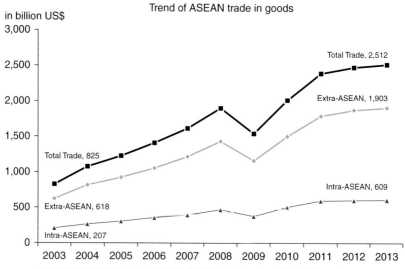

Exhibit 2.6 Intra-ASEAN Trade Flows

section, we discuss the propensity of ASEAN countries to trade and the extent to which intra-ASEAN trade has been commended thus far.

In Exhibit 2.6, we present the trend of ASEAN trade in goods. What is noteworthy is that extra- or inter-ASEAN trade between ASEAN and other countries far outpaces intra-ASEAN trade, or those within the ASEAN region itself. In Exhibit 2.7, we present specific information on intra- and inter-ASEAN trade per member country. A significant amount of intra-ASEAN trade is between Singapore and Malaysia – an issue we revisit in Chapter 11. It is not surprising that there is a clear divide between the ASEAN 5 (Thailand, Singapore, Malaysia, Indonesia, and the Philippines) that trade more extensively and the CLMV countries (Cambodia, Laos, Myanmar, and Vietnam). In Exhibit 2.8, statistics on intra-ASEAN trade are provided for priority areas, notably electronics and to a lesser extent, automobiles.

In Exhibits 2.9 and 2.10, statistics on ASEAN merchandise trade are presented for each member-country. Perhaps unsurprisingly, Singapore leads in merchandise exports, although Thailand, Malaysia, Indonesia, and Vietnam have made impressive gains recently. Compared to commercial merchandise that is visible by transport logistics and computed

Country	Intra-ASEAN trade		Extra-ASEAN trade		Total trade (in million US$)
	Value (in million US$)	Share to total trade (%)	Value (in million US$)	Share to total trade (%)	
Brunei	4,488.0	29.8	10,569.2	70.2	15,057.2
Cambodia	4,119.1	22.5	14,205.0	77.5	18,324.2
Indonesia	94,661.8	25.6	274,518.7	74.4	369,180.5
Lao PDR	3,729.3	63.4	2,155.6	36.6	5,884.9
Malaysia	119,032.2	27.4	315,196.5	72.6	434,228.7
Myanmar	9,869.0	42.1	13,576.5	57.9	23,445.4
Philippines	22,786.2	19.1	96,322.7	80.9	119,108.9
Singapore	206,672.3	26.4	576,593.2	73.6	783,265.5
Thailand	103,668.6	21.7	374,578.7	78.3	478,247.3
Viet Nam	39,531.9	14.9	225,242.1	85.1	264,774.0
ASEAN	**608,558.3**	**24.2**	**1,902,958.2**	**75.8**	**2,511,516.5**

Source: ASEAN Statistics (ASEAN Secretariat, 2014)

Exhibit 2.7 Summary of Intra-ASEAN and Extra-ASEAN Trade (2013)

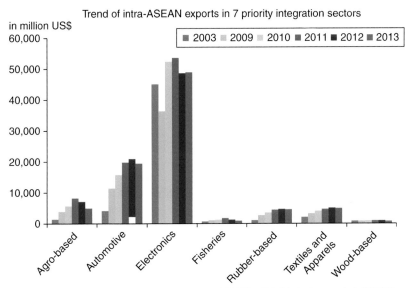

Trend of intra-ASEAN exports in 7 priority integration sectors

in million US$

2003 2009 2010 2011 2012 2013

In 2013, intra-ASEAN exports of electronic products were valued at US$48.9 billion, slightly higher than the year-ago level of US48.6 billion. The share of electronic products in intra-ASEAN exports has declined from 39 percent in 2003 to 15 percent in 2013.

Source of data: ASEAN Trade Database

Adapted from the AEC Chartbook 2014
© ASEAN Secretariat

Exhibit 2.8 Intra-ASEAN Trade in Priority Areas

	Imports (in million USD)						Exports (in million USD)					
	2008	2009	2010	2011	2012	2013	2008	2009	2010	2011	2012	2013
Brunei	2,572	2,449	2,538	3,629	3,572	3,612	10,319	7,200	8,907	12,465	13,001	11,448
Cambodia	6,508	5,830	6,791	9,300	11,000	13,000	4,708	4,196	5,143	6,704	7,838	9,300
Indonesia	127,538	93,786	135,323	176,201	190,383	187,294	139,606	119,646	158,074	200,788	188,496	183,344
Laos	1,403	1,461	2,060	2,404	3,055	3,020	1,092	1,053	1,746	2,190	2,271	2,264
Malaysia	156,348	123,757	164,622	187,473	196,393	206,014	199,414	157,244	198,612	228,086	227,538	228,276
Myanmar	4,256	4,348	4,760	9,019	9,181	12,043	6,882	6,662	8,661	9,238	8,877	11,233
Philippines	60,420	45,878	58,468	63,693	65,350	65,097	49,078	38,436	51,496	48,305	52,099	56,698
Singapore	319,780	245,785	310,791	365,770	379,723	373,016	338,176	269,832	351,867	409,503	408,393	410,250
Thailand	179,225	133,709	182,921	228,787	249,988	250,723	177,778	152,422	193,306	222,576	229,236	228,530
Viet Nam	80,714	69,949	84,839	106,750	113,780	132,033	62,685	57,096	72,237	96,906	114,529	132,033

Source: UNESCAP Statistical Yearbook for Asia and the Pacific 2014

Exhibit 2.9 Imports and Exports of Merchandise in ASEAN, 2008–2013

	Imports (% of GDP)						Exports (% of GDP)					
	2008	2009	2010	2011	2012	2013	2008	2009	2010	2011	2012	2013
Brunei	17.9	22.8	20.5	21.7	21.1	21.0	71.7	67.1	72.0	74.7	76.7	66.6
Cambodia	62.9	56.1	60.4	72.5	78.4	86.5	45.5	40.3	45.7	52.3	55.8	61.9
Indonesia	25.0	17.4	19.1	20.8	21.7	20.3	27.4	22.2	22.3	23.7	21.5	19.8
Laos	26.5	26.2	30.6	29.8	33.6	30.6	20.7	18.8	25.9	27.2	25.0	23.0
Malaysia	67.7	61.2	66.5	64.9	64.4	64.6	86.4	77.7	80.2	78.9	74.7	71.5
Myanmar	16.5	13.2	11.5	16.3	15.4	19.0	26.6	20.2	20.9	16.7	14.9	17.7
Philippines	34.7	27.3	29.3	28.4	26.1	24.4	28.2	22.8	25.8	21.6	20.8	21.2
Singapore	167.8	130.2	134.1	137.7	137.3	130.3	177.4	142.9	151.9	154.2	147.7	143.3
Thailand	61.8	47.8	54.1	62.7	64.8	63.0	61.3	54.5	57.2	61.0	59.4	57.5
Viet Nam	81.4	66.0	73.2	78.8	73.0	80.5	63.2	53.9	62.3	71.5	73.5	80.5

Source: UNESCAP Statistical Yearbook for Asia and the Pacific 2014

Exhibit 2.10 Imports and Exports of Merchandise in ASEAN (% of GDP), 2008–2013

accordingly, commercial services are less defined (Lim, 2004). Generally, services include and transportation (land, air, and sea), travel (acquired goods for lodging, health, education, and others), and commercial services (communication services, construction, insurance, financial transactions, and business-related services) (see Lim, 2004: 166; also see AEC Chartbook, ASEAN Secretariat, 2014). In Exhibit 2.11, trade statistics are presented for the ASEAN region. In assessing trade services by each

	Imports (in million USD)						Exports (in million USD)					
	2008	2009	2010	2011	2012	2013	2008	2009	2010	2011	2012	2013
Brunei	1,403	1,434	1,612	1,825	n.a.	n.a.	867	915	1,054	1,209	n.a.	n.a.
Cambodia	1,036	909	972	1,323	1,546	1,768	1,645	1,525	1,669	2,213	2,545	2,786
Indonesia	28,245	22,896	26,089	31,323	33,887	34,855	15,247	13,156	16,766	20,690	23,113	22,343
Laos	108	136	263	331	341	n.a.	402	397	511	550	577	n.a.
Malaysia	30,270	27,472	32,320	37,976	42,895	45,206	30,321	28,769	31,801	35,851	37,615	39,930
Myanmar	617	617	789	1,090	n.a.	n.a.	303	313	363	612	n.a.	n.a.
Philippines	8,557	9,020	11,864	12,085	14,009	14,628	9,717	13,951	17,607	18,740	20,322	21,685
Singapore	87,442	83,454	100,571	113,286	123,849	128,659	99,249	75,552	94,489	109,330	117,348	122,447
Thailand	45,926	36,515	45,029	52,136	53,074	55,297	33,037	30,157	34,326	41,573	49,643	58,975
Viet Nam	7,956	8,187	9,921	11,859	12,520	13,200	7,006	5,766	7,460	8,691	9,620	10,500

Source: UNESCAP Statistical Yearbook for Asia and the Pacific 2014

Exhibit 2.11 Imports and Exports of Services in ASEAN, 2008–2013

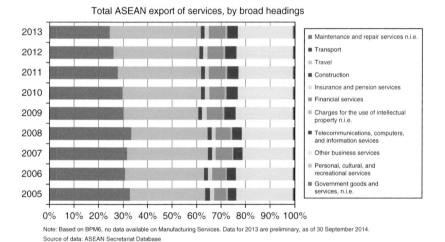

Note: Based on BPM6, no data available on Manufacturing Services. Data for 2013 are preliminary, as of 30 September 2014.
Source of data: ASEAN Secretariat Database

Adapted from the AEC Chartbook 2014
© ASEAN Secretariat

Exhibit 2.12 ASEAN Trade in Services

ASEAN member-country, with the exception of Singapore, trade in services is much lower relative to merchandise among ASEAN countries (Exhibit 2.12).

To the extent that ASEAN countries engage in trade, what is the nature of their exports across the world? Historically, as a result of their colonial legacy, the primary exports tended toward key commodities (Lim, 2004;

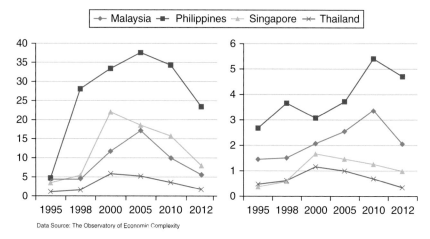

Data Source: The Observatory of Economic Complexity

Exhibit 2.13 Integrated Circuits and Semiconductor Devices as Percentage of Exports in Four ASEAN Countries (1995–2012)

Acharya, 2012). As discussed earlier in the chapter, the colonial rulers viewed their colonies, inclusive of Southeast Asia, as sources of raw materials for their consumption and industrialization (Isbister, 2006; Acharya, 2012). Up until the 1980s, this pattern of trade appears to be upheld, and we revisit this issue in Chapter 11 to discuss broader implications for ASEAN.

Moving forward into the 2000s up to the present, there is a discernible shift in the types of exports, with semiconductors, integrated circuits, electronic valves, and tubes becoming more prominent in Malaysia, the Philippines, Singapore, and Thailand (Exhibit 2.13). For some scholars, this is indicative of progress by these countries in their own industrialization and shift away from agricultural products (Lim, 2004: 168–69).

Even so, a closer examination of the nature of integrated circuits, for example, discloses a strategy by major importers (mostly semiconductor and computer firms in the United States and other developed countries) to situate more labor-intensive elements of the value chain in ASEAN countries and others (Taiwan, China). Lower-cost workers are employed to attend to meticulous pin assembly in ASEAN countries with the ultimate goal of completing the final stages in the United States (and elsewhere), in which higher value added and profits are reaped. When finished products are reimported back to ASEAN countries, the latter do not truly capitalize on the full value and purported contributions of their labor input.

As business process outsourcing (mostly call centers) has shifted from India to the Philippines and, to a smaller extent, Malaysia, a similar pattern exists where higher value added and profits are still retained by major multinationals from developed countries. Moreover, as in the case of the Philippines, in particular, the gains from outsourcing are generally confined to local firms and their attendant labor pool. However, recent developments in knowledge process outsourcing, which include higher value-added services like market intelligence, business analytics, and legal services, may soon change the dynamics for countries linked to the global value chain (Cattaneo, Gereffi, & Staritz, 2010). Nonetheless, the jury is still out on whether genuine "trickle-down effects" can adequately improve income inequality and overall economic prosperity. In all, there are implications for the establishment of regional value networks that rank among the key objectives of ASEAN – a discussion that we defer to Chapter 11.

Disparities in Institutional Development

As previewed in Chapter 1, economist Douglass North won the 1993 Nobel Award (shared with William Fogel) for his pioneering work on the role of institutions in economic development. In a widely acclaimed paper (1991), North defined institutions as "humanly devised constraints that structure political, economic and social interactions."[4] In his formulation, institution are of two types: *formal* (constitutions, laws, property rights) and *informal* (cultural norms and beliefs relating to "sanctions, taboos, customs, traditions, and code of conduct"). Institutions serve the purpose of creating stability within any society in that they reduce uncertainty and lower transaction costs. However, they can likewise be debilitating if they deter the development of an effective market system of exchange.

Although there has been a spate of studies based on or inspired by North's work, the recent work of management theorists Tarun Khanna and Palepu extended North's thesis to the context of emerging and developing countries. In their formulation, the absence of market-inducing mechanisms, such as the role of major intermediaries, creates "institutional voids" that can stifle economic development. In their work, such voids are defined very generally, extending to simple brokerage relations to wider institutions such as educational systems, openness in the media and major communication structures, and political stability.

---

[4] Quote from https://en.wikipedia.org/wiki/Douglass_North#cite_note-edegan-5 (accessed July 21, 2015).

Country	Enrollment Ratio in Primary Education						Literacy rate (%)
	Total		Girls		Boys		
	1990	2012	1990	2012	1990	2012	
Brunei	91.5 (1991)	95.7	90.4	95.1	92.5	96.2	95.4 (2011 est.)
Cambodia	82.7 (1997)	98.4	75.9	97.0	89.3	99.7	73.9 (2009 est.)
Indonesia	97.9	95.3	95.9	95.9	99.7	94.7	92.8 (2011 est.)
Laos	64.9	95.9	53.9 (1992)	94.9	62.2 (1992)	96.8	72.7 (2005 est.)
Malaysia	96.2 (1994)	97.0 (2005)	96.3	95.0 (2003)	96.0	98.5 (2003)	93.1 (2010 est.)
Myanmar	88.9	114.2 (2010)	85.4	113.6 (2010)	92.3	114.7 (2010)	92.7
Philippines	98.4	88.6 (2009)	97.5	89.5	99.3	87.9	95.4 (2008 est.)
Singapore	103.7	77.9 (2005)	102.3	77.8 (2005)	105.1	78.0 (2005)	95.9 (2010 est.)
Thailand	93.9 (2006)	95.6 (2009)	93.1	94.9	94.6	96.2	93.5 (2005 est.)
Viet Nam	97.9 (1998)	98.2	104.3 (1991)	105.1	105.5 (1991)	104.3	90-95 (2011 est.)

*Literacy rate is defined as the population at the age of 15 years who can read and write. Data from *The CIA World Factbook 2015*.

Sources:
United Nations Millennium Indicators Database Online
Secretariat of the Pacific Community National Minimum Development Indicator Database
National Bureau of Statistics China Statistical Yearbook 2013
Taipei Educational Statistical Indicators Online
UNESCO Institute for Statistics Data Centre
IndexMundi
Trading Economics

Exhibit 2.14 Enrollment Ratio in Primary Education

As applied to ASEAN, two such institutions are important: the level of education, inclusive of the talent pool (or gap), and overall human development. Termed human and social capital, such institutions underscore the importance of the long-term development of technical and social skills that meet the requirements of competition at a global level.

Educational statistics for different ASEAN countries are provided in Exhibit 2.14. The patterns vary, although it is widely regarded that there is a correlation between combined primary, secondary and tertiary education levels with the level of economic development (Lim, 2004). There has been marked improvement in enrollment for most ASEAN countries, as well as favorable literacy rates. The nations with more advanced progressions compare favorably with highly developed countries. Of course, educational levels are not sufficient per se; the type of education and the extent to which education specifically supports the technical, social, and economic requisites of economic development are the core arguments (Lim, 2004: 50–52). To be fair, such requirements apply to developed countries as well as to ASEAN.

In regard to institutional development, there is a broad array of possible measures to address this as it reflects on ASEAN. Even so, we will elect to provide an overall measure in this chapter, and discuss specific institutional voids as they apply to the ASEAN champions later in the book. Specifically, the United Nations Development Programme has developed and published over the years a Human Development Index. This

Country	HDI Index	Rank	HE	ED	IN	IE	GI	PV	EM	LS	TR	MB	EN
Brunei	0.852	30	78.55	8.68	70,883.48	n.a.	n.a.	n.a.	68.1	n.a.	112.54	0.8	22.87
Cambodia	0.584	136	71.92	5.77	2,805.43	0.440	0.505	46.79	85.8	3.9	113.58	−2.3	0.29
Indonesia	0.684	108	70.83	7.51	8,970.35	0.553	0.500	5.90	70.7	5.4	50.07	−0.6	1.80
Laos	0.569	139	68.31	4.58	4,351.27	0.430	0.534	36.82	85.0	4.9	82.27	−2.2	0.29
Malaysia	0.773	62	75.02	9.53	21,823.93	n.a.	0.210	n.a.	65.5	5.9	163.01	3.1	7.67
Myanmar	0.524	150	65.18	3.95	3,998.06	n.a.	0.430	n.a.	83.1	4.4	n.a.	−0.4	0.17
Philippines	0.660	117	68.70	8.88	6,381.44	0.540	0.406	7.26	69.3	5.0	64.79	−1.4	0.87
Singapore	0.901	9	82.32	10.20	72,371.23	n.a.	0.090	n.a.	72.5	6.5	379.14	15.0	2.66
Thailand	0.722	89	74.40	7.32	13,364.30	0.573	0.364	1.01	77.0	6.3	148.83	0.3	4.45
Viet Nam	0.638	121	75.95	5.49	4,892.41	0.543	0.322	6.45	80.9	5.5	179.98	−0.4	1.73

HE = health (life expectancy at birth, in years)   GI = gender inequality index   TR = international trade (% of GDP)
ED = education (mean years of schooling)   PV = poverty rate   MB = mobility (net migration rate per 1,000 persons)
IN = gross national income per capita in PPP $ EM = employment to population ratio EN = environment (CO_2 emissions per capita in tons)
IE = inequality-adjusted HDI   LS = overall life satisfaction index

Source: United Nations Development Programme Human Development Report 2014

Exhibit 2.15 Human Development Index (ASEAN)

index is "a summary measure of average achievement in key dimensions of human development: a long and healthy life, being knowledgeable and having a decent standard of living. The HDI is the geometric mean of normalized indices for each of the three dimensions." Specifically, it assesses life expectancy, an educational component, expected years of schooling, standard of living through gross national income per capita, and other related indices. Data for ASEAN are presented in Exhibit 2.15.

Conclusions

Any region is a product of events that are recorded in institutional histories. Southeast Asia, as a region, has been transformed from prewar colonial occupations to postwar nationalism inhibiting differing visions of regionalism. It is beyond the scope of this chapter to determine the extent to which regional integration, as conceived by scholars of this subject matter, has progressed. Yet the history of struggles in defining a collective identity has led to the founding of ASEAN, which promises collective benefits from economic, political and cultural union when its goals are fully realized (see Box 2.1).

Scholars doubt whether ASEAN has reached the potential of becoming a security community or the standard of genuine regional integration (Roberts, 2012). The extent to which economic progress can be a purveyor of eventual political integration is a question for which the jury is still out. As with any initiative toward integration, however, progress is best described in terms of a moving and evolving target. The degree to which stated goals have already been met, and the challenges of overcoming the remaining obstacles to integration, are discussed in our next chapter.

Box 2.1. The Founding of ASEAN

On August 8, 1967, five leaders – the Foreign Ministers of Indonesia, Malaysia, the Philippines, Singapore, and Thailand – sat down together in the main hall of the Department of Foreign Affairs building in Bangkok, Thailand, and signed a document. By virtue of that document, the Association of Southeast Asian Nations (ASEAN) was born. The five Foreign Ministers who signed it – Adam Malik of Indonesia, Narciso R. Ramos of the Philippines, Tun Abdul Razak of Malaysia, S. Rajaratnam of Singapore, and Thanat Khoman of Thailand – would subsequently be hailed as the founding fathers of probably the most successful inter-governmental organization in the developing world today. And the document that they signed would be known as the ASEAN Declaration.

It was a short, simply worded document containing just five articles. It declared the establishment of an Association for Regional Cooperation among the Countries of Southeast Asia to be known as the Association of Southeast Asian Nations (ASEAN) and spelled out the aims and purposes of that association. These aims and purposes addressed cooperation in the economic, social, cultural, technical, educational, and other fields, as well as the promotion of regional peace and stability through abiding respect for justice and the rule of law and adherence to the principles of the United Nations Charter. It stipulated that the association would be open for participation to all states in the Southeast Asian region subscribing to its aims, principles, and purposes. It proclaimed ASEAN as representing "the collective will of the nations of Southeast Asia to bind themselves together in friendship and cooperation and, through joint efforts and sacrifices, secure prosperity, peace, and freedom for their peoples."

It was while Thailand was brokering reconciliation among Indonesia, the Philippines, and Malaysia over certain disputes that it dawned on the four countries that the moment for regional cooperation had come – or the future of the region would remain uncertain. Recalls one of the two surviving protagonists of that historic process, Thanat

Khoman of Thailand: "At the banquet marking the reconciliation between the three disputants, I broached the idea of forming another organization for regional cooperation with Adam Malik. Malik agreed without hesitation but asked for time to talk with his government and also to normalize relations with Malaysia now that the confrontation was over. Meanwhile, the Thai Foreign Office prepared a draft charter of the new institution. Within a few months, everything was ready. I therefore invited the two former members of the Association for Southeast Asia (ASA), Malaysia and the Philippines, and Indonesia, a key member, to a meeting in Bangkok. In addition, Singapore sent S. Rajaratnam, then Foreign Minister, to see me about joining the new set-up. Although the new organization was planned to comprise only the ASA members plus Indonesia, Singapore's request was favorably considered."

And so in early August 1967, the five Foreign Ministers spent four days in the relative isolation of a beach resort in Bang Saen, a coastal town less than a hundred kilometers southeast of Bangkok. There they negotiated over that document in a decidedly informal manner, which they would later delight in describing as "sports-shirt diplomacy." Yet it was by no means an easy process: Each man brought into the deliberations a historical and political perspective that had no resemblance to that of any of the others. But with goodwill and good humor as often as they huddled at the negotiating table, they finessed their way through their differences as they lined up their shots on the golf course and traded wisecracks on one another's game, a style of deliberation that would eventually become the ASEAN ministerial tradition.

Now, with the rigors of negotiations and the informalities of Bang Saen behind them, with their signatures neatly attached to the ASEAN Declaration, also known as the Bangkok Declaration, it was time for some formalities. The first to speak was the Philippine Secretary of Foreign Affairs, Narciso Ramos, a one-time journalist and long-time legislator who had given up a chance to be Speaker of the Philippine Congress to serve as one of his country's first diplomats. He was then 66 years old and his only son, the future President Fidel V. Ramos, was serving with the Philippine Civic Action Group in embattled Vietnam. He recalled the tediousness of the negotiations that preceded the signing of the Declaration as having "truly taxed the goodwill, the imagination, the patience and understanding of the five participating Ministers." That ASEAN was established at all in spite of these difficulties, he said, meant that its foundations had been solidly laid. And he impressed upon the audience of diplomats, officials, and media people who had witnessed the signing ceremony that a great sense of urgency had prompted the Ministers to go through all that trouble. He spoke darkly of the forces that were arrayed against the survival of the countries of Southeast Asia in those uncertain and critical times.

"The fragmented economies of Southeast Asia," he said, "(with) each country pursuing its own limited objectives and dissipating its meager resources in the overlapping or even conflicting endeavors of sister states carry the seeds of weakness in their incapacity for growth and their self-perpetuating dependence on the advanced, industrial nations. ASEAN, therefore, could marshal the still untapped potentials of this rich region through more substantial united action."

When it was his turn to speak, Adam Malik, Presidium Minister for Political Affairs and Minister for Foreign Affairs of Indonesia, recalled that about a year before, in Bangkok, at the conclusion of the peace talks between Indonesia and Malaysia, he had explored the idea of an organization such as ASEAN with his Malaysian and Thai counterparts. One of the "angry young men" in his country's struggle for independence two decades earlier, Adam Malik was then 50 years old and one of a Presidium of five led by then General Soeharto that was steering Indonesia from the verge of economic and political chaos. He was the Presidium's point man in Indonesia's efforts to mend fences with its neighbors in the wake of an unfortunate policy of confrontation. During the past year, he said, the Ministers had all worked together toward the realization of the ASEAN idea, "making haste slowly, in order to build a new association for regional cooperation."

Adam Malik went on to describe Indonesia's vision of a Southeast Asia developing into "a region which can stand on its own feet, strong enough to defend itself against any negative influence from outside the region." Such a vision, he stressed, was not wishful thinking if the countries of the region effectively cooperated with each other, considering their combined natural resources and manpower. He referred to differences of outlook among the member countries, but those differences, he said, would be overcome through a maximum of goodwill and understanding, faith and realism. Hard work, patience, and perseverance, he added, would also be necessary.

The countries of Southeast Asia should also be willing to take responsibility for whatever happens to them, according to Tun Abdul Razak, the Deputy Prime Minister of Malaysia, who spoke next. In his speech, he conjured a vision of an ASEAN that would include all the countries of Southeast Asia. Tun Abdul Razak was then concurrently his country's Minister of Defence and Minister of National

Development. It was a time when national survival was the overriding thrust of Malaysia's relations with other nations, and so as Minister of Defence, he was in charge of his country's foreign affairs. He stressed that the countries of the region should recognize that unless they assumed their common responsibility to shape their own destiny and to prevent external intervention and interference, Southeast Asia would remain fraught with danger and tension. And unless they took decisive and collective action to prevent the eruption of intra-regional conflicts, the nations of Southeast Asia would remain susceptible to manipulation, one against another.

"We the nations and peoples of Southeast Asia," Tun Abdul Razak said, "must get together and form by ourselves a new perspective and a new framework for our region. It is important that individually and jointly we should create a deep awareness that we cannot survive for long as independent but isolated peoples unless we also think and act together and unless we prove by deeds that we belong to a family of Southeast Asian nations bound together by ties of friendship and goodwill and imbued with our own ideals and aspirations and determined to shape our own destiny." He added that "with the establishment of ASEAN, we have taken a firm and a bold step on that road."

For his part, S. Rajaratnam, a former Minister of Culture of multicultural Singapore who, at that time, served as its first Foreign Minister, noted that two decades of nationalist fervor had not fulfilled the expectations of the people of Southeast Asia for better living standards. If ASEAN were to succeed, he said, then its members would have to marry national thinking with regional thinking.

"We must now think at two levels," Rajaratnam said. "We must think not only of our national interests but posit them against regional interests: that is a new way of thinking about our problems. And these are two different things and sometimes they can conflict. Secondly, we must also accept the fact, if we are really serious about it, that regional existence means painful adjustments to those practices and thinking in our respective countries. We must make these painful and difficult adjustments. If we are not going to do that, then regionalism remains a utopia."

S. Rajaratnam expressed the fear, however, that ASEAN would be misunderstood. "We are not against anything," he said, "not against anybody." And here he used a term that would have an ominous ring even today: balkanization. In Southeast Asia, as in Europe and any part of the world, he said, outside powers had a vested interest in the balkanization of the region. "We want to ensure," he said, "a stable

Southeast Asia, not a balkanized Southeast Asia. And those countries who are interested, genuinely interested, in the stability of Southeast Asia, the prosperity of Southeast Asia, and better economic and social conditions, will welcome small countries getting together to pool their collective resources and their collective wisdom to contribute to the peace of the world."

The goal of ASEAN, then, is to create, not to destroy. The Foreign Minister of Thailand, Thanat Khoman, stressed this when it was his turn to speak. At a time when the Vietnam conflict was raging and American forces seemed forever entrenched in Indochina, he had foreseen their eventual withdrawal from the area and had accordingly applied himself to adjusting Thailand's foreign policy to a reality that would only become apparent more than half a decade later. He must have had that in mind when, on that occasion, he said that the countries of Southeast Asia had no choice but to adjust to the exigencies of the time, to move toward closer cooperation and even integration. Elaborating on ASEAN objectives, he spoke of "building a new society that will be responsive to the needs of our time and efficiently equipped to bring about, for the enjoyment and the material as well as spiritual advancement of our peoples, conditions of stability and progress. Particularly what millions of men and women in our part of the world want is to erase the old and obsolete concept of domination and subjection of the past and replace it with the new spirit of give and take, of equality and partnership. More than anything else, they want to be master of their own house and to enjoy the inherent right to decide their own destiny…"

While the nations of Southeast Asia prevent attempts to deprive them of their freedom and sovereignty, he said, they must first free themselves from the material impediments of ignorance, disease, and hunger. Each of these nations cannot accomplish that alone, but when they join together and cooperate with those who have the same aspirations, these objectives become easier to attain. Then Thanat Khoman concluded, "What we have decided today is only a small beginning of what we hope will be a long and continuous sequence of accomplishments of which we ourselves, those who will join us later and the generations to come, can be proud. Let it be for Southeast Asia, a potentially rich region, rich in history, in spiritual as well as material resources and indeed for the whole ancient continent of Asia, the light of happiness and well-being that will shine over the uncounted millions of our struggling peoples."

The Foreign Minister of Thailand closed the inaugural session of the Association of Southeast Asian Nations by presenting each of his colleagues with a memento. Inscribed on the memento presented to the Foreign Minister of Indonesia was the citation, "In recognition of services rendered by His Excellency Adam Malik to the ASEAN organization, the name of which was suggested by him."

And that was how ASEAN was conceived, given a name, and born. It had been barely 14 months since Thanat Khoman brought up the ASEAN idea in his conversations with his Malaysian and Indonesian colleagues. In about three more weeks, Indonesia would fully restore diplomatic relations with Malaysia, and soon after that with Singapore. That was by no means the end to intra-ASEAN disputes, for soon the Philippines and Malaysia would have a falling out on the issue of sovereignty over Sabah. Many disputes between ASEAN countries persist to this day. But all member countries are deeply committed to resolving their differences through peaceful means and in the spirit of mutual accommodation. Every dispute would have its proper season, but it would not be allowed to get in the way of the task at hand. And at that time, the essential task was to lay the framework of regional dialogue and cooperation.

The two-page Bangkok Declaration not only contains the rationale for the establishment of ASEAN and its specific objectives. It represents the organization's modus operandi of building on small steps and voluntary and informal arrangements toward more binding and institutionalized agreements. All the founding member states and the newer members have stood fast to the spirit of the Bangkok Declaration. Over the years, ASEAN has progressively entered into several formal and legally binding instruments, such as the 1976 Treaty of Amity and Cooperation in Southeast Asia and the 1995 Treaty on the Southeast Asia Nuclear Weapon-Free Base.

Against the backdrop of conflict in then Indochina, the founding fathers had the foresight to build a community of and for all Southeast Asian states. Thus the Bangkok Declaration promulgated that "the Association is open for participation to all States in the Southeast Asian region subscribing to the aforementioned aims, principles and purposes." ASEAN's inclusive outlook has paved the way for community building not only in Southeast Asia but also in the broader Asia Pacific region, where several other inter-governmental organizations now coexist.

The original ASEAN logo presented five brown sheaves of rice stalks, one for each founding member. Beneath the sheaves is the legend "ASEAN" in blue. These are set on a field of yellow encircled by a blue border. Brown stands for strength and stability, yellow for prosperity, and blue for the spirit of cordiality in which ASEAN affairs are conducted. When ASEAN celebrated its 30th anniversary in 1997, the sheaves on the logo had increased to ten – representing all ten countries of Southeast Asia and reflecting the colors of the flags of all of them. In a very real sense, ASEAN and Southeast Asia would then be one and the same, just as the founding fathers had envisioned.

SOURCE: This article is based on the first chapter of *ASEAN at 30*, a publication of the Association of Southeast Asian Nations in commemoration of its 30thAnniversary on August 8, 1997, written by Jamil Maidan Flores and Jun Abad. Reproduced in full with permission.

3   Toward an ASEAN Economic Community

Introduction

While political and economic alliances have proliferated throughout history, economic regional integration – or the aggregation of proximate or geographically clustered countries into trading blocs – is a more recent phenomenon. In fact, it is reported that Machlup (1977) could not locate such a reference before 1942 (El-Agraa, 2011: 1). Since then, regional integration has become popular and prominent, extending to all areas around the world (Bagwell & Staiger, 2002).

Regional integration has been analytically parsed in political/security, economic, and cultural/institutional terms. In practice, they – political and economic, in particular – are inextricably intertwined. Any political decision is bound to have economic repercussions, and vice versa. Even so, it should be recognized that each decision operates in a different timeframe by way of articulation, implementation, and advancement. Notwithstanding, each can provide levers for accelerating the progress of another. For example, any success in economic integration and cooperation can lay the groundwork for political/security, as well as cultural/institutional initiatives in the future (and vice versa).

In this chapter, we focus on the establishment of the Asian Economic Community (AEC), which is one of three pillars of ASEAN regional integration (the others being political and cultural). We discuss the progress of economic goals and milestones, drawing on published work by the ASEAN Secretariat as well as ancillary work by established scholars in the area. Following a discussion of progress – also termed the AEC Scorecard – we provide some implications for the role of the private sector, which lays the groundwork for our subsequent discussion of the ASEAN champions.

Defining Economic Integration

International economic integration is generally defined as "a state of affairs or a process which involves the amalgamation of separate economies into larger free trading regions" (El-Agraa, 2011: 1). International regional integration is typically classified in different structures depending on the degree of intended collaboration and the form of binding commitments.

At the most basic level, a *"free trade area"* (FTA) embodies two or more countries that agree to decrease or eliminate tariffs between them.[1] To reduce the risk of importing goods at zero tariffs in one country and reexporting them elsewhere, the rule of "certificate of origin" is enacted for participants in an FTA.

When free trade is extended to a specified region with defined boundaries but there is a common tariff on imports from nonparticipating countries, this creates a *"customs union."* When countries adopt a common currency, such as the euro, then a "monetary union" ensues as well. Even more inclusive is a *"common market"* that combines characteristics of customs unions but entails that participating countries add on the free movement of labor, services, technology, capital, and other specified elements as well.

To the extent that a common market includes shared currency (*"monetary union"*), which is typically accompanied with the coordination, if not the harmonization, of fiscal and economic policies, such additional steps toward fuller integration are achieved. One such example is the European Community. A *"complete economic integration"* posits the creation of a supranational body to oversee and resolve resolutions and possible disputes. A representative example is the United States.

As will be developed in this chapter, extensions of ASEAN (ASEAN +1, APEC) constitute a special case in that their intent is not to be discriminatory in forming charters that are completely exclusive at the expense of nonparticipating members. For example, the Asia Pacific Economic Cooperation (APEC) is organized in terms of what El-Agraa (2011: 3) terms "open regionalism," which effectively removes trade restrictions on countries that eventually join the forum.

What are the benefits of economic/regional integration? Classical (traditional) conceptions were defined by economist Jacob Viner in his foundational treatise, *Studies in the Theory of International Trade* (1937) and *The Customs Union Issue* (1950) which introduced the differences between trade creation and trade diversion. In Viner's work, trade creation takes place when a customs union leads to tariff reductions and price decreases for all, leading to a net gain for an economic union. Contrariwise, trade diversion takes place when the exchange between two unequal parties within a union occurs with the consequence of having the less efficient

[1] https://en.wikipedia.org/wiki/Economic integration. For a comprehensive treatment, see El-Agraa (2011: 1–3) and Jovanovic (2006: 21–24).

producer offers lower prices within the union but higher prices elsewhere. Nevertheless, Viner left open the possibility that some unions might work while others might not, depending on the calculus of net gain.

Subsequent empirical work attempted to elucidate on factors that induced economic refinements and more refined measures for calculating economic gains. In *The Theory of Economic Integration*, Hungarian economist Bela Balassa demonstrated not only that trade barriers decrease within an economic union but also that factor mobility enhances the demand and potential of integration that follows (Balassa, 1961: 10–15). Further validation comes from ensuing research indicating that countries gain by inclusion in economic unions, but that gains, specifically growth in GDP and productivity, are different for larger than for smaller countries (see Jovanovic, 2006).

While the above studies have focused on the performance effects of members of an economic integration, management guru Michael Porter, in his *The Competitive Advantage of Nations* (1990), accentuates the competitiveness and the gains derived from home-based, contiguous factors, such as (1) factor conditions, (2) demand conditions, (3) related and supporting industries, and (4) firm strategy, structure, and rivalry, and two exogenous parameters: (1) government and (2) chance. Although restricted to the benefits of clusters of industries, not economic unions, Porter's work provides deep insights on how economic integration can capitalize on internal factors within the partnership to develop competitive advantages in the global market. Even so, because Porter's work is heavily skewed toward selected countries and deemphasizes the role of multinationals, there is a question of the generalizability of his prescriptions (see Allio, 1990).

Although the overall effects of economic cooperation and unions tend to be positive, the eventual success of any entity depends on several factors that go beyond purely economic measures. These include political will on the part of the participants, the overall commitment of participants to the goals and objectives of integration; the scope and complexity of integration; the backgrounds and performance of participants to date; and a realistic process for mapping progress and resolving disputes. To this end, the next section reviews the formation of ASEAN and the progress that has been achieved thus far from the organization's official scorecard, and, finally, provides implications for potential participating firms.

Scoring the Progress

At the Bali Summit in 2003, the representatives unveiled the ASEAN Economic Community (AEC) as the comprehensive pillar for regional integration, along with two other pillars: the ASEAN Security

Single Market and Production Base		Competitive Economic Region		Equitable Economic Development		Integration into the Global Economy	
1.	Free flow of goods	8.	Competition policy	14.	SME development	16.	Coherent approach towards external economic relations
2.	Free flow of services	9.	Consumer protection	15.	Initiative for ASEAN integration (IAI)		
3.	Free flow of investment	10.	Intellectual property rights			17.	Enhanced participation in global supply networks
4.	Freer flow of capital	11.	Infrastructure development				
5.	Free flow of skilled labor	12.	Taxation				
6.	Priority integration sectors	13.	E-Commerce				
7.	Food, agriculture and forestry						

Data Source: ASEAN Economic Community Blueprint (2008)   Adapted from Das, 2012

Exhibit 3.1 17 Core Elements of the AEC Blueprint

Community and the ASEAN Socio/Cultural Community. Specific time-lines for implementation were set, with the AEC targeted by 2015 and the other two pillars by 2020. This declaration, signed in 2007, stipulates: *"The AEC will establish ASEAN as a single market and production base making ASEAN more dynamic and competitive with new mechanisms and measures to strengthen its existing economic initiatives, accelerating regional integration in the priority sectors, facilitating movement of business persons, skilled labour and talents, and strengthening the institutional mechanisms of ASEAN"* (ASEAN Secretariat, 2008: 2). To monitor progress, ASEAN leaders established an AEC Scorecard modelled after the EU Internal Market Scorecard aimed at "identifying specific actions that must be undertaken by ASEAN collectively and its member States individually to establish AEC by 2015" (Rillo, 2011). Also important is that the scorecard was not designed as a "compliance tool," but primarily for "evaluating the impact of these measures" (Rillo, 2013: 21). Accordingly, the structure of the AEC Scorecard with seventeen core elements of the blueprint is presented in Exhibit 3.1.

One important consideration in reading this section is that the scorecard is constantly being updated. In fact, the scorecard has been officially suspended effective December 2015. In Exhibit 3.2, we present the most recent accomplishments as of December 2015. The extent to which goals are achieved in the future will depend on many factors, some of which might not be known at the time of this writing (see Chapter 11). In this regard, we have focused on trends and developments that can influence the trajectory of progress.

Pillar 1: Single Market and Production Base

The objective of a single market and production is a commitment to eliminating tariffs among participants, as well as enhancing the mobility

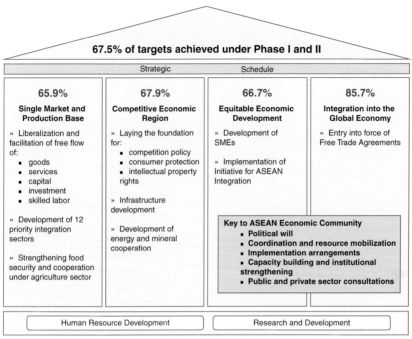

Note: As of December 2011, the implementation rates under Phase I and Phase II are 86.7% and 55.8%, respectively.
Data Source: ASEAN Economic Community Scorecard (2012)

Exhibit 3.2 Implementation of the ASEAN Economic Community Scorecard Under Phase I and II

of investment and capital within ASEAN. In short, this commitment comports with the precepts of a free-market system. Correspondingly, five core elements comprise the goal of a single market and production base: (1) free flow of goods; (2) free flow of services; (3) free flow of investment; (4) freer flow of capital; and (5) free flow of skilled labor. Exhibit 3.3 presents a recent appraisal of accomplishments relating to a single market and production base in 2012.

As of 2010, tariffs for merchandise goods are reported to have been virtually eliminated for the ASEAN-6 (Brunei Darussalam, Indonesia, Malaysia, Philippines, Singapore, and Thailand). In the CLMV region (Cambodia, Laos, Myanmar, and Vietnam), progress on tariff elimination was seen at the beginning of 2015, and further elimination of duties for the remaining 7 percent of tariff lines is expected to be completed by 2018 (ASEAN, 2015b). To date, this is acknowledged as the most successful implementation phase of the AEC.

Key Areas	Phase I (2008-2009)		Phase II (2010-2011)		Total Measures	
	Fully implemented	Not fully implemented	Fully implemented	Not fully implemented	Fully implemented	Not fully implemented
Free flow of goods	9	0	23	24	32	24
Free flow of services	10	3	13	17	23	20
Free flow of investment	5	1	5	8	10	9
Freer flow of capital	1	0	5	0	6	0
Free flow of skilled labor	–	–	1	0	1	0
Priority integration sectors	28	0	1	0	29	0
Food, agriculture and forestry	8	0	5	6	13	6
Total number of measures	**61**	**4**	**53**	**55**	**114**	**59**
Implementation rate*	93.0%		49.1%		65.9%	

*Implementation rate is calculated as the ratio of measures that are fully implemented to total number of measures targeted
(-) Indicates no measures targeted for this phase

ASEAN has implemented 65.9% of measures under Pillar I, with significant achievements in free flow of skilled labor and capital, and integration of priority sectors.
Data Source: ASEAN Economic Community Scorecard (2012)

Exhibit 3.3 Single Market and Production Base Scorecard

The removal of nontariff barriers, however, has proven to be much less successful and a more daunting challenge (Das, 2013). In the case of ASEAN, nontariff barriers include "financial control measures (e.g., multiple exchange rates) and quantity control measures (e.g., non-automatic licensing, quotas, prohibitions, and enterprise-specific restrictions)" (Ando & Obashi, 2010). Studies have reported that nontariff barriers are pervasive, in that close to 50 percent of tariff rates are related to a nontariff barrier (Ando & Obashi, 2010). In terms of industry, non-tariff barriers are relatively prevalent in the food and chemicals industries (Ando & Obashi, 2010).

To ensure timely implementation, ASEAN introduced trade facilitation consisting of the ASEAN Single Window (ASW), customs integration, harmonized standards for compliance, and enhanced information flows – all directed to facilitate ASEAN into a single market (goods, services, and investment) and a production base. The ASEAN Single Window is "an environment where ten National Single Windows of individual members operate and integrate" (ASEAN Secretariat, 2008: 8) Inclusive in this environment is "a single submission of data … single and synchronous processing of data … and single decision-making for customs clearance…" (ASEAN Secretariat, 2008: 8)

Even so, implementation remains a challenge for individual countries, although there is optimism that hurdles can be overcome in the future (Kartika & Atje, 2013: 40–41). ASEAN has also launched an ASW Pilot Project at the regional level in seven selected countries (Brunei, Indonesia, Malaysia, the Philippines, Singapore, Thailand, and Vietnam). It is likewise noted that for implementation to succeed, there is the need to reduce transportation and logistics costs and improve infrastructure – a challenge that confronts each country in various ways (Kartika & Atje, 2013: 43).

Correspondingly, the AEC Economic Community envisions the free flow of trade in services "where there will be substantially no restriction to ASEAN service suppliers in providing services and in establishing companies across national borders within the region" (ASEAN Secretariat, 2008: 10). Although implementation in this regard lags substantially behind the free flow of merchandise goods, there is still room for improvement in the case of services, where restrictions on cross-border trade have been eased in at least eighty subsectors (Rillo, 2011).

Increases in service trade are tightly related to liberalization commitments, in which ASEAN members agree to binding agreements on particular service sectors that are governed by formalized packages with specific timetables (Nikomborirak & Jitdumrong, 2013: 53–54). Moreover, the use of Mutual Recognition Arrangements (MRAs) formalizes the qualifications of professional service suppliers to hasten the flow of services in accordance with integration objectives (Nikomborirak & Jitdumrong, 2013: 55). As of 2015, eight such MRAs were accorded: engineering, architectural, nursing, accounting, surveying, medical, dental, and tourism services (ASEAN, 2015a). Earlier, as part of the AEC Blueprint, agreements were reached to remove restrictions on services for four sectors – air transport, e-ASEAN, health care, and tourism – and other type of sectors by 2015 (Nikomborirak & Jitdumrong, 2013: 57). However, as will be discussed in the following sections, the movement of labor is restricted to professionals, not unskilled labor. Moreover, agreements in regard to financial liberalization tend to be flexible and optional. In all, pundits are much less enthusiastic about the prospects of an integrated ASEAN service sector in the future.

Free Flow of Investment and Capital. The continuous inflow and outflow of investment is essential for effective international integration. The AEC Economic Community Charter states, *"A free and open investment regime is key to enhancing ASEAN's competitiveness in attracting foreign direct investment (FDI) as well as intra-ASEAN investment. Sustained inflows of new investments and reinvestments will promote and ensure dynamic* *development of ASEAN economies. ... ASEAN investment cooperation is implemented through the Framework Agreement on the ASEAN Investment Area (AIA)"* (ASEAN Secretariat, 2008: 13)

The ASEAN Comprehensive Investment Agreement "liberalizes and protects cross-border investment activities and embraces international best practices in the treatment of foreign investors" (Manila Bulletin, 2016: 1) The record yields a mixed result: Although the (ASEAN) region enjoyed its apex of foreign investment prior to the 1997-99 Asia financial crisis (5% of global stock and 20% of developing countries/total stock FDI), it is yet to surpass either of these milestones after the crisis (Bhaskaran, 2013: 81).

A good reason is that China and India have become beacons for FDI in the aftermath of the Asian financial crisis. Unsurprisingly, the devastation that accompanied the crisis eroded the confidence of foreign investors. Even so, it is reported that Southeast Asia remains one of the most profitable havens for investment, and with the inception of ASEAN, the region could become an attractive sanctuary, even with the continued attraction of China and India (Bhaskaran, 2013: 81–82).

Free Movement of Skilled Labor. The ASEAN Economic Community declares, *"In allowing for managed mobility or facilitated entry for the movement of natural persons engaged in trade in goods, services, and investment, according to the prevailing regulations of the receiving country..."*(ASEAN Secretariat, 2008: 18) In this charter, ASEAN provides for ease of issuing visas and employment passes for qualified personnel, further harmonization and standardization of services, cooperation through the ASEAN University Network, development of core competencies and qualifications for selected jobs and occupations, and strengthening the research capabilities for each ASEAN member. ASEAN also concluded a Mutual Recognition Agreement (MRA) for eight professions with the goal of easing movement within the region.

Even so, attainment of this goal remains problematic because of various remaining obstacles. Yue (2013: 121–122) cites such factors as large disparities in wages and opportunities, complications arising from geography and sociocultural-linguistic backgrounds, and uneven levels of educational development. Moreover, Yue (2013: 122–123) also addresses concerns relating to brain drains that can deplete human capital within a given country even if this might enhance the region's overall development. Hence, the perception of a "win-loss" calculus is important in assessing the future of this free movement of skilled labor across ASEAN countries.

Key Areas	Phase I (2008-2009)		Phase II (2010-2011)		Total Measures	
	Fully implemented	Not fully implemented	Fully implemented	Not fully implemented	Fully implemented	Not fully implemented
Competition policy	2	0	2	0	4	0
Consumer protection	2	0	5	4	7	4
Intellectual property rights	-	-	4	1	4	1
Transport	15	10	6	8	21	18
Energy	0	0	2	1	2	1
Mineral	1	0	7	0	8	0
ICT	2	0	4	0	6	0
Taxation	-	-	0	1	0	1
E-commerce	-	-	1	0	1	0
Total number of measures	22	10	31	15	53	25
Implementation rate*	68.7%		67.4%		67.9%	

*Implementation rate is calculated as the ratio of measures that are fully implemented to total number of measures targeted
(-) Indicates no measures targeted for this phase
Around 67.9% of measures under Pillar II were implemented as at end-December 2011, with notable progress in the areas of competition policy, IPR, and regional cooperation in minerals and ICT.
Data Source: ASEAN Economic Community Scorecard (2012)

Exhibit 3.4 Competitive Economic Region Scorecard

Pillar 2: Competitive Economic Region

The main goal of a competitive economic region is "to foster a culture of fair competition" (ASEAN Secretariat, 2008: 22) In this regard, ancillary goals include the introduction of a common competition policy within ASEAN, the establishment of a network of authorities and agencies charged with implementation, the focus on capacity-building programs, and regional guidelines for competitive policy. Specific activities cover consumer protection measures, the protection of intellectual property rights, infrastructural development, and the enhancement and improvement of taxation policies and e-commerce. Exhibit 3.4 presents recent accomplishments relating to the goal of establishing a competitive economic region in 2012.

To date, several agencies have been formed, notably the ASEAN Committee on Consumer Protection, in addition to an effort to increase awareness of consumer rights (ASEAN Consumer Complaints). Moreover, the ASEAN IPR Action Plan 2011–2015 was enacted. There have been continuing efforts to ramp up policies and measures directed at consumer protection and the security of intellectual property rights.

Yet it is the area of infrastructural development that has been accorded attention by ASEAN. As stated in the charter, *"An efficient, secure and integrated transport network in ASEAN is vital for realizing the full potential of the*

ASEAN Free Trade Area as well as in enhancing the attractiveness of the region as a single production, tourism and investment destination and narrowing development gaps. ASEAN transport is also critical in linking ASEAN with the neighboring Northeast and South Asian countries" (ASEAN Secretariat, 2008: 25)

In this regard, per the ASEAN 2015 Report, specific attention has been directed at the ASEAN Transport Action Plan, the completion of the Singapore-Kunming Rail Link, the ASEAN Highway Network, the ASEAN Single Shipping Market, the ASEAN Single Aviation Market (and the ASEAN Multilateral Agreement on the Full Liberalization of Passenger Air Services), the interconnectivity and technical interoperability of the Information and Communication Technology ICT systems, energy (ASEAN Plan of Action on Energy Cooperation) and mining cooperation, and the financing of infrastructural projects.

In their study, Abidin and Rosli (2013) report that infrastructural development still has a long way to go in terms of fulfilling milestones set for the ASEAN implementation schedule. They attribute difficulties to a lack of better coordination and integration, as well as the need for better financing schemes. Among their recommendations are "the establishment of a regional institutional mechanism for project implementations, enhancing regional planning and monitoring capacity, meeting financial needs, streamlining national infrastructure priorities with regional visions and accelerating the work to harmonize infrastructure standards" (2013: 161).

In an ASEAN Report, *Thinking Globally, Prospering Regionally: ASEAN Economic Community 2015*, additional progress is represented in the form of the ASEAN Highway Network that physically connects key roadways; six (out of sixteen) cross-border connections of the ASEAN Power Grid have been constructed and are operable, as is the Trans-ASEAN Gas Pipeline; further protocols relating to the ASEAN Open Skies have been agreed to; and telecommunications infrastructure has been enhanced.

In the 2014 World Bank's Logistics Performance, which measures the efficiency of trade and logistics, ASEAN as a region does not rank highly.[2] Only Singapore (#1) is comparable to leading countries in the world, and Malaysia (#27) and Thailand (#31) are relatively favorable. Indonesia (#43), Vietnam (#53), and the Philippines (#65) make up the second tier. Finally, Cambodia (# 81), Laos (#117), and Myanmar (#147) are placed on the third tier.

---

[2] See http://lpi.worldbank.org/international/global (accessed September 1, 2015). Brunei is not ranked because of the lack of information.

Key Areas	Phase I (2008-2009)		Phase II (2010-2011)		Total Measures	
	Fully implemented	Not fully implemented	Fully implemented	Not fully implemented	Fully implemented	Not fully implemented
SME development	1	0	4	3	5	3
Initiative for ASEAN integration (IAI)	2	0	1	1	3	1
Total number of measures	3	0	5	4	8	4
Implementation rate*	100%		55.5%		66.7%	

*Implementation rate is calculated as the ratio of measures that are fully implemented to total number of measures targeted

Pillar III has so far achieved 66.7% of targeted measures, as the implementation of various activities in SME development and Initiative for ASEAN Integration (IAI) remained generally on track.

Data Source: ASEAN Economic Community Scorecard (2012)

Exhibit 3.5 Equitable Economic Development Scorecard

Pillar 3: Equitable Economic Development

The productive growth of an economy depends on a balance between large-sized corporations and small-to-medium enterprises (SMEs). The two sectors have complementary roles. Typically, small-to-medium enterprises function as suppliers or important intermediaries for the larger firms. In many countries, smaller firms are the fount of entrepreneurship because they tend to specialize and focus on unfilled market niches not attended to by mainstream firms.

To this end, ASEAN envisioned an equitable economic development oriented to the development of small-to-medium enterprises. Within the ASEAN charter, four steps are distinguished and quoted herein: (1) "the acceleration of SME development," (2) the "enhancement of the competitiveness and dynamism of SMEs by provision of access to resources and other forms of capacity building," (3) "the strengthening of the resilience of SMEs against adverse macroeconomic conditions and financial crises", and (4) the "increase of SMEs' overall contribution to the growth of ASEAN" (ASEAN Secretariat, 2008: 31). Exhibit 3.5 presents recent accomplishments relating to the goal of establishing equitable economic development within the AEC in 2012.

To this end, ASEAN launched the ASEAN Integration in 2000 with priority areas in "infrastructure, human resource management, information and communications technologies, capacity building for regional integration, energy, investment climate, tourism, poverty reduction and the improvement of the quality of life" (ASEAN Secretariat, 2008: 32). In 2010, ASEAN implemented the Strategic Action Plan for SMEs with a targeted date of 2015. In this initiative, the ASEAN Multimedia Self-Reliant System

Toolkit Package and the Feasibility Study of the SME Service Center were undertaken. Moreover, a Directory of Outstanding ASEAN SMEs 2011 has since been published. Finally, there is recognition that, for ASEAN to succeed, economic gains from the more prosperous countries should trickle down to the smaller countries (Initiative for ASEAN Integration and the ASEAN Framework for Equitable Economic Development).

Sotharith (2013: 163–164) details the strengths of SMEs in the context of ASEAN:

SMEs are integral to the economic development and growth of the ASEAN member states, as they outnumber large enterprises in both quantity of establishments and share of the labor force that they employ. Within ASEAN, SMEs account for more than 96 percent of all enterprises and 50 to 85 percent of domestic employment. The contribution of SMEs to total GDP is between 30 and 53 percent and the contribution of SMEs to exports is between 19 and 31 percent. ... SMEs are the backbone of ASEAN and SME development is integral in achieving sustainable growth.

Despite their importance to ASEAN, and notwithstanding the initiatives to promote SMEs, this pillar is fraught with several challenges, such as financing for SMEs, the need for SMEs to be truly adaptive in the face of ever-changing consumer demands and preferences, the insufficiency of management skills, and a general weak competitive position vis-à-vis China, Japan, and Korea (Sotharith, 2013: 172–173).

Pillar 4: Integration into the Global Economy

The ASEAN Charter states, *"ASEAN operates in an increasingly global environment, with interdependent markets and globalized industries. In order to enable ASEAN businesses to compete internationally, to make ASEAN a more dynamic and stronger segment of the global supply chain and to ensure that the internal market remains attractive to foreign investment, it is crucial for ASEAN to look beyond the borders of AEC. External rules and regulations must increasingly be taken into account when developing policies related to AEC"* (ASEAN Secretariat, 2008: 33).

To achieve this goal, ASEAN adopts an "ASEAN Centrality" in its overall approach to free trade and comprehensive partnerships. Moreover, ASEAN seeks to identify and adopt international best practices and standards in production and in developing global supply networks. In addition, ASEAN has sought to develop a "package of technical assistance for less developed ASEAN Member Countries to upgrade their industrial capacity and productivity" (ASEAN Secretariat, 2008: 26). Exhibit 3.6 presents recent accomplishments relating to the goal of integrating ASEAN into the global economy in 2012.

Key Areas	Phase I (2008-2009)		Phase II (2010-2011)		Total Measures	
	Fully implemented	Not fully implemented	Fully implemented	Not fully implemented	Fully implemented	Not fully implemented
External economic relations	5	0	7	2	12	2
Total number of measures	5	0	7	2	12	2
Implementation rate*	**100%**		**77.8%**		**85.7%**	

*Implementation rate is calculated as the ratio of measures that are fully implemented to total number of measures targeted
Toward the integration into the global economy, ASEAN has achieved 85.7% of identified measures, including the ratification of various Free Trade Agreements with China, Japan, Republic of Korea, Australia, New Zealand, and India.
Data Source: ASEAN Economic Community Scorecard (2012)

Exhibit 3.6 Integration into the Global Economy Scorecard

Progress is manifested in extended networks, such as ASEAN +1, which includes China, Japan, Korea, Australia, New Zealand, and India. Moreover, ASEAN has successfully negotiated the Regional Comprehensive Economic Partnership (RCEP), which represents about 30 percent of global output, with its combined GDP of about US$ 22.7 trillion and a market of 3.4 billion people, nearly half of the world's population. Although further work on this agreement is still expected to continue into 2016, the RCEP is expected to improve market access, trade facilitation, and regulatory reform, among others, which will carve the way for ASEAN to become a more collective and proactive global player (ASEAN, 2015a). Additionally, it is reported that a survey by the US Chamber of Commerce indicated that 54 percent of American companies already have an ASEAN strategy (*Thinking Globally, Prospering Regionally: ASEAN Economic Community 2015*).

As indicated, monitoring the progress of the ASEAN Economic Community is a moving target. Scholars in this area have offered numerous suggestions on how the scorecard can be improved (see Das, 2012, 2013). Among the more salient proposals is the imperative to distinguish between goal attainment (measured in terms of partial or full accomplishment) against the impact of a particular initiative on regional integration (Das, 2012, 2013; Rillo, 2013). This was in recognition that not all initiatives have equal impact on accelerating regional integration; some have much more than others, but this was hardly noted when measures were directed at the percentage of initiatives that were implemented (see Rillo, 2013).

One important takeaway that is noted in the AEC Scorecard is the success factors that are needed for regional integration. Foremost is the collective political will by member countries to make integration possible (Inama & Sim, 2015). Because countries have varying motivations for ASEAN, it might be difficult to always act in a collective fashion, but this is a prerequisite for proper implementation. Another factor is the extent of coordination given the relatively small resources (Inama & Sim, 2015). It has been duly noted that the ASEAN Secretariat is quite small and inadequate relative to the resources allotted to the European Union, for example. Unless coordination ensues, the complexities arising from integration could overwhelm participants and could even override a lackadaisical effort at compliance. At the end it will boil down to a simple question: Will participants be involved in integration that is beneficial for them collectively but might impair their own national interests? Thus far, the key actors have been governments and their agencies. At this time, the role of the private sector, although acknowledged to be significant, is considered to be minimal. The four pillars in the ASEAN Economic Community hold important implications for current and prospective firms. This is the subject of the next section.

Implications for the Private Sector

As important as these ASEAN initiatives are, they have been largely confined at this time to national governments and their respective agencies. This is understandable. After all, complex treaty agreements and other proposals to build a production base and foster competitiveness in the form of binding agreements have to be made at the governmental level. And, as we have indicated in the previous section, these decisions are multifaceted, complex, and political. Many, if not most, fall outside the jurisdiction and control of business firms. Even so, there are particular areas that should be of interest to the private sector.

Industries Matter

While the concept of a common market is both attractive and soothing, the reality is that some industries are more amenable than others when it comes to trade. In fact, trade creates both winners and losers. In Chapter 2, statistics on intra- and inter-ASEAN trade are presented. In 2014, ASEAN trade comprised 75.7 percent of all trade with the rest of the world. Notably, Singapore, Thailand, Malaysia, and Indonesia traded more extensively with the rest of the world than their ASEAN peers did. Nevertheless, intra-ASEAN trade remains stagnant at 24 percent of ASEAN trade, with a substantial portion (estimated at 20%) representing trade between Singapore and Malaysia due to the location of Singaporean manufacturing operations in Malaysia.

Successful trading relations depend on two factors: the type of goods and services being traded (i.e., broadly represented in industries), and the relative strength and competitiveness of the trading partners. One drawback of the colonial legacies is that the colonies were generally regarded as key suppliers to the industrialization efforts of more advanced countries. Hence, in many cases, the types of commodities traded are quite similar in ways that conform to what the colonizers viewed as the comparative advantages of their colonies (Lim, 2004; Acharya, 2012). Because the exports of ASEAN countries are similar, it is hardly surprising that there is little trade between them. As indicated in this chapter, trade is also dependent on the extent to which countries are open and receptive to trade. Urata and Ando (2011) report that Singapore is very open to FDI; the Philippines, Thailand, Indonesia and Cambodia are relatively open; but Myanmar, Malaysia, Brunei, and Laos are closed.

An informative paper by two management professors, Ronald Mendoza and Charles Siriban (2014) dissects which industries might be conducive to intra-ASEAN trade when the goals of regional integration are fully realized. Among the industries to watch are banking, manufacturing, air transport, and utilities and infrastructure. Banking is particularly interesting because of scale economies that can be gained as a result of consolidation and network externalities. For similar reasons, manufacturing offers economic gains from consolidation and from production and common distribution channels and facilities. Air transport can achieve economies from less restricted air routes, as well as from shared facilities and utilities. Again, utilities such as oil, gasoline, and water can benefit from an expanded installed base and from economies of scale and scope. Furthermore, any given country might be open to trade (liberalization) but also low on facilitation.

According to Mendoza and Siriban, some winners, on the other hand, are likely to suffer or lose ground with greater liberalization. One such example is sugar, in the case of the Philippines. However, even with a projected contraction, the sugar industry could make up for losses through cheaper inputs for other goods and with expanded consumer choices (Mendoza & Siriban, 2014).

Nurturing Government Connections

It is acknowledged, perhaps begrudgingly in some quarters, that the success of some Asian countries, notably Japan, South Korea, and China of late, did not conform to the precepts of mainstream economic development. One specific divide would be the role of government in economic development. For free-market purists, government should have a minimal role, if any; one that is confined to protecting the nation from foreign enemies to supporting market institutions, such as fostering minimal infrastructure for commerce to take place. But scholars of Japan and Korea, considered to be among the recent economic miracles, underscore the role of government in not only being supportive of the private sector but also being a joint participant in firm strategies and activities (Johnson, 1982; Amsden, 1992).

Studies at the firm level, specifically an examination of surging firms that are called "rough diamonds," highlight the importance of government support and connections among the determinants of success (Park, Zhou, & Ungson, 2013). Because ASEAN negotiations have been primarily directed by national governments and their authorizing agencies in key matters of trade, production, investment, and competition, it is imperative that prospective ASEAN firms develop some type of relationship with them. In fact, not to engage in some fashion could prove naïve and foolhardy. This argument is extended and articulated in the chapters that follow.

Developing Core Competences

Trade is not simply a matter of intent but likewise a matter of competitive capacity. One firm might like to engage in trade but lacks sufficient resources to do so. The core requirements for success are a firm's trading legacy and a commitment to an export-oriented mindset. Developing a trading legacy is neither arbitrary nor expedient, but purposeful and inclusive. The success of Japanese firms in the world market, despite their late entry after World War II, was facilitated by strong government support, coordination within their industrial groupings (*keiretsu*), strong management–worker relations, and relentless support from trading organizations (Sogo-Shosha). Similarly, in the case of South Korea, a strong government mandate, a business group structure (*chaebol*), a focus on workplace excellence, and an unfathomable "can-do" attitude transformed Hyundai, Kia Motors, and Samsung from local champions to global stalwarts.

   Among ASEAN countries, only Singapore currently rates as a "five-star" export economy, although Thailand, Malaysia, and Indonesia (including Brunei because of its oil and gas exports) have promising trajectories. This does not imply that firms in favorable export environments will necessarily succeed, nor does it mean that firms in the rest of ASEAN will struggle and fail. Success will be ultimately dependent on firms that not only are visionary and can develop core competencies, but that also – perhaps more importantly – have a deep commitment to succeed such that sustained high performance over time is attained. This argument will be developed at length in the chapters that follow.

Part II

ASEAN Champions: Strategies for Enduring Success

Who are the ASEAN Champions? What characteristics distinguish them from others? What do most of them share in common?

In the next six chapters, we present detailed narratives of our ASEAN champions based on our extensive study, on-site interviews in the ten ASEAN countries, and a variety of secondary published sources.

In this research, we find that the success of our ASEAN champions stems from their ability to transform themselves into strong local players, despite highly adverse political and economic circumstances. Particularly in underdeveloped markets characterized by voids and underdevelopment, most of these firms were able to capitalize on opportunities and crafting innovative strategies. In an environment of fledgling institutions, they are able to harness human and financial resources that enabled them to embrace risks and uncertainty.

Specific strategies are parsed in six chapters: preserving institutional legacy (Chapter 4); leveraging market power (Chapter 5); pioneering market strategies (Chapter 6); deepening localization (Chapter 7); building synergy (Chapter 8); fostering internationalization (Chapter 9); and nurturing human capital (Chapter 10).

4   Preserving Institutional Legacy

Introduction

The concept of legacy is generally conceived to denote the transfer of wealth over time or the continued succession of intergenerational capital. In narratives about organizational success, the concept of wealth has been expanded and further refined to include both tangible and intangible assets. In their study of emerging transnationals, Bartlett and Ghoshal (1987, 1990) proposed a nuanced formulation – "administrative heritage" – or a confluence of history, traditions, customs, culture, and leadership successions. Specifically, administrative heritage is: *"a configuration of organizational assets and capabilities that are built up over decades; a distribution of managerial responsibilities and influence that cannot be shifted quickly; and an ongoing set of relationships that endure long after any structural change has been made"* (1987: 8).

In ensuing studies, administrative heritage has been interpreted broadly and in different ways. Occasionally, it is restricted to corporate culture – defined broadly as shared and binding beliefs, norms, and values. Even so, although corporate culture is an integral part of administrative heritage, culture is more restrictive and does not constitute legacy. Administrative heritage should likewise not be confused with strong leadership, although enduring patterns of leaders and the values that have embodied them shape and influence administrative legacy.

Administrative heritage is primarily understood in the context of a firm's overall history, specifically pivotal events that have led to its current strategy, resources (both financial and human), and competencies developed over time. As Bartlett and Ghoshal (1987, 1990) have noted, it can be an enabler of change, or it can be a constraint or an obstacle to change, assuming that the direction of change comports with prevailing norms, values, and resources.

In this study of firms in primarily developing regions that define ASEAN, administrative heritage is inextricably intertwined with institutional development. Although this connection to institutions is recognized by Bartlett and Ghoshal in a firm's internationalization strategy in relation to it external environment, institutions per se are not the focus of their work. Hence, administrative heritage in their work is primarily internal in form and development.

In ASEAN, in particular, the primary effects of colonialism and the newfound sense of nationalism after colonialism are deeply etched into institutional development. Even so, as indicated in Chapter 1, evolving institutions are the bedrock of emerging and developing economies and a key determinant of national economic development.

To accentuate the pervasive impact of institutional development, one that combines key historical events and government decisions with the development of organizations, we use the term *institutional legacy* to describe one feature of successful ASEAN champions. By this term, we refer to the amalgamation of organizational history, resources, assets, and human capital with evolving institutional features of economic development in both the country and the region. Preserving institutional legacy, highlighted in this chapter, accentuates the ability of ASEAN champions to sustain advantages deriving from legacy despite formidable odds, and thus adding context to our argument about mobilizing institutional grassroots.

What underpins institutional legacy further is our emphasis on the *coevolution* of institutions with firm development over time. In biology, coevolution can be described as changes in two interlocking bodies or entities that are mutually inclusive and reciprocal for survival and growth. One popular example is the development of bumble bees and flowers in the continuing process of copollination.[1] Bumble bees flourish with an improved stock of flora; relatedly, flora becomes more diverse with continuous pollination. Hence, one cannot survive, evolve, and thrive without the other (Wikipedia, 2011).

Applied to organizations, management professors Michael Tushman, William Newman, and Elaine Romanelli (1986) used coevolution to describe the interplay of exploration and exploitation and how strategy, structure, and processes change as a result. In the ASEAN context, institutions in highly developing economies are fledgling, underdeveloped, and in flux. Even so, pivotal changes, such as changes in government policies, can create propitious opportunities for organizations. Institutional change also involves fundamental shifts in attitudes about development.

Nevertheless, capitalizing on these opportunities is hardly a result of self-acclamation; it involves visionary entrepreneurship and a deep

---

[1] Example adopted from http://en.wikipedia.org/wiki/Coevolution, accessed July 1, 2015.

commitment to market entry, regardless of risks. With continuous changes in institutions, organizations have to learn to be responsive and adaptive to meet the requirements of new demands on them. If and when institutions change, less resilient organizations are prone to inactivity and eventual replacement by more responsive firms. Those that are successful in meeting initial institutional needs are able to create further opportunities and market demands. Governments in emerging markets often rely on these successful intermediaries to fill new market and social needs that emerge along the economic growth.

In cases and examples to follow, we describe institutional changes within particular countries and how exemplary firms are able to capitalize on such opportunities. It is in this context of coevolution that we place our concept of an institutional legacy. This does not abjure the double-edged feature of institutional legacy: Much like administrative heritage, new actions by firms can be enabled or be constrained by legacy. In fact, we argue that those firms that have been unsuccessful in addressing key opportunities were constrained by their own legacy. Hence, the ability to capitalize on and leverage institutional legacy is one factor that separates successful from unsuccessful firms. In this chapter, we describe cases of institutional legacy that have led to success. These cases and the context of their institutional legacies are previewed accordingly:

- *Holcim Philippines, Inc.* (Philippines): An innovative market leader that kept pace with developments in the nation's cement industry;
- *Siam Cement Group* (Thailand): A company that capitalized on Thailand's fledgling industry;
- *Summit Auto Body Industry Co., Ltd.* (Thailand): An innovative pacesetter in automotive and parts industries;
- *Dao-Heuang Group* (Laos): A national champion from an entrepreneurial intermediary during market reform;
- *Far Eastern University, Inc.* (Philippines): A long-standing and visionary leader in education;
- *Ayala Land, Inc.* (Philippines): A value-driven leader in land development and construction;
- *PT Lippo Karawaci Tbk.* (Indonesia): A pioneer that sets the new standard in property development;
- *EEI Corporation* (Philippines): From a producer of engineering equipment to a national behemoth in heavy industrial projects;
- *Other ASEAN Champions-Aboitiz Power Corporation (Philippines) and Adinin Group of Companies (Brunei):* Family-run legacy business.

Holcim Philippines, Inc.

Historical events have a major impact on the business environment and consequently on the development of business entities, their strategies, and their success or failure. Whether these major external shocks present opportunities or challenges to a firm depends on entrepreneurial foresight and strategic thinking as much as historical chance.

One of the first cement plants in the Philippines was set up by the national government with the help of an American contractor on the island of Cebu in 1921. The company formed the Cebu Portland Cement Company (CEPOC), became one of only two major producers of the time, and eventually accounted for more than two-thirds of the country's domestic cement output until the Japanese occupation during World War II. When the United States came to liberate the Philippines, much of the capital, Manila, was reduced to rubble by both American air raids and Japanese pillaging, becoming the second most devastated city in the world, following Warsaw. The American-led postwar reconstruction effort that followed, plus the pent-up demand for houses, buildings, roads, and infrastructure, provided promising opportunities in the cement business. In 1949, local production was at 8 million bags/year, while consumption was at 10 million (Albarracin, 1969).

In 1956, Philippine President Ramon Magsaysay sought to privatize government-owned and -operated industries, including cement. A group of enterprising Filipino industrialists under the leadership of Ramon V. del Rosario Sr. had recently formed the Philippine Investment Management Consultants (PHINMA) to take an active role in the development of the country's industrial sectors. In 1957, PHINMA won the bid for CEPOC's new plant in the La Union province, some 280 km north of Manila. This marked the first successful privatization of a government-owned corporation in the Philippines. Although other cement companies were set up by wealthy Filipino families taking advantage of the growing market, PHINMA gradually expanded its cement holdings, took control of several other cement plants, and went on to become one of the country's largest producers.

The Swiss company, Holcim, entered the Philippine market as early as 1969 by acquiring minor shares in a local cement company, but it was in 2002 when it began to expand more aggressively in the Philippines by acquiring majority stakes in the company. By this time, PHINMA had successfully diversified into other sectors, including steel, energy, paper, and real estate. In 2004, Holcim successfully entered into a merger with PHINMA's cement business, which then became officially known as Holcim Philippines.

The merger not only consolidated the company's local market leadership by affiliating the company with an international brand, but it also created dynamic synergies in market knowledge and technical expertise, which enabled Holcim Philippines to develop its product portfolio to include various kinds of cement for different applications. After five decades of focusing on cement products, the company also expanded operations to the processing of ready-mix concrete and aggregates. In addition to its cement products, Holcim Philippines currently provides concrete for roads, pavements, and housing as well as for industrial, structural, and special purposes (Holcim Philippines, 2010).

In addition to offering a wider range of products, Holcim Philippines has endeavored recently to offer more value-added services to its customers. The company has developed Holcim Helps-U-Build, or HUB, a customer support center that offers homebuilding solutions and technical support for its clients. In line with the company's trust in the triple bottom line of "people, planet, and profit," the company has also developed an alternative fuels, raw materials and waste management unit, called Geocycle, which has also grown to become a waste management solution brand offering various services such as waste coprocessing, analysis, and transport (Holcim Philippines, 2013).

Following its transparent, innovative, forward-looking, and people-oriented strategies, Holcim Philippines continues to become a well-known and trusted brand in the Philippine cement industry. What distinguishes Holcim Philippines is its ability to combine its legacy with continuous innovation that has brought the company to its position of market leadership. Throughout its history, Holcim Philippines had been able to successfully capitalize on developments in the industry and in the national economy. This success required a certain degree of entrepreneurial foresight coupled with innovative thinking in taking advantage of historical events, policy changes, and technological advancement, together with commitment to take an active role in national industrial development.

Siam Cement Group (SCG)

Like in the Philippines, the development of the cement industry in Thailand was tied to the country's national economic development. Under the leadership of King Rama V, followed by his successor, King Rama VI, Thailand sought to modernize its economy at the beginning of the twentieth century. The move toward modernization required investments in infrastructure and buildings that pushed demand for construction materials, including cement, to unprecedented levels. In 1913, King

Rama VI founded the Siam Cement Co. Ltd. by royal decree in order to decrease the country's dependence on imported construction goods, to reduce the costs of infrastructure development, and to develop local industrial capacity.

At this time, managerial talent and technical knowhow were scarce in Thailand. Thus, Siam Cement sought a joint venture with the Dutch cement production equipment and machinery manufacturer F.L. Smidth & Co. to provide them with the necessary technology alongside technical expertise. Allowing the Danish investors to acquire up to 25 percent ownership in the company, Siam Cement recognized the importance of both intellectual and financial resources provided by their foreign partner. In fact, Dutch managers held the company's top position up until 1974. The foreign partnership also helped Siam Cement leverage the local brand to match public perception that foreign products offered better quality. The company today attributes its professional management system and company culture to a synergistic combination of its royal Thai heritage, Dutch managerial effectiveness, and technological excellence.

Throughout SCG's history, investment in technology and R&D has always been a priority for the company; it set up its own laboratories and has cooperated with local and international research institutions. One of its latest collaborations is an R&D excellence center with Oxford University.

Currently, SCG has diversified beyond cement products and has ventured successfully into concrete, paper, and petrochemicals across Southeast Asia. SCG's experiences parallel those of Holcim Philippines by way of addressing the initial disadvantages of underdevelopment in terms of potential advantages and building on its relationships with the Thai monarchy. Its legacy owes much to its founding with the support of the monarchy, but also to its foreign partnerships in its effort to keep abreast of industry development. It acquires not only the critical technological expertise but also the managerial capabilities from the partnerships that set the foundation for its continuous growth as an innovative market leader in the sector.

Summit Auto Body Industry Co., Ltd. (SAB)

The former McKinsey consultant Kenichi Ohmae (1980) once described the history of progress in developing countries as a series of evolving needs in transportation, from rickety units, to bicycles and motorcycles, and eventually to automotive and modern transport. Such milestones in personal transportation can also be graded in terms of supporting or ancillary industries. The Summit Auto Body Industry Co., Ltd. was founded in 1986 in Thailand by Sunsurn Jurangkool as a wholly-owned subsidiary of his emerging Summit Group of companies, to engage in the production of automotive exhaust systems, body parts, rolled formed parts, and mechanism parts. Mr. Jurangkool had founded a motorcycle seat and automobile interior parts manufacturer in 1972 and had been involved in the automobile industry since early in his entrepreneurial career.

The 1980s were an opportune time for the auto parts industry in Thailand. Beginning in 1975, the Thai government gradually enforced stricter local content requirements, forcing assemblers to source automobile parts and components locally from 25 percent for passenger cars in the late 1970s to as much as 70 percent for diesel-engine pickup trucks by the 1990s. In the 1980s, local sourcing of specific parts including exhaust pipes, diesel engine parts, radiators, and batteries was made compulsory. As the local content requirements became stricter, automobile companies that had invested in Thailand, most notably Japanese firms, began to engage local suppliers more closely by establishing supplier networks and collaborating with local parts manufacturers (Techakanont, 2011). The Japanese were particularly interested in investing in the Thai auto industry as they sought to find new markets and an alternative production base in response to the appreciation of the Japanese Yen against the U.S. dollar following the Plaza Accord of 1985, which had increased the cost of Japanese exports to the United States.

Taking advantage of these policy developments in automobile local content requirements and the influx of Japanese investments in Thailand, SAB grew alongside the Thai auto industry. As demand for their products grew, SAB expanded by establishing subsidiaries in special economic zones created by the Thai government to take advantage of special incentives received from the Thai Board of Investments. A subsidiary was established in the Laemchabang Industrial Estate in 1994 and in the Rayong Industrial Estate in 2004.

Today, SAB is the market leader in auto body parts in the country (Summit Auto Body Industry Co., Ltd., 2005b). It has invested heavily in R&D and continuous innovation as a direct result of the legacy imprinted upon them by the stringent safety and technological requirements of international auto manufacturers. SAB has several research centers including quality test laboratories for various auto parts, dynamometer systems, and tooling capabilities. They also have developed exclusive integrated production technologies, excellent quality assurance systems, and rationalized quality and environmentally conscious management systems at par with global counterparts (Summit Auto Body Industry Co., Ltd., 2005a).

Much like Holcim Philippines, SAB took advantage of developments in the economic landscape, alongside changes in government policy. The cases of Holcim and SAB show how ASEAN champions have been quick to respond to developments in their home bases that are also affected in turn by international developments. Like Holcim Philippines and SCG, innovation has also been a hallmark of SAB's institutional legacy. SAB focused on its innovative capabilities to build and offer products that were aligned with an evolving automotive industry. In fact, innovation was an integral part of its corporate culture that was the unifying factor in SAB's successful forays into different products and extensions.

Dao-Heuang Group

Although food and beverages are essential in any economy, the underlying structure of the industry can vary substantially, ranging from small and fragmented retail establishments to large global enterprises. In developing economies, this structure typically assumes local entrepreneurial ventures that become more diversified over time. Even so, growth is not universally effective, and firms can stumble in this transition. One stalwart, the Dao-Heuang Group founded in 1991 as Dao-Heuang Import – Export Company Limited, is exemplary in meeting the evolving demands of a changing environment. The company originally dealt with the import of whisky, wine, and tobacco products. However, in subsequent years, it diversified into other areas, starting with the export of coffee beans to neighboring countries. Today, the company's main line of business includes coffee, tea, import retail, and several other ventures such as real estate rental, pharmaceuticals, and air booking services.

When Leuang Litdang, President and Chief Executive Officer (CEO), founded her company in 1991, the country of Laos was just beginning to open up to international trade as it transitioned from a socialist economy to a liberalized one (Soukamneuth, 2006). The trading company began importing tobacco products, alcoholic beverages, and perfumes from Singapore, France, and the United States. In search of export opportunities, the company looked toward Laos' agricultural sector and the country's vast tracts of available farm land. In 1998, the company tried exporting coffee beans produced by a few local growers to neighboring countries. Seeing the potential of coffee as an export product, it explored the viability of export-oriented coffee cultivation in Laos. With practically no experience or expertise in coffee production, Dao-Heuang had to look outside Laos to learn more about the business, studying international best practices and hiring Vietnamese coffee growers to teach local farmers how to grow coffee.

Since creating a new agricultural export for Laos meant job creation and economic development, the Lao government warmly supported the company's initiative. The government helped the company establish contract farming agreements with local farmers and allowed Dao-Heuang to use 65,000 square miles of fertile land suitable for growing coffee beans.

It took the company about eight years to complete intensive studies on planting methods and processing techniques, plus three more years to complete the construction of its first coffee production plant in 2008. The hard work and dedication seemed to have paid off. In 2012, with financial support from the government of Laos, Dao-Heuang successfully opened the largest instant coffee factory in Southeast Asia.

In conjunction with her company's ambitious venture into coffee production, Litdang also recognized several other investment opportunities in the newly developing Lao economy. She put up businesses in other product and service areas including retail management, property management, and pharmaceuticals. In 2007, Litdang's companies were consolidated into the Dao-Heuang Group.

After consolidation, the company conceptualized strategies for further growth. Dao-Heuang, using its agro-industry as its foundation, expanded in offering tea, beverage, and food products. The company intends to list publicly on the Lao stock exchange in five years' time.

On the surface, food and drinks are staples in any economy, developed or emerging. The differences between them lie in the development of their agricultural industry and underpinning institutions and infrastructures, and notably the functions of market intermediaries. Dao-Heuang is the classic exemplar of an entrepreneurial intermediary, as in the export-import business at a frontier stage of the business. Dao-Heuang saw promising opportunities of which it could only take advantage by getting its hands dirty and getting into the action. It saw coffee as a profitable export trading opportunity, and in the absence of a reliable supply chain, Dao-Heuang decided to establish its own. Dao-Heuang successfully transformed the challenges of underdevelopment into sustainable growth opportunities for itself and its country. Its effort to benchmark internationally and learn from leading practices nurtured strong managerial capabilities, which made it possible to capitalize market opportunities and open up new government support and business opportunities.

Far Eastern University Inc.

Educational opportunities provide a crucible for development in developing countries. Nonetheless, although education is a prerequisite for success and upward mobility, it does not guarantee it. The lack of access to education is an important institutional void. Due to its colonial past under Roman Catholic Spain and later the United States, which heavily invested in public education, the Philippines is home to a multitude of educational institutions. Although more than 70 percent of higher education institutions in the Philippines are private institutions (Commission on Higher Education [CHED], 2012), most of the country's prestigious colleges and universities are run by either religious sects or the state as not-for-profit organizations. They rely heavily on endowment for their long-term sustainability and financial success. Far Eastern University (FEU) is one of only three for-profit educational organizations listed on the Philippine Stock Exchange. The university network offers a wide range of undergraduate and graduate programs from business and law to engineering and computer studies.

FEU was formed in 1934 as a result of a merger between the Institute of Accountancy, founded in 1928, and Far Eastern College, founded in 1919. Its founder, Nicanor Reyes, recognized a void in the existing educational system that failed to accommodate working students. Higher education institutions catered mostly to students who came from higher-income families that could afford to finance their children's college education. He also noted the lack of local accountants at a time when commercial activities were increasing due to the country's economic development. American and British accountants had to be hired by large corporations operating in the country to meet their growing needs. The Institute of Accountancy was originally set up primarily as a night school for working students. In the 1930s, Reyes sought to establish the Institute as a full-fledged university, culminating in the merger with Far Eastern College, which enabled the newly founded FEU to offer a liberal arts education, with majors in accountancy and business. Several "institutes" were established thereafter: an Institute of Education in 1931, an Institute of Law in 1934, and an Institute of Technology in 1936.

The university's expansion, as well as day-to-day operations, ceased during World War II when the Manila campus was taken over by the Japanese occupying forces. The university immediately reopened in 1945. Ten years later, Institute of Nursing and Medicine was established, along with a university hospital to meet the growing healthcare needs of the country. In 1970, an Institute of Architecture and Fine Arts was established. The university entered the IT age in the early 1990s, through a joint venture with a local computer school to set up the East Asian Institute of Information Technology. Throughout its history, FEU has sought to provide educational opportunities to ordinary Filipinos to empower them to fill the needs of industries as the country progressed in its economic development.

"Our aim is to provide working students and students with lesser means a value education that is accessible, affordable, and promotes employability of the FEU graduate."
– Aurelio Montinola III, Chairman

"The vision of Nicanor Reyes is that the courses have to be empowering for the students. That was why we went into Accounting in the first place[:] because Filipinos could not practice Accounting in the Philippines and they wanted – we wanted – to show that Filipinos were just as capable as foreigners … that is one of the things that I'm thinking of right now. What other courses – what would be the equivalent of Accounting and Law in Nicanor Reyes' time, now? What is it in this new economy that would empower the Filipino?" Michael Alba, President

In recent years, the university network has sought to expand aggressively, putting up satellite campuses in Makati, the country's premier business district, and in Silang, Cavite, 54 kilometers south of Manila.

Although it is uncommon for an educational entity to be financially successful over time, FEU accentuates its legacy with continuous improvement over time with a timely focus on its constituencies. Throughout its history, FEU has adapted closely to the needs of the developing Philippine economy as much as it has helped shape the country's development story. It was the entrepreneurial insight to fill the institutional void in education and deliver necessary competencies for continuous growth of the economy.

Ayala Land, Inc.

Another key institution in national economic development is real estate and property management. In developed countries, this industry involves key intermediaries that provided important services. Given the importance of property management, it is important that services are able to support this industry through good management processes and management capabilities. In developing countries, channels for intermediaries are much narrower in scope, affecting the growth of housing and infrastructure.

As the real estate arm of Ayala Corporation, one of the Philippines' largest business groups, Ayala Land is the country's foremost real estate developer. Although Ayala Land was officially incorporated only in 1988, the company has had a long legacy under the Philippines' oldest business house, Ayala y Compania (now Ayala Corporation). The company is particularly known for developing a piece of former farmland in Makati just outside the capital city of Manila into the country's premier central business district (CBD).

The Ayala-Roxas family had purchased the farm estate or *hacienda* from the Jesuits in 1851. In the mid-1930s, a group of foreign investors led by L. R. Nielson became interested in privately developing an airport to serve Manila. When the Ayalas learned about this, they offered their suburban property as an ideal site, being still largely undeveloped and sparsely populated but very close to the growing capital city. The offer was accepted, and Manila's first airport was completed in 1937. The airport saw numerous maiden flights including that of Philippine Airlines, the oldest operating airline in Asia, in 1941. The beginning of World War II forced the airport to cease commercial operations as it was dedicated to the U.S. Air Force. Operations briefly resumed at the end of the war, but a bigger airport was opened in a different location in 1948, and ownership of the facilities was soon transferred to the Ayalas. Seizing what they saw as a real estate opportunity, the Ayala Company converted the former airport's two intersecting runways into roads, forming two sides of what would become the Ayala Triangle at the center of the company's grand commercial and residential development project. Dubbed as ambitious and farsighted when it was conceived, the Ayala Master Plan envisioned a large-scale, mixed-use, purpose-built community in what was then a sleepy, unremarkable Manila suburb.

The success of this first major venture laid the foundation for the development of real estate as one of the Ayala Corporation's core businesses. In the 1970s, the company sought to replicate its early success in Makati using the same formula of master-planned, mixed-use development in Alabang, a suburb further south of Makati and Manila. In the 1980s and through the 1990s, the company began to explore possible opportunities in Central and Southern Philippines. Some of its newer developments include Bonifacio Global City, a thriving business district developed from a former military base in Fort Bonifacio, about 4 kilometers east of the Ayala Center in Makati, and NUVALI in Sta. Rosa, Laguna, some 40 kilometers south of the Makati CBD.

As it seeks to expand market and geographical reach, Ayala Land has been engaging other real estate companies in a number of joint venture projects across the country. Most of these real estate companies are part of large conglomerates led by prominent Filipino business families. Its Bonifacio Global City project, for instance, was developed along with Evergreen Holdings of the Campos family. It has also partnered with

Aboitiz Land (of the Aboitiz family) for the development of a new business district in Cebu and with the Alcantara family's Alsons Group for a mixed-use community in Davao. Engaging in joint ventures and strategic partnerships has enabled the company to expand rapidly while reducing risk and optimizing capital (GMA News, 2013).

In all of its projects, Ayala Land has had visionary leadership in developing business and residential communities, contributing to national economic development. As President and CEO Bernard Vincent Dy articulated when he accepted the 2014 Southeast Asia Property Award on behalf of the company, Ayala Land's long-term vision has been an integral success factor, remarking that "this is truly something that has shaped Ayala Land from the very beginning – the preference of leaving a long-term legacy and the desire to create lasting value for generations" (Ayala Land, 2014). As in other case-examples, Ayala has had a continuous stream of good management and a steadfast corporate culture, intricately linked with the home country's development story. Although family management has been impaired in other firms, the legacy of successful successions among family members has been a legacy of the Ayala Group.

PT Lippo Karawaci TBK

As in the Philippines, property development has flourished in Indonesia. PT Lippo Karawaci TBK is the leading property developer in Indonesia involved in residential and urban development, large-scale integrated developments, retail malls, hospitals, hotels and leisure, and asset management. It is the largest publicly listed property company in Indonesia in terms of market capitalization, assets, and revenue, and also boasts of owning the largest diversified land bank in prime locations.

What has set Lippo Karawaci apart from the competition is its pioneering strategy of township development in Indonesia. In all of its real estate projects, the company builds comprehensive facilities such as road infrastructure, clean water sanitation, electricity transmission lines, hospitals, schools, and other basic necessities. The company's first township project, Tangerang City, some 25 kilometers west of Jakarta, has served as the model for future township development projects not just for Lippo Karawaci, but also for other Indonesian real estate developers that have begun to develop townships as well. A growing Indonesian middle-class population has fueled demand for real estate in general and has spiked demand for the company's township projects in particular, as middle class property buyers sought the higher quality of life provided by master-planned developments.

Being the first movers in township development in the country, the company initially had to source talents from abroad: American architects, Scottish township managers, and several foreign landscape architects. This expertise from abroad matched with the increasing sophistication of Indonesia's growing middle and upper class, which eagerly bought properties in Lippo Karawaci's world-class developments.

The company's success with its pioneer project, Tangerang City, required visionary leadership and faith in the country's economic development trajectory. In the early 1990s when the company planned to build the township, others viewed it as crazy given the immense scale of the operation, that is, building a city. However, its leaders viewed it as an opportunity, setting a new standard of property development in the country (Wijaya, 2014).

Established just three years earlier as a subsidiary of the Lippo Group of Companies, Lippo Karawaci acquired the rights to develop two townships near the Indonesian capital of Jakarta, Cikarang, in the east and Tangerang in the west. Both projects were thought to be highly ambitious due to costs and scale. Both townships covered an area of about 3,000 hectares each.

The company needed to find sources of capital in order to finance the huge costs of its township developments. In 1996, Lippo Karawaci was listed in the Indonesian Stock Exchange with an initial public offering of 30.8 million shares. What distinguished Lippo Karawaci – and a defining element of its legacy – was its ability to forecast emerging developments and to build internal capabilities aligned with market entry. It followed its vision and took the challenges of creating something no one had done before with new strategies and capabilities sourced from abroad.

EEI Corporation

Our final case in this chapter relates to a transformation of a company from engineering equipment to a national behemoth in heavy industrial projects. This was achieved principally by its ability to keep abreast of both industry- and nationwide developments, and by aligning internal competencies with purposeful expansion. Founded in 1931 by a retired U.S. Navy officer, the company, then known as Engineering Equipment and Supply Company (EESCO), began as a machinery and mills supply house mainly for the mining industry during the mining boom of the 1930s (EEI Corporation, 2014).[2] Today, EEI's core business is construction, specializing in heavy industrial projects.

---

[2] It was in the 1930s when U.S. colonial rule in the Philippines was at its peak. This time period also marks the boom years of large-scale mining in the Philippines, particularly gold.

EEI's growth path has been determined by the company's attitude of constantly seeking opportunities for growth and profit. Although it started in the booming mining industry, it would later take on related activities, expanding beyond machinery distribution. In 1934, the company branched out into general machine work, steel fabrication, welding and sheet metal work, and gear cutting. It was also during this time that EEI was first exposed to the international market when it successfully won contracts outside of the Philippines. In 1937, the company started doing tunneling work for the U.S. Army and built a custom cutter for the U.S. Navy in 1939. The company also got involved in the fabrication and construction of U.S. Navy coastal vessels.

When World War II broke out, the company had to close shop like the rest of the Philippine industry. Toward the end of the war, most mines were completely destroyed by the retreating Japanese forces as they faced imminent defeat. This left the Philippine mining industry virtually paralyzed (Boericke, 1945). Consequently, the company began exploring opportunities in other sectors. In 1946, EEI grew its machinery merchandising operations and delved into steel fabrication and installation. It began to cater to the government by fabricating the bodies of garbage trucks and constructing US Navy vessels. At this time, the company had begun shifting from the importation business and began focusing on its engineering shop facilities and increasing the company's capabilities as a contractor.

In 1959, Benguet Corporation, a local business group, acquired majority stake in EESCO, and in 1969, the company was renamed Engineering Equipment, Inc. (EEI). By this time, the company had ventured into fabrication for oil companies and U.S. military bases at Clark Field and had become a pioneer in the installation of power furnaces in the country and the leader in LPG tank fabrication.

In the 1970s, EEI saw opportunities in providing construction services in the Middle East and in 1974 began operations in the United Arab Emirates (UAE) and Saudi Arabia. Rising oil and energy prices throughout the decade fueled demand for construction work in the oil-rich region. By 1978, EEI had set up its Overseas Division, further diversified operations in the Middle East, and entered Malaysia. The same period marked the beginning of the overseas Filipino worker (OFW) phenomenon, with skilled construction workers and engineers taking on contractual employment in the Middle East. The new trend was facilitated by the Philippine government as it sought to remedy an increasing unemployment problem.

Today, more than half of EEI's revenue comes from overseas contracts, particularly Saudi Arabia. It has completed projects in many different countries including Kuwait, Qatar, Iraq, Singapore, Malaysia, and New Caledonia. This has been deliberate since the company specializes in heavy industrial work, of which there is limited demand in the local market.

EEI is looking to do business anywhere and is willing to go wherever the work is. Roberto Jose Castillo, President and CEO, says *"Because we are a construction company, we go where the work is."* It is neither geographically constrained nor is it limited by a preference to work in a specific industry. The company also offers a full range of construction services. This diversity and flexibility allows it to mitigate its exposure to international crises and diversify its business so that any slumps in a particular sector will not heavily damage the company. In fact, it is EEI's diversity that is credited for the company's ability to ride out the 2008 financial crisis. EEI's legacy was built on its visionary leadership in searching for business opportunities to apply its competences in industrial engineering. It pursued related diversification while developing the necessary internal capabilities and managing organizational arrangements to support the fast and broad growth across sectors and country boundaries.

Other ASEAN Champions: Aboitiz Power Corp. and Adinin Group of Companies

It is readily acknowledged that family businesses are a prominent feature in emerging and developing countries. But legacy is built on successful generational transfers in management talent and competencies, not on companies that might have excelled in one generation but failed in succeeding ones. In the cases illustrated earlier, the Ayala Land is regarded not only as one of the more successful corporations in the Philippines but among the best professionally managed companies as well. In our research, two family firms are distinguished in the management of generational talent.

Although the incorporation of Aboitiz Power Corporation happened in 1998, the Aboitiz family has been involved in the power sector since 1918 when they owned a 20 percent stake in the Visayan Electric Company (VECO), an electric company which was started by businessmen from Cebu. Through thoughtful acquisitions and partnerships that nurtured a reputation as both a family-run and a professional-led corporation, the family has since developed a leadership position in the areas of geothermal, hydro, coal and oil. Similarly, the Adinin Group of Companies, a Bruneian business conglomerate founded in 1982, is a fine example of a family-run enterprise. After progressing in the hospital where he started out as a dental technician, Haji Adnin went into a venture with his son, Musa Adnin, in order to establish Haji Adinin and Sons Co., which subsequently became Adinin Group of Companies. Haji Adnin and Musa Adnin used their entrepreneurial skills that they acquired from doing odd jobs and set them to practice in the early years of the company. It was due to their leadership, opportunity-seeking behavior, and hard work that the company diversified into construction-related services, and later into an international conglomerate.

Conclusions

In our assessment of characteristics that are common to ASEAN champions, the concept of institutional legacy is a suitable starting point because of a similar path of industrial growth and the influence of history and shared traditions. Such influences tend to be both pervasive and encompassing. Because institutional legacy covers history, industrial development, national policy, developing managerial capabilities, and ensuing strategies, it overlaps with other features of success that will be described in later chapters. Even so, we emphasize the role of pivotal historical events in the subsequent development and success of any given company. Admittedly, our treatment is biased and limited in depicting successful cases; it will suffice to say that we are not focused on failure, though we speculate that many failed cases demonstrate the lack of success in capitalizing on legacies.

In our case studies, we recognized a similar process that these leading companies applied to develop their own unique institutional legacies for sustained growth over time. There were first business opportunities due to the economic development, market transformation, and industrial policies to support local economies, and social and economic needs to overcome institutional voids. There were then entrepreneurial, visionary, and ambitious leaders who capitalized on these opportunities, which gave birth to institutional legacies setting the foundation for their growth as industrial champions. These companies emerged as key intermediaries between the government, market, and consumers facilitating the economic growth of these countries. A synthesis of variables that create and foster institutional legacy is presented in Exhibit 4.1.

Industrial development and market transformation open up the initial opportunities, but these leading companies did not stop there; they subsequently nurtured further opportunities by securing government support since they became the primary engine of the economic growth and new employment. It became possible through strong government relationships and/or pioneering strategies to build leadership in newly identified business opportunities. The legacy evolved and became stronger as the companies managed to build internal capabilities and competences

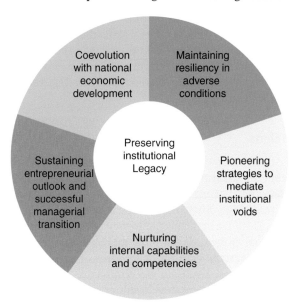

Exhibit 4.1 Preserving Institutional Legacy

that could sustain their initial success. They develop internal capabilities typically through international partnership, benchmarking of leading companies, and/or international sourcing of critical expertise. Their continuous growth into different sectors and regions was still built on the institutional legacy as the primary intermediary along the economic growth. The institutional legacy is highlighted by successful management transitions, an entrepreneurial innovative outlook, and an uncanny capability to address initial periods of high adversity. In all, firms have been able to nurture fledgling grassroots, develop core competencies during critical periods, and continue searching for opportunities across different markets and sectors. It is this context that we include legacy as part of mobilizing institutional grassroots. This feature is notable in that many other firms, including multinationals, have not fared as well in this regard.

Altogether, leveraging institutional legacy is not a guarantee of success. But because institutional development is inextricably tethered to national economic development, there are far-reaching implications on what firms can do to take advantage of opportunities that have a limited window of opportunity. In the next chapter, we elaborate on the second pillar of ASEAN champions that is related to institutional legacy but not subsumed by it – market power resulting from historical monopolies or dominant oligopolies.

5 Leveraging Market Power

Introduction

A key theoretical plank in economics and industrial organization is the study of market power. Broadly defined, this refers to the ability of a given firm to control competition by setting prices in relatively uncontested markets or those with high entry barriers. Market power is closely related to the structure of an industry. Typically, market power is associated with highly concentrated structures characterized by one dominant seller (monopoly) or when a few firms have a disproportionate level of market share (i.e., an oligopoly or oligopsony). Market power can be bequeathed by government, an outcome of a changing competitive environment or sheer good fortune.

In basic economic theory, monopolies are generally treated unfavorably and are seen as a primary cause of market failure (see Scherer, 1980: 9–27). Because a monopolist has the ability to set prices and determine its output to maximize its own profits, the resulting price and output combination may not be optimal for society, particularly when the monopolist sells at a price higher than what would have prevailed in perfect competition (see Martin, 1988: 25–290). The higher price results in a suboptimal level of sales and output, whereby fewer customers can afford to buy. And because such a firm's monopoly power rewards it with large profit margins, resources are wastefully – in a social perspective – devoted to preserving such power by erecting high barriers to entry and stifling competition.

Nonetheless, some economists and policymakers agree that in certain cases highly concentrated industries – and a monopolist, in particular – can serve the public more efficiently than a competitive market (see Martin, 1988). In the case of natural monopolies, as they are called, one very large firm or organization may be able to provide a good or service at a lower long-term average cost than several small firms because of strong economies of scale. Historically, some monopolies arise when it is considered, rightly or wrongly, by the government that one firm or organization can better serve the public good and the risk is too big for small entrepreneurial firms. To further illustrate, a firm can become a monopoly if government decrees an impassable barrier to entry for others. A national postal service has been historically defended in that having more than a single service provider would result in inefficiencies of overlapping routes, scattered customers, and multiple mailboxes. A similar logic can extend to power utilities, power generation, the railway system, and other industries that exhibit strong economies of scale. To ensure that this natural monopoly successfully serves the public good, conditions are usually set by the bequeathing government such as requiring the monopolist to serve unprofitable or economically unfeasible sectors or subjecting prices to government regulation.

Market power can also result from proprietary technology – patents and copyrights that preclude other firms from using a particular production process or producing the same product (Scherer, 1980). It is argued the profits guaranteed by monopoly power resulting from these exclusive property rights provide necessary impetus for innovation and justify expensive investment in research and development. Finally, a firm or a group of firms can benefit from access to a scarce resource (oil; precious minerals), a favorable location (distance to favorable ports and suppliers), or even managerial prowess (a prescient and visionary leader) that competitors cannot readily imitate.

Although traditional theoretical treatises treat market power in suspiciously unfavorable terms, the actual behavior of firms with market power and the effects of their dominance can vary considerably. Students of economics are socialized into thinking that a monopoly or an oligopolistic firm can raise prices above and beyond their marginal costs because of the lack of competition, resulting in inefficiency and impaired economic welfare. This logic has been used to justify anti-trust government regulations to break up highly concentrated firms and industry structures (such as the Ma Belle in the United States), or to discipline uncooperative firms (such as the steel industry in the United States) (see Scherer, 1980). Google, for example, is clearly a dominant market power in the search engine world – 68 percent of Web searches in the United States and more than 90 percent in Europe.[1] It has been accused of anti-competitive behavior by European regulators for bundling its search engine with its other commercial services, and threats have been made to weaken the company's dominance.

Similar to other Internet companies, Google benefits from network effects, whereby the development of a large user base attracts further

---

[1] "Trustbusting in the Internet age: should digital monopolies be broken up?" *The Economist.* 29 Nov 2014.

adoption and usage, resulting in exponential increases in both. Network effects create a considerable entry barrier and may stifle competition. However, network effects also reduce costs because of economies of scope and scale, and may allow the firm to reduce prices, especially when the incremental cost of production is very low or even zero. A very large and continually growing customer base for its search engine allows Google to run its advertising business profitably enough to provide users with a multiple array of free services, including the search engine. In such a case, the benefits to consumers and to society of a single firm's exercise of market power cannot be easily discounted.

This is not to say that firms that hold considerable market power cannot do harm. They have, and when they do, they are either squashed by regulators – at least in developed markets – or eventually toppled by ambitious newcomers usually armed with new technologies. In a static world, monopolists can rely on the entry barriers they have erected, simply collecting economic rent for as long as these barriers remain (Bain, 1956). However, in a highly dynamic environment, market power can wax and wane considerably.

The context of market power in ASEAN is a much more nuanced application. Particular to any fledgling and struggling national economy is the need to build critical industries literally from scratch. The reasons range from postwar rehabilitation to flawed legacies from colonialism. Even with good intentions, it is unlikely that this condition is best served with a fully functioning competitive market, spurring governments to favor significantly large and reputable firms. In context, individual firms are either bestowed monopolies or given special support to start up the process of national economic development. The scorecard is that some firms succeeded, while others failed. In context, being a monopolist or a recipient of market power is hardly a guarantee for sustained success. What differentiates our ASEAN champions is the ability to leverage market power in ways that create core competencies for current operations and for the future when competitors are likely to materialize. In this chapter, we detail the experiences of several such firms. A preview of these cases is as follows:

- *Phnom Penh Water Supply Authority* (Cambodia): a high-performing and well-respected water supply company;
- *Energy Development Corporation* (Philippines): capitalized on what was considered by government to be a strategically important industry;
- *PTT Exploration and Production PCL* (Thailand): another case where the industry was deemed to be critical for national economic security;

- *Manila Electric Company [Meralco]* (Philippines): the largest electric distribution utility in the region;
- *Philippine Long Distance Telephone Company [PLDT]* (Philippines): strong competence and innovative products and services into related areas;
- *Masan Consumer Corporation* (Vietnam): building the scale advantage through a portfolio of brands;
- *Boon Rawd Brewery* (Thailand): market dominance through proprietary technologies;
- *Other ASEAN Champions: Lao Brewery Co. Ltd. (Lao), EDL-Generation Public Company (Lao), and PetroVietnam Gas Joint Stock Corporation (PV Gas) (Vietnam):* capitalizing on their early selections as industry champions.

Phnom Penh Water Supply Authority (PPWSA)

The Millennium Development Goals (MDGs) articulated by the General Assembly of the United Nations in 2000 included a commitment to reduce by half the proportion of the world's population that is unable to reach or afford safe drinking water by 2015. At the time of the Kingdom of Cambodia's adoption of these goals as one of the developing country signatories to the U.N. Declaration, the Phnom Penh Water Supply Authority (PPWSA) was in the middle of an impressive turnaround.

Just seven years ago in 1993, the failing state-owned monopoly was able to supply water to only 20 percent of the population of Phnom Penh, the Cambodian capital city, and less than half of the city area. Water supply was unreliable – intermittently available for only about 10 hours per day – and was of questionable quality and portability. Operations were highly inefficient. New applications for water connections took months to process. Billing was often late and very inaccurate since only 13 percent of customers had metered connections. Among those billed, only about 40 percent paid their dues. Employees were generally underqualified, underpaid, and unmotivated, resulting in incompetent service.

In 1993, Ek Sonn Chan, an engineer who rose through the ranks of Phnom Penh's city government, was put in charge as Director of the PPWSA. As soon as he took office, he quickly learned that the water system he had inherited was barely a system at all. Its pipe network, dating back to the French colonial period, was old, dilapidated, and unmapped. Seventy percent of the city's water was lost to leakage or theft (Biswas and Tortajada, 2010). Among the thieves were the company's own employees as well as military men and other VIPs who profited by redirecting and selling water to richer neighborhoods (Ramon Magsaysay

Award Foundation, 2012). Mr. Ek Sonn Chan took on the daunting challenge of improving the system by completely overhauling it. He began by restructuring the bloated company, hiring more qualified staff, promoting young and dynamic personnel to senior positions, promoting a culture of transparency, engaging civil society, and investing in modern management procedures and technology (Das et al., 2010). With financial aid and technical assistance from France, Japan, the UN, ADB, and the World Bank, PPWSA laid down new pipes, repaired leaks, installed thousands of water meters, and closed hundreds of illegal connections. Instrumental to these changes was a landmark government decree granting the company full autonomy in 1996, allowing PPWSA to run as an independent business-like operation without political interference.

To achieve higher revenues and thus financial self-sustainability, Mr. Ek pushed for a gradual increase in water tariffs, but only after making sure that its customers experienced and appreciated better quality and reliable service. The tariffs increased from zero tariffs before 1983 and USD0.04 per cu.m. in 1994 for residential customers to block rates of $0.14 to 0.31 per cu.m. in 2001. These tariffs were calculated considering the company's total expenses, including operation and maintenance costs and asset depreciation. This was far from the traditional model of below-cost pricing among public enterprises in developing countries, where strong lobbies from concentrated interests (urban poor groups, unions, and political parties) and the pressure to make popular policies to maximize electoral chances keep prices inefficiently low, especially when the poor are affected (Araral, 2008).

Between 1993 and 2008, PPWSA was able to increase its annual water production by 430 percent, its distribution network by 550 percent, and its customer base by 660 percent. During the same period, it reduced water lost to leakage and theft from over 70 percent to only 6.2 percent. The number of metered connections increased by 5,255 percent, while the number of accounts handled per employee increased by 670 percent.

In 2006, Mr. Ek received the Ramon Magsaysay Award for government service for "his exemplary rehabilitation of a ruined public utility, bringing safe drinking water to a million people in Cambodia's capital city (Ramon Magsaysay Award Foundation, 2012). Two years earlier, the PPWSA was awarded the Asian Development Bank Water Prize for "dramatically overhauling Phnom Penh's water supply system and demonstrating leadership and innovation in project financing and governance." In April 2012, PPWSA became the first domestically listed company on the Cambodia Securities Exchange.

Public sector monopolies in developing countries are often associated with inefficiencies and inability to meet rapidly growing demand.

Prior to its remarkable transformation, PPWSA was a glaring example of such problems. But through the excellent leadership of Ek Sonn Chan, PPWSA has demonstrated how absolute market power can be exercised while ensuring customer satisfaction, product and service quality, and long-term financial sustainability through good corporate governance, continuous improvement, and customer-orientation.

Energy Development Corporation (EDC)

Although some firms are granted absolute market power to allow them to maximize economies of scale typical of natural monopolies, other firms may be given special treatment, leading to substantial market power based on considerations of "strategic importance," especially in a developing country context. Market power is often vested on a firm to spur the development of an industry deemed critical to economic development or national security. Special treatment may not, and perhaps must not, last forever, though.

The Energy Development Corporation (EDC) was founded in 1976 as a government-owned and -controlled corporation under the Philippine National Oil Company (PNOC), mandated by law to explore alternative forms of fuel in the Philippines. It is currently engaged in electricity generation through renewable energy sources – including geothermal, hydroelectric, and wind – and in the construction and management of geothermal power plants.

The PNOC, which founded the EDC as its subsidiary, was established three years earlier by the Philippine government to ensure a stable supply of oil in the Philippines as well as to explore, exploit, and develop all energy resources in the country, as a direct response to rapidly increasing world oil prices and the 1973 Oil Crisis triggered by an OPEC oil embargo on the United States and its allies. Realizing that the country's dependence on foreign oil imports presented a threat to both national security and sustained economic development, the Philippine government mandated the EDC to explore and develop renewable energy sources to decrease the country's dependence on foreign fuel, which was then close to 100 percent.

In the 1980s, the company discovered and developed two large geothermal reserves in Leyte and Negros in the Central Philippines, the completion of which immediately made the Philippines, the world's second largest producer of geothermal energy, behind Iceland. Today, the Philippines remains the world's second largest producer, behind the United States. Geothermal energy currently provides over nearly

11–12 percent of the country's electricity (Balangue-Tarriela and Mendoza, 2015). The rapid development of the country's geothermal resources was deemed to be of national importance, and thus received generous support from the government. Richard Tantoco, Chief Operating Officer of EDC acknowledges:

"We were fortunate to have the backing of the government and that kind of development. And that kind of context provided very strong tinder for the fire. EDC developed and progressed rapidly under those types of conditions…"

With government support, the company was able to pursue investments that would have been considered too risky by private investors. The exploration of geothermal wells in Negros early in the company's history, for example, would have amounted to between $8 and $9 million – not a small amount of investment to ask for exploration in a country new to geothermal energy.

A crippling power crisis brought about by an electricity shortage in the 1990s due to insufficient installed capacity plus pressure from the World Bank pushed the Philippine government toward privatization and deregulation in the power industry, which took away the company's monopoly over geothermal energy. Through build-operate-and-transfer (BOT) schemes, private contractors were encouraged to construct and operate power generation facilities for an assured return on investments. EDC, still then a state-owned company, took advantage of this by venturing into a BOT project with financing from the World Bank in a new geothermal plant in the Central Philippines.

During the 2000s, the Philippine government pushed strongly for the privatization of many of its state-owned enterprises. In 2007, EDC was successfully privatized. With privatization came the loss of direct government support and financial guarantees, which meant the company had to find alternative ways of financing its big-ticket projects and managing the corresponding risks through BOT schemes and joint ventures. Another challenge was that the local generation business was getting crowded and major geothermal assets had already been exploited. This led to the company's exploration of opportunities abroad. EDC is currently exploring several joint ventures in geothermal energy in Chile, Canada, Peru, Australia, and Indonesia. Most of these projects are being explored in coordination with the respective energy ministries or other related government agencies in these countries. The company has also begun to diversify into other forms of renewable energy, including hydroelectric, and later, wind power.

PTT Exploration and Production PCL

As in the previous case, the PTT Exploration and Production PCL (PTTEP) was set up by the state-owned Petroleum Authority of Thailand (PTT) to explore and exploit resources of strategic importance to the country – oil and natural gas. Also as in the previous case, the PTT, which founded PTTEP, was established by decree in 1978 as the government's response to the 1973 oil crisis. The mandate of PTT was to procure oil for domestic consumption and to lessen Thailand's dependency on oil imports through the exploitation and exploration of oil and other energy resources within the country.

PTTEP was founded in 1985 specifically to take advantage of opportunities for joint ventures with foreign companies, primarily to strengthen PTT's resource exploration capabilities. Upon its founding, PTTEP immediately bought a 25 percent stake in Thai Shell's small oil field operation in Northern Central Thailand. In 1989, the company acquired all assets held by an American private equity firm, the Texas Pacific Group, in the Bongkot gas fields in the Gulf of Thailand. The acquisition of these assets by PTTEP allowed the company to invite foreign firms to develop the area for resource exploitation.

In 1990, PTTEP brought in French company Total, British Gas, and Statoil of Norway as partners in a BOT scheme to develop the Bongkot gas fields. Under this scheme, Total was to manage operations for the first five years, after which all operations were to be transferred to PTTEP. This was intended to allow PTTEP to maximize knowledge transfer and to learn best practices from its international partners. Through this and succeeding joint ventures in the development of local natural gas and oil reserves, the company was able to raise its capacities for exploration and operations to global standards.

Banking on its local success, PTTEP has pursued opportunities outside Thailand since the early 2000s. Its first successful venture outside the country was a joint project with Chevron to develop gas fields in Myanmar, which today services both Myanmar and Thailand's energy demands. The company has also ventured into Vietnam, Indonesia, Canada, Brazil, Algeria, Egypt, Mozambique, Kenya, Oman, and Australia. Although currently, only 10 to 20 percent of income comes from international operations, PTTEP expects the share of overseas income to increase to 20 to 30 percent by 2020.

The establishment of state-owned monopolies and the awarding of special government support in areas of "strategic importance" is common practice in the early years of industrial development across many developing countries – even those that generally welcome free market capitalism. What distinguishes our ASEAN champions is their ability to masterfully develop their own competencies so that they eventually "grow up" enough to be weaned off government support and to go out into the world to compete on an international level.

Manila Electric Company (Meralco)

Some of our champions have used their core businesses where they are able to exercise significant market power as a springboard for innovation and diversification. The Manila Electric Company was founded in 1903. Today, it is the largest electric distribution utility in the Philippines, exclusively powering more than 5 million customers across Metro Manila and surrounding areas. Apart from its core business in distribution, the company, through its subsidiaries, also engages in power generation, transmission and energy-related services.

Meralco gained its early advantage with its entry into the electricity sector made possible by its acquisition in 1904 of La Electricista, a Spanish-American electricity company that began providing electricity to residential consumers in Manila in 1892. By the turn of the century, La Electricista had been serving three thousand customers and provided street lighting services in parts of the city.

By being a first mover in a naturally monopolistic industry, the company was able to position itself toward becoming the Philippines' leading electricity provider early on. In 1925, the company was bought by Associated Gas & Electric Company (AGECO) of the United States. This allowed Meralco to purchase existing utilities such as small diesel-powered generators and consequently expand its operations beyond Manila and into its surrounding suburbs that would later form part of Metropolitan Manila. In 1961, a consortium of Filipino businessmen led by Eugenio Lopez Sr. bought Meralco from its American owners, becoming one of the first American firms in the country to be "Filipinized." A period of expansion and capacity building ensued in the areas of power generation and distribution. By 1969, Meralco became the country's first billion-peso company (Paterno, 2010). In the 1970s, the Philippine government nationalized power generation, forcing Meralco to sell its generation assets. Now focusing on electric distribution, the company tripled its franchise area by the mid-1980s (Paterno, 2010).

Although Meralco's franchise area is only 3 percent of the country's land area, it is by far the biggest distribution utility, serving 25 percent of the population and accounting for 55 percent of all electricity consumed, while the second-biggest power distributor accounts for less than 10 percent.

The sheer size of its exclusive franchise area – the entire national capital region plus the neighboring provinces, which in total make up about 25 percent of the country's population and 55 percent of all electricity consumed – has provided Meralco with a competitive advantage over other electric utilities and power generators in the country.

Moving forward, Meralco is intent on not only further strengthening its core distribution business and expanding its power generation capacity to ensure reliable supply for its customers, but also introducing innovations to create greater customer value. Toward the latter objective, the company has created a Corporate Technology and Transformation Office to encourage innovative solutions to promote customer centricity and enhance reliability. Meralco is embarking on a "smart grid" journey – putting in place a communications network layered on its electric grid – to provide real-time information regarding network conditions. This enables Meralco to optimize overall grid performance and provide rate options for more efficient use of electricity, including demand response and the handling of distributed energy sources like solar and wind.

From a customer standpoint, smart grid allows for the offering of prepaid electricity. Meralco's prepaid service, branded Kuryente Load, is the world's first electric service integrated with a telecommunications platform. Customers can load their meters in exactly the same way they load their mobile phones. Its product roadmap includes an enhanced postpaid service that will provide near real-time consumption data accessed by customers through an online account.

In parallel, Meralco is exploring renewable energy, battery storage, and even electric vehicles, supporting initiatives by the Asian Development Bank and various local government units to deploy electric tricycles and jeeps versus the conventional vehicles that cause pollution.

Philippine Long Distance Telephone Company (PLDT)

In the 1920s, several small telecom companies, each with its own system, served the Philippine archipelago. This meant that a call can only be made within an island or region, with zero connectivity between competing networks across the islands. To address this issue, the Philippine Commonwealth government passed a law creating the Philippine Long Distance Telephone Company (PLDT) to merge four competing telecom companies serving Eastern Visayas, Bicol Peninsula, and Samar Island. The law granted PLDT a 50-year charter and the exclusive right to establish telephone lines in specific parts of the country within a 40-year time period, creating a legal monopoly for the company over its franchise areas. The aim was to facilitate quick communication and delivery of services as a means of promoting economic development.

With this mandate, the company began to acquire other small telecom companies across the country, in order to hasten the interconnection of previously separate intercom systems into one nationwide network. The Second World War disrupted operations, but operations had resumed to prewar levels by the early 1950s. From its founding in 1928, PLDT ran as a private corporation, but in the 1970s, the company was nationalized by President Ferdinand Marcos. In 1982, the Philippine government acquired the company's only remaining competitor and integrated it into PLDT, making the company a national monopoly. With the toppling of the Marcos government in 1986, PLDT was soon re-privatized but remained a nation-wide monopoly until the Philippine government deregulated the telecommunications industry in 1995. The company experienced rough times during the 1997 Asian financial crisis, but this provided an opportunity for Manny Pangilinan of the Hong Kong-based First Pacific Co. Ltd. to acquire a 17.5 percent stake in PLDT, through which Mr. Pangilinan became CEO. Under Mr. Pangilinan's leadership, PLDT began to pursue more aggressive strategies.

In 1999, the company acquired Smart Communications, then and now the Philippine's largest mobile phone operator. This acquisition has proven to be a clever move as Smart now contributes greatly to PLDT's bottom line, buffering the effects of declining revenues from the landline business.

In 2000, PLDT started to venture into information and communications technology through the establishment of ePLDT. Services eventually offered by ePLDT have included data, data security, call centers, and e-commerce. In December 2000, ePLDT launched Smart Money, the world's first bank-issued reloadable electronic payment card linked to a mobile phone. Smart Money serves as what is now popularly known as an electronic or digital wallet that allows the user to pay bills (including third-party transactions), reload phone credits, and transfer money using a Smart mobile phone. PLDT's Smart Money arguably pioneered mobile money services, which have now become very popular in a number of African and Latin American countries. The famous M-Pesa was launched by Safaricom in Kenya, where about 25 percent of the country's GDP flows through electronic money (The Economist, 2013), more than six years after the launch of Smart Money. Other innovations introduced by PLDT include electronic mobile phone credit reloading for Smart and prepaid landline service.

Today, PLDT is focused on continuing to build its local subscriber base and preparing its services for international markets. With regard to the former, the company continues experimenting with new value-added services while strengthening its e-commerce services, particularly Smart Money. One of their latest new services is a joint project with the Philippines' SM Group and South Korea's Samsung in an online retail venture targeting overseas Filipino workers. The new service will allow overseas Filipinos to purchase retail products online and have the products delivered directly to their recipients at home using Smart Money (Manila Bulletin, 2014). For its internationalization strategy, the company has set up PLDT Global to seek opportunities abroad, specifically emerging markets. In 2014, PLDT bought a 10 percent stake in Rocket Internet, a German Internet business incubator, to codevelop innovative online payment solutions to be introduced in low-income markets in other countries.

PLDT has demonstrated how a company that has secured considerable market power by being a first mover and by taking advantage of economies of scale and scope can leverage its market strengths to develop pioneering innovations that create greater value for its customers and contribute further to its longer-term profitability. It continued building its competences through international alliances and mergers and acquisitions, which led to stronger marker positions by launching innovative products and services in related market sectors.

Masan Consumer Corporation

Although power and water utilities, telecommunications, and oil and gas exploration are more often considered natural monopolies, food and beverage companies also have the potential to develop and exercise market power. The economies of scale and scope linked to food and beverage processing and distribution, coupled with the potential for building household brands, provides an opportunity for firms to grow into powerful market players. When a company is able to hinge on the progress of its host country and its growing consumer market, such development potentiates its market power further.

Masan Consumer Corporation is the largest subsidiary of the Masan Group, one of Vietnam's top three private sector firms, with a market capitalization of over $3 billion. Masan manufactures and distributes food and beverage products including soya sauce, fish sauce, chili sauce, instant noodles, instant coffee, instant cereals, and bottled beverages. The company traces its origins to an import-export trading company founded in 2000, which was later merged with a food processing and seasoning firm in 2003.

Masan's initial success can largely be attributed to the rapid economic development experienced by Vietnam in the last two decades. The country's food and beverage industry has been on the rise due to improving living standards and rapid urbanization, leading to a substantial increase in the population's spending power. Masan Consumer has been able to successfully leverage this progress, allowing it to thrive quite remarkably. And this progress is expected to continue. In 2011, per capita expenditure on food and nonalcoholic beverages in the country still stood relatively low compared to its Asian peers, promising huge potential for further growth. Currently, the potential size of the food and beverage category is estimated at $500 million (Masan Group, 2014b). It is therefore not surprising that the company has taken an aggressive acquisition-led expansion path.

To help fund its expansion activities, Masan opened its doors to foreign investment. In 2011, Masan received $159 million from the U.S.-based multinational alternative asset manager Kohlberg Kravis Roberts & Co. LP (KKR) for a 10 percent stake in the company. This was followed by another $200 million in 2013, making KKR's investment in Masan Consumer the largest private equity transaction in Vietnam to date (Kohlberg Kravis Roberts & Co. LP, 2011; Reuters, 2013).

Masan has acquired several brands in recent years to diversify its growing portfolio. Being especially keen on the beverage sector, the company bought 50 percent of Vinacafe, the country's market leader in instant coffee in 2011, and bought additional shares to gain a majority stake the following year. Masan also bought into and later also gained a majority stake in a bottled mineral water company in 2013 (Masan Group, 2014a). Masan also bought stakes in an animal feed manufacturer in 2012 in a bid to join the protein-based food market.

Taking advantage of a rapidly growing domestic market has been a key to the success of Masan Consumer Corporation. As expected, the company is very determined to continue growing alongside the rapidly growing Vietnamese market and to further establish itself as the market leader in Vietnam's food and beverage sector. It managed to build scale and scope advantages to capitalize on the fast growth by acquiring key assets and a portfolio of well-recognized brands.

Boon Rawd Brewery

When a rapidly growing domestic market provides an opportunity for business, being a first mover no doubt boosts a company's market power potential. When proprietary technology is involved, the market power potential is multiplied even further. A company that successfully leverages such power can have a bright future ahead of it.

Boon Rawd Brewery was founded in 1933. It is currently the largest beverage company in Thailand. It produces, distributes, and export beverage products under several brands, including the famous Singha and Leo Beer brands. It has also ventured into other interests such as agriculture and real estate.

In 1929, Boonrawd Sresthaputra, the company's founder, fancied the idea of brewing a homegrown Thai beer after having sampled a number of imported brews. The following year, he requested permission from the monarchy to set up the first beer brewery in Thailand. It took three years for the permission to be granted by the King. While waiting, Mr. Boonrawd went to Germany and Denmark to study different techniques of beer-making (Soravji, n.d.). He brought back German brewing technology, which allowed him to produce high-quality beer on par with foreign brews.

Boon Rawd became the first beer brewery in Thailand when it began operations in 1934. The absence of local competition from being a first mover plus protection from imports provided by the Thai government allowed the company to grow virtually unchallenged for years. Local sales steadily increased through the decades. By the 1970s, Boon Rawd had started exporting to the United States, triggered by demand from returning soldiers who had tried Singha beer in Vietnam during the war. From then on to the 1990s, sales increased even more rapidly. In 1998, Boon Rawd introduced Leo Beer at a lower price point than Singha.

The company started expanding into the overseas market more aggressively in the 2000s. In 2010, Boon Rawd sought global partnerships with the football clubs Manchester United and Chelsea and the Formula One Red Bull Racing Team to promote the Singha brand (Businessweek, n.d.). Boon Rawd has also sought to diversify into snack products, fruit juices, and even Korean food, through several acquisitions. The company has also recently expanded into real estate and packaging (Businessweek, n.d.).

These expansion activities demonstrate how Boon Rawd has successfully leveraged its market power to expand its portfolio and move into both related and unrelated segments that present promising opportunities for the company both locally and overseas. This was a case that a company solidified its first-mover position in a market by acquiring unique proprietary technologies no other competitors had, which resulted in dominant market power for a long time.

Other ASEAN Champions: Lao Brewery Co. Ltd., EDL Generation Public Company, and PetroVietnam Gas Joint Stock Corporation (PV Gas)

In any discussion of market power, it is easy to overemphasize the impact of monopolies derived from state-owned or state controlled companies, or from fortuitous circumstances favoring the first firm to have access to critical resources. But the extension of such market power would not necessarily occur without concomitant management skills to continue to build and nurture core competencies. In our research, two firms provide graphic testimony to these arguments. From 1975 up to the early 1990s, large corporations in Lao were nationalized by the government. This included Lao Brewery, where foreign owners of the company surrendered their shares to the government. It was during this period of nationalization that Lao Brewery attained monopoly status, being the sole beer producer in Lao until the early 1990s, when the Lao government initiated market reforms. Since then, Lao Brewery has capitalized on its partnership with the Carlsberg Group to become one of the most successful and innovative companies in the country and is noted for its product quality, diversification, and unrivaled distributorships.

Another Lao company, EDL Generation Public Company, is a newcomer in the power generation industry but has already earned accolades from pundits for its leadership in the generation, distribution, and wholesale of electricity (primarily through its parent company), as well as in the construction of transmission lines. To understand the company's performance, the Mekong River is considered to be an important geographic landmark in Laos that connects the Tibetan Plateau to China's Yunnan province going through Indochina (Wikipedia, 2015). The majority of EDL Generation's hydropower plants relies on the Mekong River's presence in the country (EDL-Generation Public Company, 2015). In fact, EDL-Generation is the only company in Laos that constructs and operates hydropower plants. Even so, the company has leveraged knowledge about the industry as it has sourced its technology from Japan, France, and England and is now on track to become a key player in the region.

In a similar fashion, the PetroVietnam Gas Joint Stock Corporation (PV Gas), the current market leader in Vietnam's gas industry, was initially supported by the government under the auspices of its parent company, PetroVietnam. Being the first and sole distributor of dry gas in the country bore early benefits, and the company rose into prominence as the market leader. With the prospects for the Vietnamese gas industry looking favorable for its products and infrastructure. More importantly, the company seeks to further develop its technology and research activities to enhance processes and the quality of gases it provides. It plans to invest more on integrated, state-of-the-art infrastructure for its R&D institutions as well as enhance international cooperation ties with foreign companies, research institutions, and universities around the world (PetroVietnam, 2012; PV Gas, 2013).

Conclusions

Although often maligned as unfair or derided as unwieldy and inefficient, market power can be a highly enabling success factor both for the firm exercising it and the country whose socioeconomic development coevolves with it. It is a double-edged sword. Market dominance, control over prices, and weak or inexistent competition can lead to complacency and inertia. On the other hand, economies of scale and scope, deeper pockets, and in some cases, special government support can provide a springboard for innovation and international growth, contributing to long-term success.

Our ASEAN champions have successfully leveraged the market power that they have either secured for themselves by pioneering the industry or been entrusted with by the government in an effort to develop an industry of strategic importance for economic development or people's welfare. They have used their market power to develop competencies that have enabled them to sustain long-term profitability even with the arrival of competition and, for some, to venture into related and unrelated activities both local and abroad. A synthesis of these characteristics is presented in Exhibit 5.1.

Market power is of course neither unique nor confined to emerging and developing countries. In fact, its study occupies a prominent position in economics and industrial organization that has focused largely on developed economies. What is notable in ASEAN is the coevolution of market power and economic development. Many of our ASEAN champions have had market power that was secured through government edict as a national strategy to harness resources and to provide critical services in pivotal times of a country's history. Like Meralco, Electricite du Laos (EDL), although founded in 1961 as a private company, was nationalized by the government of Laos in 1986, and like PLDT, was tasked to consolidate several provincial public utilities under its supervision. In 2011, with strong government support, its subsidiary EDL-Generation Public Company became the first company to be listed in the Laos Stock Exchange – part of the government's efforts to offer Laos as a promising

Exhibit 5.1 Leveraging Market Power

frontier market for investors. Meralco, EDC, PPWSA, PTTEP, PLDT, and PetroVietnam Gas were all government-created monopolies.

Our ASEAN champions have been successful and continue to have promising futures because of how they have maximized their potential, having been bequeathed their market power early on. Champions like PPWSA have embraced good governance and corporate discipline to foster efficiency and a strong commitment to public service. Without such discipline, monopolies can quickly succumb to inefficiency and incompetence. Monopolies, especially those that had been given the privilege of government support early on, must build internal competencies and "grow up" sooner rather than later to sustain long-term success. EDC and PTTEP are shining examples of government supported monopolies that weaned themselves off special treatment and developed the competence to venture and succeed overseas.

Building internal competencies, developing human capital, and cultivating productive assets can be made easier when a firm holds market power. What sets our champions apart is their ability and conscious decision to use their strengths to innovate and create greater value for their customers. Meralco and PLDT turned their first mover advantage into strong innovative capabilities that set the basis for their strong international presence.

A rapidly growing domestic market, often characteristic of developing countries, is a boon to any firm, especially one that captures a large share of the market. Masan Consumer Corporation, for example, has grown alongside Vietnam's thriving consumer market. Its growth potential is as bright as the country's promising development prospects. As Vietnam's economy prospers, Masan can secure a growing customer base for as long as it preserves its market share by continuously upgrading product quality and variety to meet increasingly demanding consumer preferences as consumer incomes rise. In particular, it successfully acquired key assets and established a portfolio of well-known brands to sustain its dominance.

Commitment to product excellence and development of brand equity can come a long way in a company's push toward internationalization. Boon Rawd Brewery took advantage of foreign proprietary technology combined with market power bequeathed by the Thai monarchy early in its history to develop resources and build competencies, which it then used to invest in exploring markets overseas and building a global brand as it embarked on an internationalization strategy. In all, our arguments relating to market power are much more expansive in terms of understanding marketing in underdeveloped contexts. Market power is distinguished from marketing strategies. Although market power is a product of both endogenous and exogenous factors, firms that employed exemplary marketing strategies tend to arise from primarily internal or endogenous factors. Such firms are discussed and portrayed in detail in our next chapter.

6   Pioneering Marketing Strategies

Introduction

Economic development can be viewed from the historical prism of market transactions. Markets have been in existence since the first exchange and trade, but they are formally chronicled only as far back as the eleventh century, which ushered in chartered markets and new towns (Casson & Lee, 2011). Markets have foreshadowed development and have defined the human condition throughout history. Markets predate capitalism and corporations (Roxas, 2000).

Marketing management, on the other hand, is a relatively recent phenomenon, dating back to pre–World War II conditions to a strong producer orientation epitomized by Henry Ford's dictum that buyers could buy any car in "any color they want, as long as it is black" (Lutz & Weitz, 2005: 89). With more customer knowledge and awareness, this dictum shifted to a consumer orientation or a focus on customer needs and requirements. Stanford's professor Theodore Levitt, in his influential paper "Marketing Myopia," argued that businesses fail when they are more concerned with the product and lose sight of broader marketing/consumer needs (Levitt, 1975). More recently, there is a further shift to what Alvin Toffler (1980) called "prosumer" or its modern variant, co-creation, defined as deep engagement by the customer in defining the form and function (i.e., co-creating) of a product or service (Mills, 1986; Prahalad & Ramaswamy, 2004a, 2004b).

With respect to emerging markets, marketing management can be conveniently parsed into three stages of strategic decisions: (1) what market to enter, (2) how to market, and (3) when to enter. In this chapter where we highlight the experiences of successful ASEAN firms, our focus is on the first and the third decisions. The argument underlying marketing excellence is that such ASEAN champions outdo their peers in these two phases (market entry and timing), despite facing formidable odds and constraints. The second question – how to enter – is more nuanced and treated in the next chapter (deepening localization).

Deciding on which markets to enter typically involves considerations of potential size, access, and responsiveness. Size is important in determining the level of market penetration and anticipated revenues. However, access is likewise pivotal in that even highly attractive but inaccessible markets can significantly raise costs and entry and ensuing operations. Finally, responsiveness of customers to various marketing attractors, such as the 4Ps (place, price, product, and promotion), will determine the potential effectiveness of a given marketing strategy.

As applied to developing markets, such as ASEAN, considerations of size, access, and responsiveness can be potentially discouraging. The limited size of markets, the difficulty in gaining entry, and the lack of receptiveness – characteristics of a relatively underdeveloped economy – leads to a calculation where costs far outweigh benefits. Unsurprisingly, many multinationals shy away until they think that a market has developed substantially. Intuitively, such reticence can become opportunities for local firms, particularly if they are attuned to local market conditions and have the ability to respond to market needs.

In a previous study of successful local firms, called the "rough diamonds," it is reported that they capitalized on these opportunities but are at considerable risk (Park, Zhou & Ungson, 2013). Nascent market niches are not easy to identify, and even if they are, the risk is that consumers who populate these niches might not grow significantly, nor will they necessarily respond to market cues and strategies. Hence, not only do prospective firms need to recognize the potential, but they must be prepared to invest and nurture the segment themselves. In this context, we call this "filling unserved market niches."

Closely related to this decision is when to enter, or the general issue of timing. Observers suggest that the timing of entry is oftentimes the more difficult decision when compared to identifying which markets to enter, given that windows of opportunities tend to be brief and uncertain. In the mainstream marketing literature, this decision is included in the topic of first and secondary mover advantages.

First-mover advantages accrue when leaders are able to build their reputation, secure logistics and materials, garner government support, and build entry to barriers (Lieberman & Montgomery, 1998). On the other hand, followers can gain the advantage if they are able to learn from the mistakes of the leader, capitalize on the demand created by the leader, and offer better products and services than the leader (Lieberman & Montgomery, 1998). In all, there is no conclusive empirical evidence that either decision holds an absolute advantage (D'Aveni, 1994; Lieberman & Montgomery, 1998).

This finding holds true when applied to developing markets, such as ASEAN, with some firms developing competitive muster as first movers, while others follow a successful growth path as followers and learners. Success depends largely on how well a particular decision is implemented and supported by the entire organization.

Because ASEAN presents such diverse markets, new models for capturing value in a meaningful manner have become an imperative (Bhasin, 2010). In *Think New ASEAN!*, scholars Philip Kotler, Hermawan Kartajaya and Hooi Den Huan (2015) argue for a further shift from consumer to human centricity. In cases that we present in this chapter, we address some of these issues and present the nuances of these marketing decisions. A preview of these cases is as follows:

- *Bangkok Cable Company Limited* (Thailand): sustained growth through international collaboration and related product and market diversification;
- *Thai Metal Trade Public Company Limited* (Thailand): total steel solution provider with high value-added service across the entire supply chain;
- *Pruksa Real Estate Public Company Limited*(Thailand): correctly forecasted market needs and built a formidable market position;
- *PT FKS Multiagro Tbk* (Indonesia): first company to use whole fish to produce food oil and import soybeans to meet fast-growing local needs;
- *Keppel FELS Limited* (Singapore): built a competitive edge by addressing local needs;
- *TC Pharmaceuticals Industries Co., Ltd.* (Thailand): first to market energy drink to blue-collar workers;
- *PT Solusi Tunas Pratama Tbk* (Indonesia): led the market growth with right technologies and business model;
- *Other ASEAN Champions: Tien Phong Plastic Joint Stock Company* (Vietnam), *PT Ultrajaya Milk Industry and Trading Company Tbk* (Indonesia), *and Cebu Air, Inc.* (Philippines): displaying the benefits of first mover and secondary mover advantages.

Bangkok Cable Company Limited

Bangkok Cable Company Limited was founded in 1964 by Mr. Sompong Nakornsri, who heads the company as Chief Executive Officer. Currently, it holds a formidable market position in several products: wire and cable products including copper cables, PVC wires, aluminum cables, telecommunication cables, and fire safety cables. The company also exports its products to neighboring countries such as Myanmar, the Philippines, and Bangladesh.

But, like many other ASEAN champions, the company's success was based on its ability to understand the economic needs at the time and its willingness to shape the market. In the 1960s, Thailand received increased demands in electricity generation and consumption, resulting in the construction of more power plants within the country (Country Studies, n.d.). Moreover, Thailand had shifted from 110 voltages to 220 voltages. This meant that wires had to be changed, increasing the demand for new copper wires that were compatible with 220 voltages.

Mr. Nakornsri was able to identify this opportunity in the cable market. He sought to produce copper wires to support the growing market of Thailand and the infrastructure of the country. A visionary in this respect, he secured one of the first contracts to produce copper wiring. At first, the company focused on supplying homebuilding installations and catered mainly to the provincial markets (Bangkok Cable Co. Ltd., 2014) whose demands for electricity were growing rapidly (Country Studies, n.d.). Later on, the company expanded its market to the government and private sectors.

In addition, collaboration with Japanese companies in technical and academic matters gave Bangkok Cable a comparative edge in developing and producing various types of cables and wires. These advantages included technology transfers and the sharing of best practices which made the company more competitive and that facilitated the company's diversification into PVC wires.

By the late 1980s, the company pursued a joint venture with Phelps Dodge Thailand Co. Ltd. to produce copper rods, complementing its other ventures with Japanese firms. By the year 2000, the company opened its fire- and flame-testing laboratory for cables. This included Bangkok Cable's production and distribution of fire safety cables.

Currently, the company mainly exports its products with neighboring countries such as Myanmar. Most of Bangkok Cable's overseas customers concentrate on government infrastructures, since such projects require large amounts of cables and wires. It is expected that demand for such products would go up, especially since various Southeast Asian countries continue to pursue several infrastructure projects (OECD, 2014). In all, Bangkok Cable combines its previous expertise in marketing along with technological adaptations to continuously enhance its market position in the industry.

Thai Metal Trade Public Company Limited

One element shared by many ASEAN champions is the ability to creatively combine technological prowess with market savvy. Thai Metal

Trade Public Company Limited, a total steel solution provider, engages in the distribution, processing, and production of steel. The company aims to provide all-inclusive steel-related services to their favored sector – medium-sized companies – according to client specifications.

Thai Metal's marketing strategies resulted from its recognition of early market needs as well as an astute reading of competition. At the time of the company's inception, the value of steel in Thailand was relatively the same, reflecting its commodity status, which was advantageous for the company's larger competitors. The company made the bold move of differentiating itself from other trading companies by offering value-added services. Nevertheless, initiating a differentiation strategy in a commodity market was a risk. The company needed to convince its customers to buy steel from the company by including additional services besides distribution of steel.

In order to support this strategy, Thai Metal established steel center functions to penetrate new market bases mostly including medium-sized companies. Furthermore, the company improved its distribution systems such as through warehouse expansions (Thai Metal Trade PCL, 2010). By 1992, the company was renamed as the Thai Metal Trade Co., with a vision for a radically new business model. In light of its success in offering various services beyond basic steel, the company strove to become the fully integrated steel service center.

Mr. Soon Tarasansombat, the current CEO, was able to visualize Thai Metal as an integrated steel company that would not only concentrate on steel trading, but also on steel servicing and manufacturing. He saw that the company could not survive on steel trading alone, particularly since there were larger steel companies in Thailand that concentrated on the same service. Instead, he decided to focus the company's services toward medium-sized companies that were willing to pay for Thai Metal's services over other larger companies so long as additional services were provided.

Mr. Soon Tarasansombat used his vision of an integrated steel company in order to capture this niche market. In an interview, he opines:

"We're just a small company. And then step by step we [increased] some sales then [expanded] our market. We tried to penetrate in some other markets that we didn't cater before. … We [expanded] some other functions. We setup steel center functions." – Paisal Tarasansombat, Chief Executive Officer

In 2004, the company ventured into the fabrication industry. Unlike the general construction industry where it concentrated on cement-based construction such as buildings, warehouses, and factories, the fabrication industry concentrated more on steel components such as car parts, truck assemblies, and so on. For the company's steel component, Thai Metal concentrated more on producing pipes for which local demand was high. Through this venture, the company established its own pipe manufacturing plant, where Thai Metal gets 50 percent of its sales.

Thai Metal partnered with Metal One of Japan in 2007 – a partnership that reaped further synergies through Metal One's experience and expertise combined with Thai Metal's marketing force and capabilities. Because Thai Metal owns a complete supply chain of steel – ranging from steel production and distribution to servicing – the company is able to tweak the strength and durability of its steel depending on specific requests by customers. This is further supported by the company's proactive approach in servicing its customers, ensuring Thai Metal's loyal consumer base among medium-sized companies (Thai Metal Trade PCL, 2014).

Currently, Thai Metal Co. is primarily targeting medium-sized companies, as these types of firms require more support as opposed to larger-sized firms. Through this strategy, the company is able to carve out its own market share separate from larger competing companies. Furthermore, Thai Metal cannot just distribute steel because the market price of said product tends to be the same regardless of the company source. Due to this price competition, medium-sized companies tend to source their steel from larger companies that provide steel at the same price. Thai Metal was able to prevent this when it offered not only to distribute steel but also to guarantee customers of its steel products based on customized quality specifications. Thai Metal continues to build marketing competencies based on its shrewd understanding of technological developments.

Pruksa Real Estate Public Company Limited

Among the few cases that exemplify industrial marketing is Pruksa Real Estate Public Company Limited. Founded in 1993 as a residential developer by Mr. Thongma Vijitpongpun, the company's primary business is the construction and development of low-cost housing, but it has recently diversified into the development of high-end real estate projects. Its housing products include the construction of townhouses, duplexes, and single detached houses for low-cost housing, along with villas and condominiums for their high-end real estate projects.

In the 1990s, the real estate market in Thailand was gearing toward townhouses. The Thai government promoted low- and middle-priced housing in 1993 through reducing corporate income taxes for developers who constructed low-cost housing projects. Along with this, the Thai government also increased civil service salaries and liberalized the banking sector in Thailand, allowing commercial banks and other financial institutions to provide more housing loans to its customers. The reforms made by the Thai government created a new market of consumers interested in low-cost housing, due to the increase of salaries and better loan programs contributing to Thailand's middle class growth at that time (Kritayanavaj, n.d.).

Real estate developers in the early 1990s were not too keen on undertaking low-cost housing projects due to low margins of return. Seeing the opportunity in terms of the potential market growth for low-cost housing, Mr. Thongma founded Pruksa Real Estate in 1993 in order to take advantage of the new niche market of middle-class customers looking for affordable and low-cost housing. In order to keep revenues sizeable, Mr. Thongma implemented a high-volume model for his company's low-cost housing projects, supported with new and innovative construction processes.

Pruksa Real Estate was founded in 1993, riding on the back of government incentives provided to real estate developers offering low-cost housing. It was during this period that the low-cost housing market was still in its infancy. Several Thai customers were looking for houses with affordable rates. Pruksa Real Estate decided to develop town houses to capture the growing demand for low-cost housing.

It was right after the company's founding that Pruksa Real Estate was able to develop several townhouses and duplexes. These projects included Baan Pruksa, Pruksa Town, The Reno, and Villette Citi. Subsequently, the company expanded beyond constructing townhouses.

New market demands meant that the company had to adapt. In Thailand's case, the real estate market had an increase of demand for low-cost housing, with demands going as high as eight hundred thousand units in the industry from the years 1993 to 1997; and reaching a demand of ninety thousand units per year after the Asian Financial Crisis (Kritayanavaj, n.d.). Pruksa Real Estate decided to capitalize on this venture.

The company decided to increase its production in order to meet growing demands for low-cost housing in Thailand. Pruksa Real Estate established in 2005 a new precast concrete factory so that it could increase its production, supporting several low-cost housing projects (Pruksa Real Estate PCL, 2014a). The construction of Pruksa's precast concrete factory was supplemented by knowledge and skill-transfer programs from Germany (Pruksa Real Estate PCL, 2014b).

Besides the construction of its precast concrete factory, the company also completed its precast fence and pillar factory in 2005. The construction of the said factory amounted to 150 million baht (Pruksa Real Estate PCL, 2014a). The company's investments in constructing its precast factories allowed Pruksa Real Estate to increase its market share in the Thailand housing industry by guaranteeing construction materials for the company's projects.

Furthermore, the company continues its strategy of not only constructing and developing its own projects, but also managing the projects after completion. This means that the operations of Pruksa's projects are also operated by the same company. This practice by Pruksa is seen to be different from other real estate developers, since the usual practice for real estate development companies is that they spearhead construction, but not the operation of projects once completed.

In order to accommodate its long-term growth both in the construction, development, and management of its real estate projects, the company adopted a strategic business unit (SBU) structure to minimize costs and sustain the company's growth (Pruksa Real Estate PCL, 2014a).

The company rebranded itself in 2010, by changing its English name from "Preuksa Real Estate" to the current Pruksa Real Estate brand. The brand change aimed to reflect the evolution of the company's services. One of these changes is the development of condo projects targeted at high-growth areas within and in proximity of Bangkok (Pruksa Real Estate PCL, 2014a). The move to developing condominium projects is one of the key strategies of the company in pursuing diversification.

In order to minimize costs, the company created an integral strategy to grow its market share. While other real estate developers hire contractors for construction, it was decided by the company that it would manage its own construction projects. This strategy allowed Pruksa Real Estate to implement total quality management policies in order to keep costs at a minimum and manage time effectively.

PT FKS Multiagro Tbk

As indicated in the previous chapter, food and agribusiness constitute a critical industry in the early stages of economic development. FKS Multiagro is engaged in the food and feed industry. Its three business activities are fisheries, feeds, and trading. In 1970, before FKS Multiagro, its founder created a trading company based in Jakarta that exported agricultural commodities. From that time until the 1980s, the business engaged in the trade of spices and exportation to Europe, the United States, and China. The company also expanded its operations throughout the country by establishing branches in other parts of Indonesia.

In 1992, FKS Multiagro was incorporated as PT. Fishindo Kusuma Sejahtera. It commenced commercial operations in 1993, engaged in the production of feed ingredients, and was the first company in Indonesia that used whole fish in the production of fish meal and fish oil. In 1998, the company expanded its manufacturing facilities by increasing its capacity to process whole fish and including the processing of poultry feathers for the production of feather meal. Despite the Asian Financial Crisis and the depreciation of the Indonesian Rupiah, exporters found an opportunity given the weaker currency. Despite a fall in domestic demand, export activities enabled the company to boost its revenue and net income.

In 2000, the company underwent a period of re-evaluating its core business and the change from El Niño to La Niña weather patterns exposed the company's reliance and vulnerability to the availability of fish. Thus, the company decided to lessen its reliance on the manufacture of feed ingredients and explore opportunities in the import of feed ingredients. Given that the largest feed ingredient imported at the time was soybean meal, the company decided to go with this.

In 2002, the company decided to list its shares on the Jakarta Stock Exchange, now known as the Indonesian Stock Exchange. In 2005, the company installed a cold storage facility with a capacity of 300 MT. It was in 2006 when the company changed its name from Fishindo Kusuma Sejahtera to FKS Multiagro. This was done to represent the transition the company had undergone from industrial fisheries to a broader feed ingredient base. FKS also stands for the three product lines of the company, namely fisheries, kernel (corn), and soya. Also in 2006, the company crossed the 1 trillion Rupiah mark in terms of revenue.

The reason for the company's decision to include soy in its portfolio was mainly foresight. The company had observed that Indonesians consume soy on a regular basis in the form of Tahu Tempe. Furthermore, there is inadequate production of soybeans within the country. With the country's growing population, it is anticipated that the demand for soybeans will continue to increase.

The current strategy of the company is to continue with prioritizing the import of healthy foods, particularly soy beans. It sees that local consumption per capita of meat and poultry is still relatively low while consumption of tempeh and tofu are quite high. The company believes that given the lack of local production of soybeans relative to the demand of consumers and small and medium producers of food in which soybeans are a major ingredient, FKS Multiagro will find soybean import continuously profitable. This is only expected to increase given the growth of the middle-class sector (PT FKS Multiagro Tbk., 2014).

PT Solusi Tunas Pratama Tbk

In another example of industrial marketing, Solusi Tunas Pratama ranks as one of the leading telecommunications infrastructure providers in Indonesia. Since its founding in 2006, Mr. Nobel Tanihaha has led the company as its President Director. Solusi Tunas engages in providing, managing, and leasing Base Transceiver Station towers.

When the Indonesian government issued eleven licenses to telecommunication (telecom) operators, most of the telecom operators initially refused to share their Base Transceiver Station (BTS) tower networks with one another. This presented problems for Indonesia as it would be considered a logistical nightmare if all eleven telecom operators built BTS tower networks independent from one another. This provided an opportunity for Solusi Tunas to operate as a telecom infrastructure provider independent of the eleven telecom operators, especially the big three operators of Indonesia. Ever since, leasing out BTS towers has been the core business of Solusi Tunas.

It was during its founding that the Indonesian government was trying to convince telecom operators to allow their BTS towers and other networks to be accessed by other local competitors. These telecom operators included Indonesia's Big 3 companies in the local telecom industry: Telkomel, Indosat, and XL Axiata (Oxford Business Group, n.d.).

While the Indonesian government was negotiating with the Big 3 and other telecom operators, Solusi Tunas decided to join its first bid to buy a BTS tower. Mr. Nobel Tanihaha mentions that:

"... I came back to Jakarta, set up a company, went to the bidding then I lost. I lost to the biggest tower company now in Asia. They [became] the biggest because they won that [bid] first."

Losing its first bid did not stop Solusi Tunas from pursuing its core business. The company started to build its first BTS towers right after said bidding. In 2007, Solusi Tunas signed a contract with PT Ericsson Indonesia for the construction of 528 towers to build and have subleased to PT Axis Telecom Indonesia. Subsequently in 2008, the company entered into a master lease agreement with PT Bakris Telecom Tbk (PT Solusi Tunas Pratama Tbk, 2014).

However, Mr. Nobel Tanihaha realized that building BTS towers alone was both financially and logistically unfeasible. He along with the entire company decided to adapt their strategy by acquiring BTS towers from telecom operators themselves.

In 2009, the company bought 543 towers from PT Indosat Tbk., PT Smart Telecom, and PT Telekomunikasi Indonesia (Persero) Tbk. To pursue its expansion, Solusi Tunas signed Master Lease Agreements with PT Axis Telecom Indonesia, PT XL Axiata Tbk., PT First Media Tbk, and PT Hutchinson CP Telecommunications. As of 2010, the company was the fourth largest tower provider in Indonesia, with its portfolio containing 650 BTS towers in Jakarta and approximately 500 more in the Greater Jakarta region and other locations in the country (Borroughs, 2012). In 2012, Solusi Tunas acquired PT Platinum Technology, a company that owns fiber optic network investments and microcell poles (PT Solusi Tunas Pratama Tbk, 2014).

Using newly acquired PT Platinum Technology as its subsidiary, the company has established small data centers using fiber optics. Solusi Tunas is considered to be one of the pioneers in the telecom provider industry to use microcell posts as a means of rolling out its fiber optics expansion. The company expects that Indonesia's growing middle class would fuel the expansion of the telecom industry, hence the need for upgrading its networks using fiber optic technology to meet this demand in the next few years (PT Solusi Tunas Pratama Tbk, 2014).

This is further supported by the increasing usage of LTE technology in Indonesia's big cities. Hence, a fiber optic-based infrastructure is necessary to meet the increase of data usage expected in LTE-based technologies. Moreover, the company has used innovative tactics in adding value to its service. One of these innovations is the company developing a software application for telecom providers to share and distribute code division multiple access (CDMA), a channel-access method integral to communication technologies (PT Solusi Tunas Pratama Tbk, 2014).

Solusi Tunas strategy is centered on increasing profit margins and portfolio expansion. In terms of increasing profit margins, the company continues to take advantage of its lease agreements with telecom companies, along with benefiting from its IPOs. This has allowed Solusi Tunas to increase its revenues in 2012 by 60 percent as compared to the previous year (PT Solusi Tunas Pratama Tbk, 2014).

In terms of portfolio expansion, Solusi Tunas aims to expand its capacity for bigger data networks. The company is aiming to concentrate on areas with larger density of data users as opposed to increasing coverage. By focusing on areas with larger density, the company will be able to increase its profit over time due to the increase of data traffic (PT Solusi Tunas Pratama Tbk, 2014).

In aid of this expansion, the company is seeking to grow its portfolio through acquisitions of towers from other independent tower providers or from existing telecom operators. Solusi Tunas uses a selective acquisition process that enables the company to strategically increase its portfolio. An integral focus of tower operators is having strong balance sheets to support large capital expenditures needed for the construction of new towers since companies cannot simply rely on tower acquisition alone (Grazella, 2013b). Expansion of portfolio requires strong financial capacity, hence why Solusi Tunas's current strategy is focused on increasing profit margins in supporting portfolio expansion. Solusi Tunas senses the market needs and makes dynamic adjustments ahead of the market. It aggressively expands the tower portfolio, acquires necessary technologies, and establishes market positioning according to impending market changes while addressing internal financial conditions.

Keppel FELS Limited

To be the first mover in oil rigs reflects not only marketing gravitas but also a calculated risk because of the high investment. Keppel FELS was founded in 1967 and is the largest rig builder in the world today. It specializes in mobile offshore drilling rigs that can be used in deep waters and harsh environments (Bloomberg Businessweek, 2014). Keppel FELS is listed as a subsidiary of Keppel Corporation and leads Keppel Offshore & Marine's (Keppel O&M) offshore operations. Its core activities are the design, construction, fabrication, and repair of offshore drilling rigs and production facilities as well as other offshore support facilities. Mr. Wong Kok Seng has held the current Managing Director position since October 2012.

"[Mr. KC Lee] built the first oil rig in Asia; that was the first in the market. The advantage at that point was that they were the first in the market then so the early bird catches the worm in this case." – Wong Kok Seng, Managing Director

Far East Shipbuilding Industries Limited (FESL), later renamed as Far East Levingston Shipbuilding (FELS), was born in 1967. It was a family-owned offshore yard founded by Mr. Lee Khim Chai or "KC Lee." Toward the end of the decade, there was an expectation of offshore exploration expansion in the waters of Southeast Asia as more areas came under lease or concession agreements. Mr. KC Lee saw an opportunity to enter the rig-building business as the demand for oil rigs was anticipated to increase due to heightened exploration in the region. Furthermore, the estimated amount of time that companies were expected to carry out exploration in offshore concession areas in Southeast Asia was about 10 years.

Shortly thereafter, in the 1970s, ARCO of Indonesia kick-started the business of oil exploration in the Southeast Asia region. At the time, all the rigs used for this purpose originated from Western companies since rig building in the region was practically nonexistent during this period.

Moreover, the dominant players in the market were from the United States of America. Being the first rig-builder in Asia, Keppel FELS benefitted from the first-mover advantage. The costs of constructing a rig in the West and transporting it to Southeast Asia where it was to operate were immense, which is where Mr. KC Lee saw an opportunity for his company to enter the market.

Mr. KC Lee sought to gain knowledge from American rig-building industry leaders concentrated in the areas of Mississippi and Texas. The three big players in the business during this time were Bethlehem, Levingston, and LeTourneau.

The 1970s was a successful year of learning and capacity-building for the company as they sought to augment their knowledge and expertise in rig building and were able to achieve the delivery of quality rigs to their clients, all the while still remaining a contract manufacturing company. The subsequent years of 1971–1973 were tough on FELS, and its profits were affected by the cyclical nature of the industry. While 1974 marked a year of prosperity for the company, it was cognizant of the dangers of focusing solely on rig building. The company decided to diversify into related products such as platforms, heli-rigs, jack-up legs, and derricks, among other steel structures.

The years of 1975 and 1976 were record-breaking years for the company in terms of profits with shareholders earning 25 percent dividend. True to the cyclical nature of the industry, this was followed by a slowdown in the demand for rigs and ships. The company's diversification strategy allowed it to keep its yards busy for that year despite a slowdown in operations. However, it would not be able to sustain them for long: FELS reported its first loss in 1978 and its second in 1979.

In the late 1970s, rig-building companies that carried original designs such as LeTourneau and Bethlehem set up operations in Singapore. FELS was now faced with competition from these original manufacturers because it was now operating in the same region as them. FELS had to find its competitive edge in order to continue to thrive in the industry. FELS also decided to license designs in order to remain competitive with companies with original design capabilities. FELS licensed a rig design from Friede & Goldman, an American engineering company that designed rigs but had no building capacity.

While Keppel Shipyard had a majority stake in the company since 1973, it was only in 1980 that Keppel took over the management of the company and started looking at changing the corporate strategy. When Keppel management came in, an upward climb was ahead of them. Although the company was profitable for the most part, current projects were delayed and the current cost management system in place was inefficient. The new management was able to turn things around and transform the company into an efficient organization. Furthermore, market outlook was positive as the rise in oil exploration led to an increasing demand for rigs. The company's revenue in 1980 doubled. By 1981, it had achieved a record net profit of S$42.7 million, had a steady flow of projects in the works, and was completing jobs ahead of schedule.

In 1982, FELS bid for a Soviet Union contract to build two turnkey projects, one of which was a harsh environment rig which the company had never built before. After seven months of negotiation, FELS won the bid; both projects were completed by 1984. The subsequent years marked a period of downturn in demand for rigs; however, the company foresaw a pickup in 1986 and in anticipation of this, decided to build the Friede & Goldman MOD V jack-up rig that could withstand harsh environments and was capable of operating in deep waters. In less than a year after completion, the rig was bought by Santa Fe International Services. Mr. Frank Connor of Santa Fe said, *"Against the European, Chinese, and American shipyards, FESL wasn't always cheaper, but they were the best in terms of delivery times."*

In 1993, FELS signed two Build-Own-Operate agreements with the National Power Corporation of the Philippines, marking its first power generation undertaking. FELS was commissioned by then President of the Philippines, Fidel V. Ramos, to build a floating power plant. This was built in Singapore and towed to Batangas. In 1994, a second order came in that was to be towed to Manila. Power generation helped boost the company's bottom line, and this became the second most important business for Keppel FELS. Later on, once the contracts with the Philippine Government had ended, these barges were refurbished and deployed to Brazil.

Since the integration of Keppel FELS, Keppel Shipyard, and Keppel Singmarine under Keppel Offshore & Marine in 2002, the three companies have been able to reap synergies. For example, before the integration, Keppel AmFELS used to be under Keppel FELS while the yards in the Philippines were managed under Keppel Shipyard; this led to different managerial practices that served a narrow set of interests. However, under the umbrella of Keppel Offshore & Marine, the companies are able to apply standardized managerial practices and purse a common vision.

Keppel FELS and Keppel Offshore & Marine believe in the "near market, near customer" approach that allows them to better cater to customer needs and contribute to local content. In line with this, Keppel Offshore and Marine has established offices in various parts of the world such as the United States, Brazil, the Netherlands, Azerbaijan, Indonesia, China, and Japan (Keppel Offshore and Marine, 2014).

Integration has also helped Keppel O&M to pursue their "near market, near customer" strategy. Keppel O&M is able to better reach customers through its network of yards and the presence of local teams worldwide. Also, customers with varying projects have the ease of working with a single entity to provide a range of services. Though each yard has its own areas of specialization, Keppel O&M allows greater rationalization of resources by allowing sister companies to utilize facilities and workforce all over the world (Seatrade, 2012).

Mr. Wong has identified sustainable energy as a potential growth area for Keppel FELS. Given the company's design capabilities and expertise in construction coupled with a growing long-term demand for off-shore wind energy in Europe, he believes that Keppel FELS is in an optimal position to maximize opportunities in this area. For instance, the European Wind Energy Association (EWEA) anticipates that by 2030, 120 gigawatts of offshore wind energy can be attained. In line with this, Keppel FELS has tailored solutions for installation and maintenance vessels to support offshore wind farms (Lee, 2013). Its continuous success comes from its market-based value that emphasizes building advantages by addressing local needs. It applies the same value in its international operations looking for business opportunities from local practices and needs.

TC Pharmaceutical Industries Co., Ltd.

Diversification can be an integral part of any marketing strategy. While this subject is treated in depth in later chapters, one company that successfully integrated marketing as a part of its diversification strategy is the TC Pharmaceutical Industries Co., Ltd. It is engaged in the manufacturing and marketing of nonalcoholic beverages and snacks. Its product line includes Kratingdaeng (Red Bull), Zolar energy drink, Puriku white tea, Sponsor sports drink, and Sunsnack. Saravoot Yoovidhya, son of founder Chaleo Yoovidhya, is the Managing Director of TC Pharmaceutical Industries Co., Ltd.

The company was founded by Chaleo Yoovidhya in 1956. Mr. Yoovidhya was a self-made man from humble beginnings. He was a bus-ticket collector, a duck farmer, and a fruit trader before arriving in Bangkok to work as a salesman for a foreign pharmaceutical company (The Red Bull Beverage Co. Ltd., n.d.a). Mr. Yoovidhya pursued unrelated diversification by expanding his business to include the manufacturing and retailing of products used by consumers in their daily lives (The Red Bull Beverage Co. Ltd., n.d.b). In 1976, Mr. Yoovidhya created the Kratingdaeng (Red Bull) formula. After a year in the market, Kratingdaeng outsold all of its competitors except for Lipovitan – D. The following year, Red Bull would outsell this too to become the number one energy drink in Thailand.

The reason behind Kratingdaeng's success was that Mr. Yoovidhya was able to strategically market and to position his product in order to appeal to blue-collar workers (Fernquest, 2012). Not only did he tap laborers by building his brand through distributing free samples and heavily advertising to the target market, but he made the decision to target provincial areas of the country first. This strategy was unique at the time and distinguished Kratingdaeng from other products on the market (Horn, 2012). In 1978, the company changed its name to "TC Pharmaceutical Industries Co., Ltd."

In 1985, Sponsor – an electrolyte beverage marketed as a "Sports Drink" – was launched by the company (TC Pharmaceutical Industries Co. Ltd., 2011). Today, Sponsor is Thailand's most popular sports drink (DKSH, 2014). The beginnings of Kratingdaeng's internationalization trace back to 1987 when Dietrich Mateschitz, an Austrian cosmetics salesman, and Mr. Yoovidhya entered into a partnership to create Red Bull GmbH, an Austrian-based company independent of TC Pharmaceutical Industries (Onkvisit and Shaw, 2009). Mr. Mateschitz discovered that Kratingdaeng was useful as a cure for his jetlag and after getting in contact with Mr. Yoovidhya, each of them put up $500,000.00 to create the western producer of Red Bull.

TC Pharmaceutical's Red Bull is exported to foreign markets and is the market leader in the Asia Pacific Region. In terms of energy drinks, it ranks first in China and second in Thailand. In 2012, it recorded a market share of 81.2 percent in off-trade volume in China. However, in markets such as the Philippines and Indonesia, TC Pharmaceuticals has been unable to take full advantage of opportunities as brands such as Asia Brewery's Cobra and PepsiCo's Sting of the Philippines have been considered to be more dynamic and heavily marketed and advertised in comparison to TC's Red Bull. Although TC's Red Bull has a long history in the region, customer interest is waning due to this (Euromonitor International, 2013).

TC Pharmaceutical Industries is looking to launch its sports drink "Sponsor" in Vietnam. The sport drink segment has been growing at double-digit rates in the country due to the public's increasing interest in fitness and health. Sponsor aims to appeal to those who are involved in sports, outdoor or industrial workers, office workers, and students with active lifestyles. In 2014, TC Pharmaceutical Industries teamed up with DKSH to bring this product to Vietnam (DKSH, 2014).

Red Bull sponsors various concerts and racing events to promote its brand, such as the international racing event called "The Race of Champions," which was created in 1988 and was jointly sponsored by the brands Red Bull and the Boon Rawd Corporation's Singha in Thailand in 2012. The event is the only motorsport event which brings together drivers from various motorsport categories to race in identical cars. In the same year, the company sponsored the Kratingdaeng Fat Fest Bangkok, a concert showcasing over 100 bands on five different stages.

TC Pharmaceutical emerged as an ASEAN champion based on its unrivaled marketing and sales capabilities rooted in thoughtful diversification. Its founder had rich experiences and knowledge in establishing the energy drink business by accessing the right channels, identifying the right target consumers, and building the internationally recognized brands.

Other ASEAN Champions: Tien Phong Plastic Joint Stock Company, PT Ultrajaya Milk Industry and Trading Company Tbk, and Cebu Air, Inc.

While first-mover advantages confer initial advantages for a given firm, sustaining this advantage can become more difficult with the subsequent entry of competitors. The Tien Phong Plastic Factory was borne out of a resolution by then Ministry of Light Industry in December 1958 to construct the first plastic factory in Vietnam. Having been the first plastic manufacturer in Vietnam, the company was easily able to gain dominance in the market. With its origins as a state-owned enterprise, the company enjoyed a lot of government support in its early years, especially since the Vietnamese government has been aggressively promoting its plastics industry – due to it being a fast-growing export industry, among other strengths (Vietnam Trade Promotion Agency, 2011). Far from resting on these laurels, the company shifted away from plastic pipe products for water supply and construction projects by establishing a number of subsidiaries and joint ventures, expanding production facilities, forging partnerships with Sekisui Chemicals of Japan, and planning expansion in selected Asian markets.

Initially a family business in 1960, the PT Ultrajaya Milk Industry and Trading Company (Ultrajaya) currently produces the largest share of liquid milk products in the Indonesian market. Just a few years later, in 1975, it earned distinction as a pioneer in Ultra High Temperature

(UHT) technology and aseptic packaging in the Indonesian market (Ultrajaya, 2014). The UHT technology involves heating raw materials at 140 degrees centigrade for 3–4 seconds. It is known to sterilize products by killing bacteria while at the same time preserving the drinks' nutrients. Aseptic packaging, meanwhile, ensures long life of the products without the addition of preservatives (Ultrajaya, 2014). Being a pioneer in this efficient technology, the company was able to establish itself as a market leader in the liquid milk segment (Ultrajaya, 2012). With the growing popularity of its products for Indonesian consumers, the company is on the forefront of extending its market-oriented strategies to international markets.

As indicated, being a follower can lead to competitive strategies, provided that such a firm can learn from the lessons borne from the first mover. In certain cases, such learning can arise out of adversity. Cebu Air (Philippines) commenced commercial operations in 1996 with a "low fare, great value" strategy (Cebu Air, 2014). Its market scope was limited to daily flights from Manila to Cebu and Iloilo daily with only a few aircrafts. Early on (Steinmetz, 2011), Cebu Air's fares were pegged at around 40 percent lower in price than that of the country's flagship Philippine Airlines (Flightglobal, n.d.). However, with increased oil prices, Cebu Air could not sustain its cost-leadership position. Undaunted, the company also went on a campaign to win rights to international locations. It solidified its marketing strategy by forwarding its image as a fun and lively airline. It tapped into new markets and began to capture segments such as those that would travel inter-island and would traditionally use ferries to do so. In a bold move, the company tapped overseas Filipino workers and Filipino residents abroad. Currently, the company is a huge contributing factor to the Philippine airline market growth, which was at about two million passengers in 2005 and, as of 2011, had increased to 12 million (Flightglobal, n.d.).

Conclusions

While market power can lead to dominant firms, either by bequeathing them with monopolies or by sheer access to favorable resources, marketing entails strategic vision, commitment, and keen insights on market trends. The questions for firms relate to what markets to enter and the timing of entry. Our cases indicate that firms explore market niches that are largely unfilled because demand is not manifest or because the size of the niche does not justify the investment. The firms are hence called pioneers in that they assume the risk of overinvestment should market niches not become full-fledged markets. In our cases, the firms

Exhibit 6.1 Pioneering Marketing Strategies

were entrepreneurial in fashioning opportunities into enterprises. These characteristics are summarized in Exhibit 6.1.

These companies illustrate uncanny abilities to sense the market trends and emerging consumer needs. They recognize unmet needs in the local market or for the fast-growing middle-class customers. Their market dominance owes not only to this market-sensing ability and foresight to lead the market, but also to their innovative business models and technologies. Once they identify a niche or target a new consumer group, they were able to come up with innovative business models (e.g., Sumber Alfaria's minimart for convenient service of low-to-middle class consumers, Solusi Tunas's leasing of BTS towers, or Thai Metal's total steel solution provider approach) or new technologies (e.g., Multiagro's use of the whole fish for fish oil and Solusi Tunas's fiber optics to be ready for bigger data needs by the fast-growing middle class) to solidify their market positions. The sustained growth of these champions was then possible due to their operational improvement. They acquired the necessary capabilities through international alliances and acquisitions for brand building and channel management in their newly identified markets (e.g., TC Pharmaceuticals) and developed a vertically integrated steel supply chain for high-value-added service (e.g., Thai Metal). These companies often start with strong marketing-based corporate value that guides their strategic directions. Following its vision of "Near Market, Near Customer," Keppel FELS focused on appealing to the specific needs of local consumers in every country in which it operates.

In regard to the second issue – the timing of entry – decisions are inextricably related to entry into niche markets. ASEAN champions principally assumed the role of first movers and took advantage of circumstances surrounding their decision. Rarely did the firms wait for markets to fully blossom before they entered them. In some cases, firms entered unfilled niches (e.g., Bangkok Cable's entry into copper cables); in others, firms astutely combined marketing and technology (e.g., Thai Metal's integrated service model); in other cases, firms set the standard for future competition (e.g., Solusi Tunas's BTS tower leasing or TC Pharmaceuticals' minimart). What is not as evident is the hard decision undertaken by these firms to invest heavily in products and industries that were considered risky at the time. The ability of firms over time to exploit the early advantages in the niches they have entered is further illustrated in our next chapter.

7   Deepening Localization

Introduction

The term "localization" prompts both traditional and contemporary narratives. In marketing theory, localization might simply mean attending to the demands and preferences of a given local market or segment. It is generally taken that such local adaptation or local responsiveness, although compelling, does not radically alter the value proposition of the firm. Thus, if Starbucks, the market leader of coffee products, decides to add sushi to their offerings in Japan, the company sees this as an ancillary offering that does not change its image as a leading coffee provider. In global strategy, the term "transferable marketing" is used to define the ease and the cost of adapting particular product features to accommodate local preferences (Yip, 1995).

Even so, in markets that are predominantly local and valuable for added breadth, the characteristics of the local segment can overwhelm considerations of a marketing strategy that are traditionally global or multidomestic. When, in fact, local adaptation becomes the overriding objective, and if a firm decides that minor adjustments do not suffice to meet local demands, then a different interpretation of localization becomes more appropriate.

Localization goes beyond changes in the product or services that add value to a prospective customer. In their study of surging firms in emerging markets, Park, Zhou, and Ungson (2013) reported that, in addition to simply hiring local talent, successful firms also had to invest and train local workers. Thus, localization transcends transferable marketing and local adaptation and will entail more significant commitment and investment, given the growing affluence of the middle-classes in China and India. For example, a follow-up study by Park, Ungson, and Cosgrove (2015) found that successful firms used an assortment of multibrand and -product extensions to afford breadth and choice to an idiosyncratic middle-class consumer in addition to an investment in human capital. In short, localization is not confined to extending marketing strategies or locational decisions that were largely formulated in the context of advanced economies, but to financial investments and human resource management focused on the needs and aspirations of a growing and viable local market segment. Collectively, localization entails a deep commitment on the part of the firm to a local population.

Within ASEAN, the conventional wisdom was that firms succeeded on account of favorable protectionist policies, access to critical resources and supplies, and simply cheap labor. Although this might have been valid in the past, our study discloses that sustained success also depends on the ability of local firms to meet the requirements of local responsiveness, in many cases ahead of foreign multinationals. In fundamental ways, the needs of localization go counter to globalization of a "flat world" of large and homogenous market segments. Localization impels its own logic and creates its own contingencies. It challenges firms to uncover deep and previously recessed needs of nascent consumer groups. It requires an immersion in the nature, culture, and very being of the markets they serve. Even so, localization is not a universal strategy that works in all cases. There is the risk that a firm might err by overinvesting, in which case over-localization creates higher costs and commitment than expected. Hence, as in any effective strategy, the costs and benefits of localization have to be considered, and this is what differentiates high from low performance.

In this chapter, we describe specific localization strategies of ASEAN champions in their quest for national prominence. A preview of these cases is as follows:

- *Jollibee Foods Corporation* (Philippines): Outcompeting McDonald's by catering to local flavor, culture, and values
- *Vietnam Dairy Products Joint Stock Company [Vinamilk]* (Vietnam): Building the best brand by making dairy products part of the local diet
- *PT Mitra Adiperkasa Tbk.* (Indonesia): Leading the trends as premium lifestyle retailer
- *SM Prime Holdings, Inc.* (Philippines): Becoming the largest mall developer through innovative responses to market needs
- *PT Summarecon Agung Tbk.* (Indonesia): Developing townships for prosperous local economies and communities
- *PT Sumber Alfaria Trijaya Tbk* (Indonesia): Mini-marts deeply entrenched in the local community
- *Other ASEAN Champions – Lafarge Republic Inc.* (Philippines) *and Yoma Strategic Holdings Limited* (Myanmar): Adapting closely to business and community needs

Jollibee Foods Corporation

If there was ever a poster child for localization, it would be the Jollibee Foods Corporation. Widely known as a popular Filipino food chain, Jollibee is involved in the operation of various fast food restaurants. From its humble beginnings as a small ice cream parlor in the 1970s, the company has successfully grown to become the largest quick-service restaurant in the Philippines with a market capitalization of $4.4 billion and now aims to become one of the top five restaurant groups in the world. The company expects to do this by expanding the existing operations of its global portfolio of restaurant chains, including Greenwich Pizza, Chowking, Red Ribbon Bakeshop, Mang Inasal, Burger King (Philippines), and three fast food chains in China, as well as by forging joint ventures and pursuing acquisitions in the Philippines, China, and the United States (Jollibee Foods Corporation, 2013; 2014a).

Filipino-Chinese entrepreneur Tony Tan Caktiong opened his family ice cream parlor in 1975. Three years into its operation, Mr. Tan Caktiong decided to diversify into sandwiches after realizing that events triggered by the 1977 oil crisis would almost double the price of ice cream. The Jollibee hamburger, made to the family's home-style Filipino recipe, quickly became a customer favorite. A year later, with seven stores in metropolitan Manila, the family incorporated the Jollibee Foods Corporation. The company expanded quickly and gained considerable market share without facing serious competition until the early 1980s, when American fast food chain McDonald's entered the Philippine market. McDonald's was the behemoth of the global fast food industry, unsurpassed in global competition. Indeed, McDonald's commanded such a reputation that it had set the standard not only for fast food operations, but even as a desired family destination.

Rather than back down and give way to the global giant, Jollibee decided to compete with McDonald's head on. The company leveraged on what they believed was their strongest advantage: the preference of Filipino consumers for the taste of Jollibee burgers, which was slightly spicy and more flavorful than McDonald's American-style plain beef patty. Counting on developing products that were more friendly to the Filipino palate, Jollibee broadened its menu to include Chickenjoy fried chicken, a larger premium single-patty burger called the Champ and meant to compete directly with the McDonald's double-decker Big Mac, Filipino-style Jolly spaghetti, which was slightly sweet and contained ground meat and hotdog slices, and even a unique peach-mango dessert pie, all developed to local consumer tastes. In 1983, Jollibee launched a TV ad campaign containing what has become famous among Filipinos as the Jollibee trademark, "Langhap Sarap," which loosely translates to "smells good, tastes good."

Around the same time, Jollibee introduced today's widely popular Jollibee mascot to depict its vision of its ideal employee as a bee working happily and efficiently with other jolly bees. Taking advantage of the Filipino penchant for celebrations and family gatherings, Jollibee pioneered offering children's birthday party packages. The company did all of this while making sure to keep its prices lower than McDonald's by maintaining tight operations management (Tran, 2005; Bartlett & O'Connell, 1998). Despite the growing foreign and local competition, Jollibee secured its place as market leader by 1985 (Jollibee Foods Corporation, 2014b).

The company ambitiously ventured into overseas markets quite early, starting in Singapore in 1984 and Taiwan in 1985, but issues with local partners undermined its success (Alfonso & Neelankavil, 2012). Consequently, Jollibee focused on local expansion throughout the Philippines and was largely successful. In 1993, the company went public through an initial public offering, raising $8 million, but the family maintained majority ownership. The following year, the company began its diversification by acquiring Greenwich Pizza Corporation and then entered into a joint venture with Deli France bakeshop in 1995. Since then, Jollibee has gradually expanded its own brand internationally and has acquired other quick-service restaurant chains locally and abroad. As of the end of 2013, the company operated more than 580 stores overseas in eight countries and territories: Brunei, Singapore, Vietnam, Hong Kong, Qatar, Kuwait, Saudi Arabia, and the United States. It is also currently looking into entering the Indonesian, Malaysian, and Canadian markets (Alfonso & Neelankavil, 2012; Morales, 2013; Rivera, 2014a; 2014b).

Vietnam Dairy Products Joint Stock Company (Vinamilk)

Most people would agree that food is primarily local. Different countries, and different regions embedded in them, have different tastes, needs, and expectations regarding what they eat. Dairy is no exception, despite the common perception that milk is a staple experienced the same way by everyone in the world.

Vinamilk is the biggest dairy company in Vietnam, and with a market capitalization of roughly $4.88 billion, it is the second most valuable business in the country after PetroVietnam Gas, another one of our ASEAN champions. The company's products include fresh milk, condensed milk, powdered milk, yogurts, ice cream, cheese, and nondairy products such as soya milk and fruit juices.

Vinamilk was set up as a state-owned enterprise in 1976. Immediately after being established, the company sought to consolidate the industry through the nationalization of several dairy factories. Although it essentially was a government monopoly with virtually no local competition, the company adopted a strong consumer focus early on, trying to better understand local needs and attitudes toward dairy products. After all, dairy was relatively new to the Vietnamese diet, and the country did not have a tradition of dairy farming. Vinamilk sought to gradually integrate milk products into the Vietnamese diet. In 1990, average annual milk consumption was just half a liter per person. By 2013, this had surged to 18 liters per person per year. The secret? Add a little vanilla to make the milk taste sweeter, which the Vietnamese loved.

The company grew steadily as the local market welcomed more dairy into their lives. In 2006, Vinamilk went public through an initial public offering in the Ho Chi Minh City Stock Exchange. In the same year, it launched its first large-scale dairy farm, which allowed the company to produce its own milk. Prior to this, it had depended on powdered milk imported from China and Australia. Vinamilk continued to expand thereafter, setting up a number of large-scale dairy farms.

On all of its farms, Vinamilk made sure that high quality standards were strictly met, while keeping operation costs down. In order to reach as many Vietnamese homes as possible, the company established a wide local distribution network that covered more than 224,000 retailers (Vinamilk, 2014).

The company today enjoys 50 percent market share for milk, 80 percent for condensed milk, and 90 percent for yogurt. The Vinamilk brand is now one of the best known in Vietnam, but it is not stopping there. The company aims to boost sales from $1.65 billion in 2014 to $3 billion by 2017, and join the ranks of the world's fifty biggest dairy companies. It has recently entered into a joint venture in Cambodia set to begin operations in 2015. It is also looking to expand into Europe and the Middle East.

PT Mitra Adiperkasa Tbk.

Like culinary taste and diet, localism applies to clothing preferences, fashion, and lifestyle. Dubbed the number-one premium lifestyle retailer in Indonesia, Mitra Adiperkasa (MAP) operates fashion and lifestyle stores, food and beverage establishments, department stores, and super-markets. It is known as a premium retailer of branded clothing, acces-sories, shoes, bags, toys, and sports equipment, and as the local operator of Starbucks. The company currently manages more than 1,800 outlets across 64 Indonesian cities and boasts a portfolio of over 150 world-famous brands, including Zara, Marks & Spencer, Topshop, Lacoste, Adidas, Reebok, SOGO, SEIBU, Debenhams, Galeries Lafayette, Domino's Pizza, Burger King, and Krispy Kreme.

Starting with a single sports store in the 1990s, the company quickly diversified into the fashion and lifestyle segments, achieving phenomenal growth in the last two decades. A lot of this success can be attributed to the company's decisive action in taking advantage of partnership opportunities with foreign brands wanting to take a piece of the growing Indonesian pie. This meant a balance of recogniz-ing what the market currently wanted and predicting what it would want in the future. For example, when MAP introduced the Next and Lacoste brands to the market, most Indonesians did not know any-thing about them. Soon after their introduction, however, Indonesian shoppers were eagerly flocking to their stores (PT Mitra Adiperkasa Tbk., 2014).

The company briskly expanded, and by the time of its initial pub-lic offering in the Indonesia Stock Exchange in 2004, MAP had a net-work of 448 stores selling various premium brands. After the 2000s, the company realized that Indonesia's growing middle class was an even larger and faster growing segment than the affluent bracket. In recent years, MAP has "recalibrated" its portfolio to include more brands that catered to middle-class consumers (Grazella, 2013a). They have also recently been pursuing e-commerce to cater to its increasingly tech-savvy customer base.

MAP is intent on growing its local business even further, aiming to achieve 20–25 percent growth each year. In particular, it is seek-ing to expand outside Jakarta and into smaller cities like Makassar in South Sulawesi and Balikpapan in Eastern Kalimantan, seeing massive potential in areas outside the Indonesian capital where competition is already tight (Grazella, 2013b). The company is very optimistic about the local market and aims to bank on Indonesia's consistently high consumer confidence levels and growing middle class. Although MAP currently operates a small-scale enterprise in Thailand, it remains deliberately focused on the Indonesian market, choosing to "localize" deeper into the smaller cities across the Indonesian archipelago, where the size of the middle-class and affluent population is expected to dou-ble in less than a decade.

SM Prime Holdings, Inc.

A casual stroll through a shopping mall anywhere in the world reveals several typical features: multiple floors of shops and restaurants, lounging areas, ample parking spaces, air-conditioning, and perhaps an activity center. Yet walking through one of fifty-three SM malls in the Philippines will surprise the most avid international shopper with uncommon amenities, such as a chapel where daily masses are offered – although perhaps one should have expected this in a country where about 90 percent of the population is staunchly Roman Catholic. SM Prime Holdings Inc. engages in the development, operation, and maintenance of shopping centers, amusement centers, cinemas, and also, after a recent consolidation with the SM Group's real estate subsidiaries in 2013, the development of residences, offices, hotels, and convention centers. The company currently operates over fifty malls in the Philippines and six in China.

When Henry Sy Sr., today the richest man in the Philippines with an estimated net worth of over $12 billion (Forbes n.d.), opened the first "ShoeMart" in downtown Manila in 1958, he envisioned an inviting, upscale shoe store to cater to Manila's up-and-coming consumer class – it was the first fully air-conditioned shoe store in the hot and humid Philippine capital. Increasing local demand for shoes, matched by Mr. Sy's pioneering innovations in store layout, sales, and merchandising, some of which he had picked up from practices he observed in the United States, led to the early success of ShoeMart (SM Shoemart n.d.). The business expanded, branching out into a store chain, and in 1972, ShoeMart opened its first full-line department store, changing its name to SM. This shift to the department store business sprung out of both an opportunity in the market and the challenge brought about by the inability of local shoe suppliers to catch up with ShoeMart's rapid expansion. Since suppliers could not provide more shoes, Mr. Sy decided to start selling apparel and other merchandise in his stores.

The department store business thrived, and SM began opening new branches. However, another roadblock soon emerged, as the lack of adequately large leasable retail spaces in metropolitan Manila limited the company's expansion. Again, Mr. Sy converted this challenge to an opportunity, venturing into real estate as he decided to develop his own shopping center in suburban Quezon City just outside the city of Manila. After two years of construction, SM launched the country's first "supermall" in 1985. This pioneering introduction would soon change the face of the Philippine retail industry, one that SM would naturally take the lead in. Soon after the mall's launch, SM further diversified its retail business into supermarkets and appliance stores to complete the roster of anchor tenants in its mall and fulfill the promise of its now-famous tagline, "We've got it all for you." Today, the company takes pride in making sure it provides everything that customers want when they come to its lifestyle malls, including international brands that Filipinos have been exposed to abroad.

"Our focus is on our customers – we understand what they need and want when visiting the malls. About five years ago, we see a lot of Filipinos going to Hong Kong and Singapore to shop in Uniqlo, Forever 21 and H&M. What we did was to bring these brands to the Philippines for their convenience." –Jeffrey Lim, Executive Vice President

With the success of its first mall project, the company soon began building more malls around metropolitan Manila and later ventured outside the capital and into provincial cities. From 1991 onward, the number of SM malls all over the country has grown exponentially, and in 2001, SM opened its first mall outside the Philippines in Xiamen, China.

Looking to the future, SM intends to continue expanding in the Philippines outside metro Manila wherever it sees a significant rise in disposable income. They are also keen on continuing to expand in China.

What SM has done is to closely cater to the evolving needs and wants of the Philippine consuming class, pioneering concepts borrowed from abroad while introducing tweaks and innovations uniquely suited to the local market. The SM story is deeply entrenched in the development history of the Philippine retail industry, both as a visionary pioneer and a recognized market leader.

PT Summarecon Agung Tbk.

No company can exist in a vacuum. Even Internet-based companies have multiple points of contact to the ground, whether in hiring manpower, dealing with suppliers, or engaging its customers. To different extents, companies, because they are grounded in specific locales, will have to invest in the specific areas and communities that they operate in. Some companies are more heavily invested than others.

When Mr. Soejipto Nagaria founded Summarecon Agung in 1975, he started with 10 hectares of undeveloped marshland in Kelapa Gading in what was then the backwaters of Jakarta. Since then, Summarecon has managed to transform the subdistrict into one of the most affluent residential and commercial areas in metropolitan Jakarta. And over the years, Summarecon has built a reputation as one of the leading real estate companies in Indonesia, especially in the development of townships.

During the 1970s, there was very little interest among investors in developing the swamp lands of Kelapa Gading, as most developers preferred to work with arable agricultural land. As a result, Mr. Nagaria was able to acquire the land at a very low price (Ellisa, 2014). Originally, the intention was simply to speculate on future increases in land prices, but increasing demand for housing among the growing Indonesian middle class presented a development opportunity for the company. The company began with just thirty townhouses, but later expanded to three hundred. Soon, Summarecon started buying more land in the area but had to acquire properties parcel by parcel given the small landholdings in the district. The company painstakingly had to consolidate the small parcels into larger blocks to form a large-scale development project. By 1978, it had acquired a total of 30 hectares in the area.

This allowed the company to develop the area as a township. Unlike most developers at that time, who sought to target the upper classes by building upscale housing alongside traditional upmarket amenities such as golf courses, Summarecon envisioned a fully functioning neighborhood that placed an emphasis on public life and setting up facilities as "trigger factors" that would attract affluent inhabitants. In line with this, Summarecon created a master plan that accounted for the building of commercial spaces and facilities such as a market, schools, a commercial and food center, and a sports center in addition to residential housing (Ellisa, 2014).

Determined to provide residents all the services and facilities they needed within Kelapa Gading, Summarecon set up a primary school in 1979 and an Islamic school in 1983. The establishment of these private schools effectively boosted the image of Kelapa Gading as a reputable residential neighborhood since private schools did not only serve the residents of the neighborhood but also brought in students from other areas as well. Today, several top-notch private schools are located in Kelapa Gading, namely BPK Penabur, North Jakarta International School, Jakarta Taipei International School, and Don Bosco (Ellisa, 2014).

In 1984, Summarecon built Pasar Mandiri, a retail complex anchored by a supermarket and surrounded by an assortment of commercial shops, patterned after Singapore's modern market concept.

"The key thing … for a township to survive is that it has to grow. To be successful there must be a local economy. In each location we develop, we must create a local economy. Because without a local economy, no one's going to live there." – Michael Yong, Finance Director

Providing a conducive environment for the local economy to develop and prosper became a key priority of Summarecon Agung in each of its projects. This was the reason for the building of shopping arcades early on in the development of each of its townships. Later, these shopping arcades would give way to full-sized malls.

In the same year that the shopping arcade was opened, the company also launched a sports club in Kelapa Gading, the first of its kind to be built within a housing complex in Jakarta. Finally, in 1990, the first phase of a full-sized mall was completed. By this time, Summarecon had practically built a new town from scratch, attracting residents from Jakarta and neighboring cities, to a new, well-planned township will full amenities.

Soon, Summarecon ventured into developing other townships using the same successful formula. In 1991, they entered into a joint venture to develop another township in Gading Serpong, an area spanning 1,500 hectares located 21 km to the west of Jakarta. The following year, they began development of Summarecon Bekasi, located 21 km to the east of Jakarta. In all of these projects, Summarecon invested heavily in infrastructure, including roads and sewerage, as well as schools, markets, and leisure centers alongside residential, commercial, and office developments. At the core of its real estate development strategy has been a commitment to the development of the local economy and community.

PT Sumber Alfaria Trijaya Tbk

Not all companies have the rare opportunity to build their locale from the ground up. Others have to find their place and purpose in a well-established local economy and community with established preferences and resources. At the age of 17, Djoko Susanto began managing his parents' small grocery food stall inside a traditional market in Jakarta. Taking advantage of the increasing smoking habits of Indonesians, the young Mr. Susanto started selling cigarettes in the family stall alongside grocery items. This proved to be very profitable. Soon, he was opening a few new stalls in different locations. Putera Sampoerna, a local tobacco tycoon, noticed the success of Mr. Susanto's stalls, and partnered with him to open several more stalls and eventually a discount supermarket chain.

From these beginnings came what is now known as PT Sumber Alfaria Trijaya Tbk, founded in 1989, today a $1.6 billion retail empire of more than nine thousand AlfaMart convenience stores across Indonesia with sales of $3.37 billion in 2014. Sumber Alfaria was originally founded as a consumer goods trading and distribution company, functioning as a subsidiary of Sampoerna's tobacco company. In 1999, the company opened its first Alfa Minimart. This was a different retail format, bigger than a traditional grocery stall or convenience store, carrying more household goods and basic foodstuffs including vegetables and meat, unlike regular convenience stores, but smaller than a full-sized supermarket.

"If you come to our stores, you will see that it's basically a very small supermarket... Why did we develop this format? At that time, the infrastructure in Indonesia was not very good with heavy traffic congestion in the city. People were not willing to go too far away from their homes to buy daily needs. They wanted stores that offer convenience and easier accessibility." – Hans Prawira, President Director

The minimart concept catered to families, who found it difficult to buy daily needs in supermarkets far away from residential areas. Most of its customers belonged to the lower- to middle-income class segment, which constituted the majority of the local population. The minimarts were located primarily in residential areas, away from the high-traffic business and commercial centers where most of its competitors, mainly convenience stores, were located. Unlike convenience stores that offered mostly ready-made, ready-to-eat products, Alfa Minimarts sold mainly groceries and foodstuffs. In essence, the Alfa minimart was a cleaner, brighter, more modern version of the traditional Indonesian *warung*, or neighborhood store.

The format proved successful among its customers. However, an early challenge emerged in the recruitment of store staff. The company initially found it difficult to recruit enough workers with experience in the retail industry and the level of customer orientation that the company required. Furthermore, the long and unconventional shifts required in the operation of a 24-hour minimart were a relatively new idea to the local labor force. To meet the increasing human resource requirements of its rapid expansion, Sumber Alfaria had to invest in human resource development early on. It prioritized hiring store staff from the local community, offering both part-time and full-time positions. To elevate their employees' level of competence, the company instituted comprehensive training programs for them and encouraged more senior employees to mentor and share best practices with their newer counterparts. The company also provides e-learning programs and scholarships for employees who wish to seek further education at various universities and technical institutes in the country.

Sumber Alfaria's "localization" was not limited to tweaking their business model and store format to cater to local needs. Its deep localization involved commitment to the local community in which each store was embedded. The traditional *warungs* held a special place in many Indonesians' hearts, especially because of their personal relationships with store owners and managers, and their familiarity with fellow patrons. Building on this special function of the *warung* in the local community, the company envisioned each of its thousands of Alfamart stores as local "community stores." About 140 Alfamart stores have invested in "community zones" within store premises that serve as function rooms for the local community. These rooms are made available for free to the community for birthdays, special occasions, and public meetings, as well as to local government for official business. The company has also provided community boards for local announcements. As an added service to its customers, Alfamart began accepting bill payment services and train ticket purchasing in its stores in 2008. This has since been expanded to other services, such as the purchasing of airline tickets and payment of motorcycle installment fees in most Alfamart stores.

Alfamart has ventured into online shopping recently, allowing customers to shop on the web and have their purchases delivered or readied for pick-up in the most convenient Alfamart store. In 2014, Sumber Alfaria partnered with SM Prime Holdings, the largest retailer in the Philippines and another of our ASEAN champions, to bring the Alfamart brand to the country. As of mid-2015, the joint venture had opened thirty stores in the Philippines as part of a "pilot test" of the market. One of the changes the company is considering for the Philippine market is the introduction of dine-in meals and amenities, which are common features among the local competition but alien to the original business model. It will be very interesting to see how Alfamart's localization efforts will proceed in this new market, especially since the two companies involved in this joint venture have both been highlighted for their success in understanding and catering to local needs.

Other ASEAN Champions: Lafarge Republic Inc. and Yoma Strategic Holdings Limited

From food to retail services to real estate, the cases discussed so far showcase how some of our ASEAN champions have espoused a strategy of deep localization to take full advantage of the local economy and community in which they operate. Localization requires paying close attention and adapting to local customer needs, preferences, and developments. Deep localization involves integrating these factors in one's strategy and business model, rather than mere tweaks in product or service features. More importantly, deep localization involves solidarity with the local economy and community – a commitment to its codevelopment. Although we have focused on the cases above, there are other examples among our ASEAN champions worth briefly mentioning here.

Lafarge Republic, Inc., engaged in the manufacturing, development, exploitation, and sale of cement, marbles, and other types of construction materials in the Philippines, is a notable example. The company traces its origins to a local cement company founded in 1955 that pioneered the dry process of manufacturing cement in the country. In general, cement manufacturing is strongly grounded in its locale, both for its supply of resources and demand for its output. Each of the company's plants is situated near basic raw-material sources and primarily depends on these sources for its production. At the same time, it relies on the local labor force to supply its workforce needs. Acknowledging the importance of the local communities in which their plants are embedded, Lafarge Republic has integrated corporate social responsibility in its business strategy, making sure that it "gives back" to the communities it operates in, offering scholarships, engaging with local government in support of its projects, and responding in times of local disasters. In 2013, when a super typhoon hit the central Philippines, flattening coastal towns and destroying thousands of homes and hundreds of millions of dollars' worth of infrastructure, Lafarge Republic quickly responded by developing a special low-price cement product to aid in the reconstruction efforts and made it available directly to NGOs. As part of its commitment to serving its Filipino customers best, the company has invested in developing cost-efficient products as well as green technologies such as alternative fuels (including local waste products) in its manufacturing process to not only provide what local customers need, but also to help ensure the preservation of the local environment.

Some companies are wholly invested in their locales such that their company's success is ultimately tied with the success of their relatively small but budding local market. Yoma Strategic Holdings of Myanmar is a prime example. Yoma was set up in 2006 by Hong Kong businessman Serge Pun and listed on the Singapore stock exchange to allow international investors to invest in Myanmar, a developing economy of 50 million people that had just recently opened up to foreign investors and was often described as a frontier market. Yoma has ventures primarily in real estate and construction, but it has also ventured into agriculture, logistics, automotive, retail, and luxury tourism as it actively builds itself into a local conglomerate. By venturing into multiple sectors of the developing Myanmar economy, it believes that it is able to gradually build expertise, strengthen its competencies, and develop human capital among its employees. Banking on this, Yoma believes that it has become the ideal business partner among multinational companies wanting to invest in Myanmar. As the company has developed alongside the local economy and the skills and competencies of its people, Yoma has decided to share its gains through an employee share option scheme, a pioneering move in the very young private-sector economy.

Exhibit 7.1 Deepening Localization

Conclusions

Localization is increasingly being viewed as an imperative for profitable growth in emerging markets, but the term's meaning has transformed. Going local does demand stringent attention to the needs and requirements of a targeted local sample. However, localization now also means uncovering the cultural attitudes and values that are not all that transparent in the local sector. Moreover, it impels firms to carefully align their product/service mix in ways that incorporate these underlying attitudes and values. A synthesis of our findings is presented in Exhibit 7.1.

When current local preferences or customs do not perfectly match a company's offerings, it must learn to adapt to them, but it may also seek to shape local preferences to create demand for its products. Jollibee Foods Corporation clearly demonstrated how catering to the local palate (with a tastier burger or a sweeter spaghetti sauce) and providing for local needs (birthday party packages) was key element of success even against bigger foreign competition. Vietnam Dairy Products Joint Stock Company, more popularly known as Vinamilk, faced a developing market that did not consider dairy a dietary staple. But by working with the government to introduce dairy products to the Vietnamese diet for their nutritional value, innovating products to make them more palatable to local tastes, and developing a wide distribution network to facilitate ease of access among the growing consumer class, Vinamilk had succeeded in growing its local customer base and is now aggressively looking at expansion opportunities aboard.

Sometimes opportunities do come from the outside. When premier Indonesia retailer Mitra Adiperkasa (MAP) first brought in foreign brands like Lacoste to the local market, customers barely knew anything about them. But the company had insight into changing trends in customer tastes and behavior. They saw the rise in disposable income among the growing Indonesian upper and middle class as a sign of things to come – an increased desire for imported lifestyle brands among increasingly sophisticated buyers. And as this trend continues outside the primary cities, MAP is venturing more locally into second-tier cities in the provinces, bringing imported clothing brands, restaurants, and cafes – including Starbucks. Success in retail often requires insight to ever-shifting local trends. And as successful as MAP has been in bringing foreign brands to Indonesia, a company in the Philippines, SM Prime Holdings, was successful not just in bringing in international brands but also in bringing in the international phenomenon of the shopping mall. SM pioneered the development of full-sized malls in the Philippines back in 1985. Its success demonstrates how a company can cater to local needs while introducing foreign concepts to differentiate itself from local offerings, resulting in a final product that is both local and world class.

PT Summarecon Agung deeply committed itself to the development of Kelapa Gading, the site of its first real estate venture, beginning with a 10-hectare property in undeveloped swampland just outside Jakarta. Today, the subdistrict is a prestigious residential and commercial area, known for its urban planning and abundant amenities, including schools, hospitals, hotels, commercial centers, and entertainment destinations – a benchmark for township developments across Indonesia. Finally, PT Sumber Alfaria has demonstrated what deep localization fully entails. Not only does it involve catering to the local retail needs of Indonesian households, upgrading the traditional *warung* or neighborhood store, and providing for the basic food and grocery needs of its customers at a high level of service and quality assurance. More importantly, it involves a company immersing itself in the local communities it operates in. It must not just coexist but also codevelop with these communities. It must help build local human and social capital just as much as it takes advantage of it. It must give back to the community in which it thrives as much as it expects that community to contribute to its long-term profitability and success.

It is not all too surprising that local firms are able to understand, cater to, and influence local needs and wants more so than an average multinational firm. Because local firms are themselves embedded in the local culture, they are in a better position to do all of this. Nevertheless, identifying underlying cultural values and even managing to influence them is not enough; successful local firms have to make a deep commitment to serving and (aiding in) sustaining the local sector, and they must do this in ways that build distinctive competitive advantages.

8   Fostering Internationalization

Introduction

Historically, the question confronting firms has been whether they should internationalize or not. Because the world keeps getting smaller, in today's economic environment, the emerging mantra among firms is no longer whether they should, but when they should do so. Without unjust implications, globalization has been welding a highly interconnected world that is paced by international trade, lowered trade barriers, strategic partnerships, and the transfer of technology. Social media has ushered in a new conduit for information exchange and retrieval in almost instantaneous fashion, creating numerous windows of opportunities for entrepreneurial ventures. New market segments, particularly the global youth, have emerged with more market power than before. These segments dare organizations to change and respond, or remain inert and risk being changed.

The history of international business is essentially one focused on the strategies and experiences of multinational firms located principally in developed countries in their quest to open up new international markets. Each stage of globalization is punctuated by the emergence of new technologies – railroads, steel, electricity, information exchange, automobiles, and microprocessors – that accelerate international trade and commerce. Accompanying each stage are new forms of enterprise that predefine the nature of multinational activities. In his groundbreaking work, historian Alfred Chandler (1962) reported the rise of large-scale organizations with requisite strategies and structures that support core activities. This work has spawned a number of follow-up studies designed to replicate the findings and to assess its generalizability in other cultural settings (Stopford & Wells, 1972). While there are differences among multinationals from the United States, Europe, and Japan, it is evident that sustaining growth trajectories remains a complex and daunting undertaking.

Today's multinationals have grown in prominence so much that their strategies and experiences have formed a plethora of material in any international business course. Simply defined, multinationals are "large enterprises with substantial resources to perform various business activities through a network of subsidiaries and affiliates located in multiple countries" (Cavusgil, Knight, & Riesenberger, 2014:13). Whereas globalization is examined across different levels – world, country, industry, and the firm – it is at the level of enterprise that specific applications can be readily accessed. Currently, a global firm is a multinational with highly interlocking activities across several countries that create value through scale and scope economies (Yip, 1992, 1995). In Yip's work, Wal-Mart, Coca Cola, Samsung, Sony, ABB, Nike, Exxon, and Procter & Gamble are among many established multinational firms that fall within the "globalized firm" category.

Recently, attention has been directed at multinationals from emerging and developing countries, which has been referred to as "Emerging Multinationals" or "Born-Again Multinationals" (Cuervo-Cazurra & Ramamurti, 2014). This new breed of multinationals has distinct differences from their older brethren in terms of their ability to transform local into global brands, leverage local skills into international competencies, excel in a narrow but scalable market segment, employ local resources more effectively than foreign stalwarts, and innovate a business model that does not directly conflict with erstwhile market leaders (The Economist, 2008). In an incisive study of upcoming firms termed as "rough diamonds" from Brazil, Russia, India, and China, management professors Seung Ho Park, Gerardo Ungson, and Nan Zhou (2013) extol related competencies such as the ability to capitalize on changing governmental policies and industry conditions, aggressively fill untapped market niches, develop distinctive operational excellence, and create a pathway for profitable growth.

As applied to ASEAN economies, many if not most ASEAN champions do not meet the full requirements to be truly global multinationals. Although these firms are most certainly market leaders in their respective countries, few would qualify as "regional champions." Nevertheless, a number of firms have already paved the way for internationalization in the foreseeable future. A preview of these firms is as follows:

- *Dutch Mill Co. Ltd.* (Thailand): Internationalizing into neighboring countries from a strong domestic position
- *Thai Union Frozen Products PCL* (Thailand): Global expansion in seafood business through partnerships and acquisition
- *Thai Beverage Public Company Limited* (Thailand): Achieving global vision through professional management and learning

- *Sembcorp Marine Limited and Keppel FELS Limited* (Singapore): Integrating regional and global value chain for marine and offshore platforms
- *Other ASEAN Champions: Charoen Pokphand Foods PCL* (Thailand), *PETRONAS Dagangan Berhad and DIALOG Group Berhad* (Malaysia), *and TOA Paint (Thailand) Co., Ltd.* (Thailand): Strong global presence with full-scale local operations

Dutch Mill Co. Ltd.

When a group of food scientists from Kasetsart University, an agricultural university in Bangkok, established the company that would later become Dutch Mill Co. Ltd., their singular interest was to provide quality dairy products to the Thai people to improve their nutrition and health. Thirty years later, the company has become the largest dairy producer in Thailand, and has successfully introduced its brand in nine out of the ten ASEAN markets, targeting to penetrate its last untapped market (Brunei) by 2016. Today, it envisions itself as one of the best dairy companies in ASEAN.

The company's initial success may be partly attributed to several developments in the local dairy industry in the 1980s. The Thai government passed several policies promoting dairy farming and milk consumption. In particular, the creation of the National Milk Drinking Campaign Board in 1985 significantly boosted milk consumption in the country (Chungsiriwat & Panapol, 2009). Following its early success in milk products, the company diversified into producing flavored yoghurt drinks, which the company is particularly known for across the region today.

Dutch Mill's entry into the Southeast Asian market began in 1996, when it began exporting its yoghurt drink products to Singapore rebranded under the trademark of an established Singaporean company. Shortly after this, the company began developing its own Dutch Mill brand for export to nearby Vietnam, Cambodia, Laos, Myanmar, and Southern China. This export strategy was primarily motivated by the large surplus capacity the company had in its newly built production facilities. However, the growth of its export markets soon encouraged the company to take on internationalization more deliberately. In 2001, Dutch Mill entered into a joint venture with a Chinese beverage and ice cream company to set up local production and avoid the high import duties slapped by the Chinese government on imported dairy products then. Today, Dutch Mill has several production plants across the region, including plants in the Philippines and Myanmar.

In order to strengthen its R&D capabilities and raise itself to global standards, Dutch Mill partnered with French multinational food and beverage giant Danone in 2007. Danone, on the other hand, was particularly interested in Dutch Mill's knowledge of the regional market and its regional distribution network.

Despite beginning with humble roots and modest aspirations, Dutch Mill has emerged as a regional player in Southeast Asia and is intent on expanding export markets further.

Thai Union Frozen Products PCL

Although some firms originally targeted domestic consumers then saw the opportunities presented by overseas markets, others embraced an international strategy from the onset. Thai Union Frozen Products PCL (TUF) is today the leading seafood producer and exporter in Thailand and one of the largest in the world. It produces and exports a wide variety of products including frozen tuna loin, shelf-stable tuna, sardines, and mackerel, frozen salmon; and frozen cephalopods, as well as baked goods, pet food, and frozen ready-to-eat meals. Among the company's internationally recognized brands are *Chicken of the Sea* (USA), *Hyacinthe Parmentier* (France), and *Mareblu* (Italy).

Around the time of the company's founding in 1988, American fish companies were looking to transfer their canning operations overseas to reduce production costs. Thailand's low wages attracted American business to the country. The father-and-son team of Kraisorn and Thiraphong Chansiri, founders of TUF, grabbed the opportunity. Previously, the two had run a smaller operation that would later become a subsidiary of TUF producing and exporting canned sardines and mackerel. To become internationally competitive, the company consciously held product and process quality up to global standards. In 1992, they partnered with two major Japanese clients/dealers, Mitsubishi Co. Ltd. and Hagoromo Foods Co. Ltd. to develop products suitable for Japanese and global tastes and quality standards.

To ensure product quality and operational efficiency along the supply chain, TUF sought to vertically integrate its business, setting up subsidiaries in various related businesses: can manufacturing, label printing, packaging, and marketing (Cohen, 2006; Thai Union Frozen Products PCL, 2012). It also acquired a frozen shrimp packaging business in southern Thailand, which later evolved into what is now Thai Union

Seafood, producing and distributing the company's second-largest product segment (Cohen, 2006; Thai Union Frozen Products PCL, 2012).

TUF has sought to expand internationally through mergers and acquisitions. In 1996, it established its U.S.-based subsidiary, Thai Union International, through which it bought into Tri-Union Seafoods LLC, producer and distributor of seafood products under the popular US brand name "Chicken of the Sea." Three years later, TUF fully acquired Tri-Union, solidifying its entry into the U.S. market (Cohen, 2006; Thai Union Frozen Products PCL, 2012). After establishing itself in North America, the company went on to pursue more acquisitions in the subsequent years and began to enter other major markets, including China with its acquisition of Century Union (Shanghai) Foods in 2005 (Cohen, 2006). With its international acquisitions, TUF was able to acquire a number of world-famous brands and widen its geographical reach into a truly global network (Thai Union Frozen Products PCL, 2014). Most recently, TUF announced acquisitions of Norway's King Oscar, one of the world's largest suppliers of canned fish, and MerAlliance, Europe's leading producer of chilled smoked salmon (Bangkok Post, 2014; Jittapong, 2014).

Through strategic partnerships and acquisitions of international brands, TUF has successfully expanded its global reach, establishing operations in multiple countries and penetrating international markets.

Thai Beverage Public Company Limited

Thai companies are among the most internationalized on our list of ASEAN champions. Most of them have embraced internationalization as an integral part of their overall strategy, and many have embraced the whole of Southeast Asia as their market base. In their strategic roadmap for the next six years laid out in 2014, the Thai Beverage Public Company Limited or ThaiBev, maker of Chang beer, announced its intent to solidify its position as the largest and most profitable beverage company in Southeast Asia. Established in 2003 in a consolidation of fifty-eight small alcoholic-beverage producers into a single corporation, ThaiBev is today the largest beverage producer in Thailand, and is in fact already one of the largest in Asia. Chang Beer, the company's flagship product, enjoys a 60 percent market share at home. Their other products include spirits, other beers, nonalcoholic beverages, and food.

Although Chang Beer remains the company's largest revenue earner, it has diversified into other segments to both secure new markets and at the same time develop new competencies. In 2004, they launched Beer Archa, targeting younger Thais who preferred products with lower

alcohol content. This required new marketing and product positioning that was different from its flagship product. In 2008, they launched
Federbrau, a German-style premium beer. Federbrau was the only locally
brewed beer that met the German Purity Law, which strictly prescribed
the use of natural ingredients, a German-based manufacturing process,
and a unique fermentation method (Thai Beverage PCL, 2008).

In 2012, ThaiBev bought into Fraser and Neave (F&N), a Singaporean
food conglomerate (Koh, 2012), seeking to gain access to its R&D
and marketing assets as well as its experience in overseas operations.
Subsequently, the company has tapped F&N resources to supplement
its international trading arm, International Beverage Holdings Limited
(IBHL). IBHL has offices in several countries all over the world, including the United States and Australia.

As this and our previous cases have shown, producing world-class
quality products through the adoption of international standards and
investment in R&D, and establishing wide regional distribution networks
are essential to successful internationalization. But equally important is
the development of an international outlook, a culture of profession-
alism, and good governance on par with some of the world's leading
multinationals. Since its founding, ThaiBev has actively sought to profes-
sionalize itself in order to transform the local beverage industry. This was
necessary to successfully harmonize the operations, resources, and organizational capabilities of over 50 formerly independent companies into a
single corporation. It did this by emphasizing the need for good corporate governance and transparency. These efforts were highly instrumental in ThaiBev's early success in achieving its aspirational goal of being
listed on the Singaporean Stock Exchange in 2006. In the same year,
it was a finalist in the award for "Most Transparent Company" among
newly listed firms, and in 2009 it won the award among foreign listings
from the Securities Investors Association of Singapore.

Sembcorp Marine Limited and Keppel FELS Limited

Singapore is perhaps more popularly known for its reputation as the business and financial hub of Southeast Asia. It is however, also the regional
hub for the marine and offshore platform construction industries. Two of
our ASEAN champions from Singapore, Sembcorp Marine and Keppel
FELS, are in the marine and offshore platform engineering industries.
These two companies are good examples of how firms in ASEAN have
fostered internationalization not only by offering products and services
to the wider international market, but also by integrating operations
across countries into a regional or global value chain.

Sembcorp Marine is an integrated marine and offshore company that offers the entire spectrum of engineering solutions such as shipbuilding, ship repair and conversion, rig building and repair, as well as offshore construction and engineering. The company has a network of six yards in Singapore and is present in six other countries worldwide.

Its early roots tracing back to a joint venture between Singapore's Economic Development Board and Ishikawajima-Harima Heavy Industries Co., Ltd. of Japan, what eventually in 2000 would become Sembcorp Marine Ltd. started acquiring foreign assets, although indirectly, in the late 1990s. With its acquisition of another Singaporean shipyard company in 1997, it acquired partial ownership of shipyards in Indonesia and China. In 2001, the company bought into Cosco (Dalian) Shipyard in China. Three years later, they acquired a 30 percent stake in the greater Cosco Shipyard Group, which operated five shipyards in China. In 2005, they ventured into the United States by acquiring Texas-based Sabine Industries. The following year, they acquired two more shipyard companies in Indonesia. They also began making minor investments in India. In 2008, the company entered into a partnership with a shipyard company based in Rio de Janeiro, Brazil.

Today, Sembcorp Marine has overseas shipyards in six different countries: Brazil, Indonesia, China, India, the United States, and the United Kingdom. The new shipyard in Brazil will enable Sembcorp Marine to construct drillships, semi-submersibles, jackup rigs, platforms, and supply vessels once it is completed by the end of 2015. Meanwhile, the company's investments in the United Kingdom will allow them to provide services to clients who operate in the North Sea. They are currently exploring opportunities in Saudi Arabia.

Sembcorp Marine has embraced internationalization as central to its long-term growth strategy, which involves not only its strategic expansion in overseas hubs but also its continued investment to strengthen its position and capabilities in Singapore.

Another example of success in internationalization is that of Keppel FELS (also profiled in Chapter 6). We focused on Keppel FELS's success in pioneering market strategies earlier, but its success in overseas expansion is also worth noting here). From its early roots as a family-owned offshore yard founded in 1967, the company has made a name for itself in the global offshore and marine industry.

One of its earlier ambitious international ventures was in the Gulf of Mexico in 1990, with the company buying a 60 percent stake in a shipyard in Texas creating AMFELS. The following year, they won a bid to design and construct a semi-submersible oil production platform for Petrobras, the Brazilian national oil company. Meanwhile, they were one of the first to recognize opportunities in the Caspian Sea which had one of the world's largest oil discoveries in the last 20 years, leading the company to set up an office in Azerbaijan in 1996, and a yard in 1997. The North Sea was another important region and in 2002, to strengthen its presence to serve the North Sea, the company acquired a 100 percent stake in the Verolme yard in Rotterdam, the Netherlands, which was renamed Keppel Verolme.

As a guiding principle, Keppel FELS has adopted a "Near Market, Near Customer" approach, which the company believed allowed it to better cater to customer needs and contribute to local content. This was the rationale behind the establishment of representative offices in countries all over the world, including the United States, Brazil, the Netherlands, Azerbaijan, India, Indonesia, China, and Japan (Keppel Offshore and Marine, 2014). The company needed to have these offices as close as possible to clients, deployment sites, and shipyards that can provide products and services. Nonetheless, although each yard had its own areas of specialization, the company encouraged optimal utilization of resources by allowing sister yards to utilize its facilities and workforce anywhere in the world.

Because of the company's network of twenty shipyards all over the world, an order can come in from one part of the world, and the closest shipyard may provide the bulk of required services to be able to coordinate with the client closely and deploy rapidly, but shipyards from another part of the world also provide complementary products/services as part of a regional or global production network.

Other ASEAN Champions: Charoen Pokphand Foods PCL, PETRONAS Dagangan Berhad and DIALOG Group Berhad, and TOA Paint (Thailand) Co., Ltd.

Only a small number of our ASEAN champions may be categorically named "multinationals," especially by Western standards, but many of them have indeed explored opportunities outside their domestic markets, and quite a number of them have successfully laid the path to greater internationalization by establishing a presence overseas through representative offices, fully functioning subsidiaries, or joint ventures. Thai companies have been particularly enthusiastic in expanding their reach, especially across ASEAN. Dutch Mill, TUF, and ThaiBev are some examples. Another is Charoen Pokphand Foods (CPF), the agro-industrial and food subsidiary group of Thailand's largest conglomerate.

CPF does business in feeds, farms, food, and food service worldwide, from the Philippines to Sweden. Tracing its roots to a small seed-manufacturing business in 1954, the company successfully rode the wave of rapid growth in the Thai poultry industry in the 1980s, which motivated an expansion into livestock and then aquaculture. The company first went overseas in 2002 with the establishment of a subsidiary in the United States for the distribution of seafood products in the American market. In the same year, it set up CPF Europe to import and distribute products in the EU. Within the next five years, investments were made in the United Kingdom, China, Turkey, Malaysia, India, Russia, Laos, and the Philippines. Since then, CPF has embarked on a path of rapid internationalization, as it envisions itself as the "Kitchen of the World," investing heavily in expansion activities aimed at sustainable growth through an expansion of food businesses, market diversification, and the expansion of distribution channels in Thailand and overseas, particularly in high-potential countries.

Another modern necessity, petroleum, has allowed other ASEAN champions to make promising inroads on the path of internationalization, such as PETRONAS Dagangan Berhad and DIALOG Group Berhad of Malaysia. PETRONAS Dagangan Berhad (PDB) is the retail and marketing arm of the Malaysian oil and gas giant, Petroliam Nasional Berhad (PETRONAS) of the famed twin towers that distinguish the Kuala Lumpur skyline. PDB is engaged in the sales and marketing of downstream petroleum products, including petrol, liquefied petroleum gas (LPG), and lubricants in Malaysia and several other ASEAN countries. The company now has the second-largest market share of LPG over the central and southern Philippines, and is looking to grow its presence in the North and in metro Manila. PDB is also growing its LPG business in Vietnam. Meanwhile, the company has focused on selling lubricants in Thailand.

The DIALOG Group Berhad provides integrated technical services to the oil, gas, and petrochemical industry. It provides engineering and construction services, logistics, plant maintenance, and IT solutions. After earning an impeccable reputation at home, the company gained a partnership with New Zealand's Fitzroy Engineering Group, opening windows of international opportunities for the company. Over the years, DIALOG's overseas network has grown to span three continents. The company currently has offices and facilities in Singapore, Thailand, Indonesia, China, Australia, New Zealand, India, United Arab Emirates, Saudi Arabia, and the United Kingdom.

Another company that is meritorious in our research is Thailand's TOA Paint, which systematically transformed itself from a small family enterprise into a fledgling international firm that currently operates in several ASEAN countries. It is currently the largest paint manufacturer in

Thailand, owning about 50 percent of shares in the market, with a product range that includes decorative paint, wood coating, marine protective coating, construction chemicals, automotive coating, and spray paint.

The company started to expand its geographical reach through overseas markets in 1994 with the establishment of several subsidiaries in Vietnam and Malaysia as well as branch offices in Vietnam and China (TOA Group, 2010; 2013). Today, the company is present in seven ASEAN countries, namely Vietnam, Indonesia, Malaysia, Laos, Cambodia, and Myanmar (TOA Group, 2014). It also exports its products to Singapore, Brunei, and more than forty other countries across the globe (Gujarat Money, 2010).

Beyond ASEAN, TOA Paint is also looking to expand to South Asia and the Middle East. In 2010, the company founded its Indian subsidiary, TOA India Private Limited, and announced the construction of a manufacturing facility with a 3-million-ton annual capacity in the state of Tamil Nadu in South India (Business Standard, 2010). It also opened a representative office in the southwest city of Kerala the following year (The Hindu Business Line, 2011). Furthermore, another plant is to be constructed in West India, set to commence operations after 2015. The company has been expanding aggressively in India due to its huge paint market. In a 2011 interview with then-President Jatuphat Tangkaravakoon, it was mentioned that the company's strategy for expanding overseas is through gradual and selective product offerings (ISN Hot News, 2011).

"In the initial stage, due to our small customer base we'll have to start out by following the market leader and overtake them when the opportunity arises. We'll need to focus on particular products so that people become attached instead of focusing on a variety of products where there is no focus point." (Tangkaravakoon, 2011; as cited by ISN Hot News, 2011)

Conclusions

As indicated, internationalization is closely related to diversification in that broadening market vista would invariably entail international expansion. In this chapter, the focus is on firms with a clear strategic intent to go global in order to gain more competitive advantage, tap into foreign markets, establish global value chain, and acquire advanced competences.

Our ASEAN champions have made inroads on the path of internationalization by investing in product quality and adopting international standards, acquiring local firms in overseas markets, establishing regional distribution networks, initiating integrated regional value chains, and

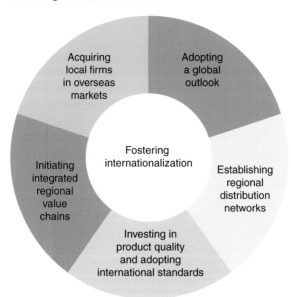

Exhibit 8.1   Fostering Internationalization

adopting a global outlook. Dutch Mill and TUF have demonstrated how ASEAN firms have begun to think global beyond local. Realizing that their commitment to customer satisfaction and high-quality products is universally appreciated, these companies have found overseas opportunities for their world-class products and services. To further enhance their capacities to provide products that meet global standards, they have forged partnerships with foreign and global companies to learn best practices and benefit from their experience and expertise in foreign markets. But internationalization does not just require meeting global product standards; it also means adopting globally accepted processes and good corporate governance. Companies like Thai Beverage have invested in internal processes and the development of a corporate culture that values integrity, transparency, and corporate sustainability – well beyond the common expectations for developing-country firms. Firms like Keppel FELS and Sembcorp Marine have embraced a fully global outlook, bringing their business closer to their international clientele and creating a truly global presence. A synthesis of our findings is presented in Exhibit 8.1.

Even so, these firms would not be regarded as multinationals according to the standards set by renowned firms from developed countries.

Although these firms are champions in their national settings, they are still fledgling multinationals in the global sense.

This evaluation should not be taken as a disparagement of the international operations of these firms, but as a starting point in their evolution into full-fledged multinationals in the future. The progress at this time reflects the difficult circumstances of any developing economy. It also indicates how these firms had to first develop domestic strengths and market leadership before they were able to compete with multinationals that typically have more experience and resources. Currently, the firms profiled in this chapter are national powers, with some emerging as regional players. With ASEAN and the AEC, however, the jury is out whether some of these firms can leverage their capabilities and become ASEAN multinationals. To meet this requirement, these firms will need to muster their full capabilities. One such capability is building synergy, which is the subject of the next chapter.

9   Building Synergy

Introduction

The subject of diversification has a long history in management strategy and international business. Generally regarded as a growth strategy, diversification refers to expanding a firm's line of business, specifically with a new product offering in an existing market or tapping completely new markets. Typically, entering new businesses requires building new capabilities internally or obtaining these skills externally through acquisitions. Because entry into new markets involves the development of new skills and capabilities, it can be expensive, and it generally leads to higher risks (Ansoff, 1957).

Even so, a distinction should be made between operational and financial risk (Klein & Saidenberg, 1997). Operational risk generally arises from uncertainty in procedures and processes. However, diversification can reduce financial risks because investments are not placed in one single nest, but mediated within a varied portfolio. Hence, any loss in one business can be compensated by profits made elsewhere.

Diversification is generally classified as either related, when new products and markets are similar to existing businesses, or unrelated, when new products and markets do not fall in any categories of a firm's given portfolio. Unrelated diversification is considered riskier and more complex than related diversification. Diversification is also closely related to horizontal (expanding into new product or market areas) or vertical (internalizing supplier or retailer activities) growth.

Whether diversification poses more risks than gains is a subject of empirical inquiry and verification. On one hand, diversification is regarded as a part of an evolving successful growth strategy that, if supported by appropriate structures and processes, may contribute to long-term profitability (Chandler, 1962). In regard to financial risks, there is evidence that diversified financial portfolios have advantages in terms of holding less capital and issuing more loans, but not necessarily being more profitable (Klein & Saidenberg, 1997). Yet in another study of diversification records of thirty-three U.S. companies from 1950 to 1986, Porter (1987) reports that these companies are generally unsuccessful: they divested more acquisitions and their strategies failed to create value during the study period.

Where there is common ground in many of these studies is a recognition that high performance will depend on the ability of firms to remain efficient, specifically the ability to control and coordinate the complexity that results from having multiple businesses. Thus, while diversity is good, it can also detract attention from core strategies.

To reduce organizational inefficiencies, firms need to build *synergies* across different lines of business. In all, synergies can be financial (creation of value through good portfolio management), operational (honing economies of scale and scope across the different product/business lines), or organizational (the ability to learn through diverse offerings and structures and build slack and capacity).

This objective can be nuanced when applied in the context of firms in emerging and developing markets. Among the distinguishing elements of success in Japan and South Korea is the ubiquity of large diversified business groups. Once derided as politically riddled and hopelessly inefficient, Japan's *zaibatsu* that flourished before World War II was forced to dismantle but resurrected in a looser form of conglomeration called *keiretsu*. The growing success of Japanese firms in the 1980s even kindled an interest in framing some type of counterpart in the United States (Gerlach, 1990). In South Korea, the resurgence of a postwar economy was explained in large part by mostly family-led conglomerates called *chaebols* (Amsden, 1992; Ungson, Steers, & Park, 1997).

Among observers and pundits, mostly from developed economies, these large-scale conglomerates were still held in suspicion and occasionally denigrated in terms of importance and influence. In the case of Korea, the *chaebol* was also disparaged as being anti-competitive and detrimental to the full development of small and medium-sized enterprises and became the subject of structural reform by one Korean administration. Rebuttals came by way of arguments that in developing economies the size of a business mattered for both reliability and security, and that diversified conglomerates operated as an internal market that funneled much-needed capital to smaller affiliated firms that would otherwise have been denied it (Ungson, Steers, & Park, 1999). According to McKinsey, conglomerates made up 80 percent of the largest fifty companies by revenue in Korea over the last decade to 2014, and their revenues grew by 11 percent per year on average. In India, conglomerates constituted 90 percent of the top fifty companies, excluding state firms, and had average revenue growth of 23 percent per year. Their continued success seems to negate the notion that they exist as mere second-best alternatives when institutional voids exist or when markets are largely undeveloped.

In our study of ASEAN champions, we determined that diversified structures mattered in determining high performance for so long as synergies were built along with diversity. Admittedly, many of these firms would hardly resemble the size and function of *keiretsu* and *chaebol* and may not be considered by observers as "conglomerates," but many of the advantages and benefits arising from a broad operational portfolio gave rise to distinctive features and favorable financial results. In cases we profile in this chapter, we pinpoint how these firms were able to develop synergies to match their diverse product/market offerings. A profile of each firm is as follows:

- *PT Indofood Sukses Makmur Tbk.* (Indonesia): Building a total food company through related diversification
- *PT Global Mediacom Tbk.* (Indonesia): Creating an integrated media platform around the core business
- *WCT Land Sdn. Bhd.* (Malaysia): Building a holding company that links construction, property development, and property management
- *PT Malindo Feedmill Tbk.* (Indonesia): Vertical growth from its core across the entire industry chain
- *Yoma Strategic Holdings Limited* (Myanmar): Managing an investment conglomerate to capitalize on multiple business opportunities
- *Bangkok Dusit Medical Services PCL* (Thailand): Managing a network of health care service businesses
- *Mudajaya Corporation Berhad* (Malaysia): Developing a network of engineers with deep industry expertise
- *Other ASEAN Champions: QAF Brunei Sdn. Bhd.* (Brunei), *Adinin Group of Companies* (Brunei), and *Advanced Info Services PCL* (Thailand): Building profitable businesses through unrelated and related diversification

PT Indofood Sukses Makmur Tbk. (ISM)

Indofood, through its highly popular brand Indomie, is the world's largest producer of instant noodles. The company was born out of Liem Sioe Liong's group of companies, more popularly known as the Salim Group, today Indonesia's largest conglomerate and one of the largest in the region. The company that would eventually become known as Indofood was established in 1971 as part of the Salim Group's early diversification strategy into food, textiles, banking, and later, cement, automobiles, wood products, and real estate, born out of its highly profitable commodity-trading business. The Salim Group had become particularly known for its expansive diversification strategy, which peaked before the Asian Financial Crisis of 1997, with 280,000 employees organized into 12 divisions ranging from food to computers (Dieleman, 2007).

Embedded in this strategy of expansive horizontal diversification was the irresistible opportunity to ride the wave of favorable government policies that allowed firms like the Salim Group companies to develop market power in order to jumpstart local industry and to reduce the country's import dependence. However, although from an observer's standpoint the group may seem to have entered every industry it could get itself into, what makes the Indofood subsidiary quite exemplary is how its related diversification has taken advantage of synergies across its products and services. The company today has five core business segments, namely consumer branded products (CBP), bogasari, agribusiness, distribution, cultivation, and processed vegetables.

The CBP segment is the company's main food processing arm, producing its trademark *Indomie* noodles, dairy products, snack foods, food seasonings, nutrition and specialty foods, as well as beverages such as ready-to-drink tea and coffee, bottled water, carbonated soft drinks, and fruit juice. Under the same group, Indofood operates two subsidiaries in the business of corrugated and flexible packaging, which serve other divisions within Indofood as well as third-party customers in Indonesia and overseas. Bogasari, which has been with the Indofood Group from the start, is still one of the top flour producers in the country, and is the largest pasta producer in Indonesia and the whole Southeast Asia. Meanwhile, Indofood's agribusiness subsidiary, IndoAgri, owns and operates nearly 300,000 hectares of oil palm plantations in Sumatra and Kalimantan. The company also cultivates and processes rubber, sugar, cocoa, and tea. IndoAgri's edible oil and fats division, in turn, manufactures and markets the downstream products of the agribusiness plantation division. Among its products are cooking oil, margarine and crude coconut oil, some of which are leading brands in Indonesia.

The company's distribution segment, which has the most extensive network in the country distributes majority of Indofood's products, and serves third-party customers as well. Finally, the cultivation and processed vegetable segment is overseen by China Minzhong Food Corporation, an integrated Chinese vegetable processing company acquired in 2013.

Indofood has adopted diversification as a key strategy toward its vision of becoming a "total food solutions" company, from planting and processing of raw materials to the production of final products and the distribution of such to retailers (Afriani, Dewi, & Mulyati, 2012).

PT Global Mediacom Tbk.

Synergy across business activities was demonstrated in the previous case along both vertical and horizontal lines. The next case shows synergy across diversified products and services on multiple media platforms.

Global Mediacom is Indonesia's first and largest integrated media, broadcasting, entertainment, and telecommunications company. It produces and distributes media content, broadcasts TV and radio channels, publishes newspapers, magazines, and tabloids, and develops mobile content and value-added services. It is currently the market leader in both free-to-air and pay television.

Founded in 1981, Bimantara Citra, the company that would later become Global Mediacom, was involved in various unrelated ventures in broadcast media, telecommunications, IT, hotels, chemicals, infrastructure, and transportation. As the years progressed, however, the company's success in broadcast media convinced its leaders to focus on media as its core business, and the company soon divested itself of its other assets. Through a number of acquisitions, the company expanded its broadcasting reach on television and began partnering with international content providers like the popular music channel MTV Asia. By 2005, the company had fully acquired two major television networks and soon focused on building its media content, both by acquiring programs and developing in-house productions. It also put up four radio stations and began its print media business by acquiring a local tabloid publisher.

The following year, the company introduced value-added services to TV viewers, including SMS Call TV that allows viewers to participate in game show quizzes or vote in reality/talent shows through phone calls or SMS text messages. In the same year, the company acquired majority ownership of its third TV network. Following these developments, the company officially changed its name to PT Global Mediacom Tbk in 2007 to strengthen its image as a leading integrated media company. In the same year, Global Mediacom acquired majority ownership in a Singapore-based company offering content and value-added services. With this acquisition, the company launched its online news and entertainment media portal, okezone.com. By this time, Global Mediacom had fully divested itself of its non-core assets, including its shares in a mobile telecom company. This signaled the company's commitment to focusing on media as its core business. It did not mean, however, that the company was not intent on expanding its activities. On the contrary, Global Mediacom embarked on an aggressive expansion in the media broadcasting, content, and value-added services business.

Expanding to new media, such as mobile and Internet, Global Mediacom has ventured into PC online gaming and mobile gaming. Through a joint venture with Chinese Internet services giant Tencent, the company has begun offering the mobile and social networking application, WeChat, and is collaborating with them on developing other online communication and entertainment products. It has also ventured into online shopping through a joint venture with the Japanese e-commerce company Rakuten, as well as 24-hour home TV shopping through a joint venture with South Korea's GS Home Shopping Network.

Global Mediacom shows how a company can diversify without losing focus, and in fact, build synergies across integrated platforms as demonstrated in its multimedia business. Through several acquisitions and international partnerships, the company has broadened its reach and increased its depth of product and service offerings, cementing its market leadership in Indonesia.

WCT Land Sdn. Bhd.

What Global Mediacom did in media, WCT Land demonstrated in real estate and property management. WCT Land is the property development and management arm of WCT Holdings Berhad, a leading investment holdings company also engaged in engineering and construction. The company's portfolio includes townships, luxury homes, high-rise residences, industrial properties, offices, mixed commercial developments, concessions, hotels, and shopping malls – covering a total area of over 300 hectares of development projects across Malaysia.

WCT Land was founded in 1996 by its parent company, then named WCT Berhad, as it ventured into property development. WCT Berhad, founded in 1981, was then primarily a civil engineering and construction company, specializing in earthwork, highway construction, and other infrastructure developments. Seeing opportunities in real estate development brought about by the highly favorable economic conditions of the early 1990s, including the liberalization of financial markets in the region, WCT jumped into the real estate bandwagon with a pioneer project in the Bandar Bukit Tinggi Township in Klang, a high-growth city west of the capital, Kuala Lumpur. Although the financial crisis that plagued the region in 1997 and 1998 was a major setback for most real estate developers, WCT bounced back strong at the turn of the decade. Synergies between WCT Berhad and WCT Land proved highly valuable, as WCT Land's township development, which involved the construction of buildings, roads, and waterworks, required resources and expertise that WCT Berhad was strong in.

In 2006, WCT Land diversified into property investment and management through the launch of the Bukit Tinggi Shopping Center in its Bandar Bukit Tinggi township. In the same year, the company won a concession for the construction and management of an integrated complex at the new low cost carrier terminal (LCCT) of the Kuala Lumpur International Airport. It also won concessions in India for the Durgapur and Panagarh-Palsit Expressways through its parent company, which are now also being managed under WCT Land. In 2010, the company launched its first hotel venture also in the city of Klang. In 2012, it launched The Landmark, a premier development aimed to serve as the corporate hub of its Bandar Bukit Tinggi township. From construction (through its now-sister company, WCT Berhad) to property development and on to property management, WCT Land has taken full advantage of synergies across the real estate and property segments, and it has now extended these synergies to overseas ventures in Vietnam.

PT Malindo Feedmill Tbk.

Although some firms take advantage of synergies horizontally, as Global Mediacom has done across media platforms and WCT Land has done across real estate projects and properties, other firms have no less remarkable success in harnessing manifest synergies vertically along the value chain.

PT Malindo Feedmill Tbk, another Champion from Indonesia, is in the business of producing animal feed, growing poultry, and processing poultry products. Founded in 1997, the company's sales have grown 18 percent every year for the past 5 years, exceeding the industry average of 11 percent (Mayagita & Eslita, 2014). The company started as an animal feed producer of corn and soybean meal, but in 2001, Malindo acquired an 80-hectare chicken farm, realizing the obvious complementation between its feed mill business and the production of day-old chicks (DOCs). The company pursued more acquisitions of other feed mills and DOC farms thereafter. In 2007, Malindo entered the broiler chicken business, which was the next stage in the poultry meat value chain after DOC production. Broiler farms raised DOCs until they were fully grown and ready for meat harvesting.

In 2013, Malindo ventured further down the value chain into food processing through the creation of a new subsidiary. The new company was expected to produce synergies with the on-farm segment of the Malindo group, thus Malindo intends to further increase its investments in commercial broiler farms in order to augment its supply of raw materials for the new subsidiary (World Poultry, 2013).

Moving forward, the company has announced that it will continue to expand its market reach across Indonesia so that the products of its core businesses, namely the production of animal feed, day-old chicks, and commercial broilers, span the entire country. Malindo also aims to further develop its downstream and upstream businesses to support and further strengthen its core businesses. The trend of increasing chicken consumption among Indonesians continues to motivate Malindo to eagerly pursue its geographical expansion and vertical integration as it leverages on the synergies among its businesses along the value chain.

Yoma Strategic Holdings Limited

Tarun Khanna of Harvard Business School has argued that conglomerates in developing countries have thrived because businesses need to compensate for the underdeveloped nature of the local market. Whether this implies that conglomerates are a transient phenomenon or that by maximizing early opportunities and securing a sizable chunk of the market they are able to maintain their dominance in the long run is not the subject of this chapter. However, the opportunities presented by the carte blanche nature of very young markets do offer fertile ground for rising conglomerates to develop synergies across related and perhaps even seemingly unrelated businesses.

In the early 1990s, when Serge Pun, founder of Serge Pun and Associates (SPA), decided that it was time to invest in Myanmar, the country of his birth, he came armed with years of experience in the real estate business, having had success in Hong Kong, Thailand, China, and Malaysia. But the business environment in Myanmar, having just recently begun to open up to private-sector development and foreign investment was very different from the more developed markets he had previously operated in. Rather than being daunted by the unique challenges presented by doing business in a transition economy, Mr. Pun saw the opportunity to take part in the creation of new markets and the founding of new industries.

Originally, SPA's venture into Myanmar was focused on real estate through the establishment of First Myanmar Investment Co. (FMI) in 1992. However, Serge Pun soon realized that various sectors in Myanmar provided opportunities for investment. Yoma Strategic Holdings was set up to take advantage of these opportunities. Mr. Pun recalls how new business opportunities presented themselves in conjunction with the company's real estate business.

"...We built the first gated community in Myanmar and it required security guards, so we hired about 60 to 70 guards. The neighbors thought we were doing a pretty good job. They came to us and said, 'Will you do security for our factory?' 'Will you provide security for our building?' Soon, we had a company employing 830 security guards, providing security services for factories, embassies, executive homes, and other properties." – Serge Pun, Executive Chairman

Besides its own security agency, Yoma Strategic Holdings also had to set up its own landscaping company that would meet the high quality requirements of its premium real estate developments. Soon, this company also began providing service to third parties in the same way that it turned out for the company's security agency. In 2013, the company entered into a joint venture with Dragages Singapore Pte Ltd, a large-scale international construction company, to build FMI developments to world-class standards. These ventures, borne out of necessity, proved to be highly complementary to the company's core real estate business and provided Yoma Strategic Holdings with a strong competitive advantage from the synergies formed across them. From real estate development and building construction to landscaping, security, and property management, subsidiaries under the Yoma umbrella working together guarantee the premium quality promised by the company in each of its projects.

In 1993, the company established Yoma Bank, one of Myanmar's first private banks and today one of its largest. Among the bank's key products are housing loans, for which buyers of FMI properties enjoy better deals. In the following year, the company ventured into motorcycle trading through a joint venture with Suzuki. In 1997, it entered into a joint venture with Nissan and Sumitomo, acquiring exclusive distributorship of Nissan automobiles in Myanmar.

In 2007, Yoma diversified into the biodiesel industry through the harvesting of Jatropha curcas – a plant that can produce oil for biodiesel production. The company has also ventured into retail, luxury tourism, and logistics, while continuing to expand its operations in auto trading, construction, and real estate.

Bangkok Dusit Medical Services PCL and Mudajaya Corporation Berhad

Because narratives about synergy tend to focus on the financial and operational aspects of benefits and risks, it is rare to locate cases in which synergy is obtained from organizational structures and internal processes. And yet, Bangkok Dusit Medical Services PCL, a leading provider of health care services in Thailand, and Mudajaya Corporation Berhad in

Malaysia provide illuminating examples in our study. The company was founded in 1969 by a group of forty medical practitioners and pharmacists (Bangkok Hospital, 2015). The original founders were friends studying at the same college, and the establishment of the company's first hospital was made possible through each doctor's contacts and experiences. At the time of establishment, scarcity marked the Thai health care industry, with only public hospitals operating in Thailand. Seeing that the health care providers are not enough, the founders of BDMS set out to establish Bangkok Hospital in 1972, which became the first private medical institution in the country (Bangkok Hospital, 2015).

As the operations of the company's first hospital improved, BDMS started to look into the goal of creating a network of hospitals in a continuous bid to provide more options for health care in Thailand. Although the company continued to expand its Bangkok Hospital group, it also began to acquire other local hospital brands, starting with the acquisition of the Samitivej Group in 2004.

A year later, in 2005, BDMS launched its two specialist hospitals, the Bangkok Heart Hospital, which specializes in cardiac diseases, and the Wattanosoth Hospital, specializing in cancer treatment (Tris Rating Credit News, 2014).

In 2011, the company's portfolio significantly increased as a result of a share-swap merger with Health Network PCL (HNC), the major shareholder of two well-known local hospital brands, Phyathai Hospital and Paolo Memorial Hospital. In the same year, the company acquired minor shares in Bumrungrad Hospital PCL, an internationally accredited, multispecialty hospital in Bangkok (Bangkok Dusit Medical Services PCL, 2014; Tris Rating Credit News, 2014).

Additionally, in the past decade, the company has also diversified into complementary businesses such as medical laboratories, saline production, and pharmaceuticals. Most recently, BDMS purchased shares in Save Drug Center Co. Ltd. through subsidiary Bangkok Save Drug Co. Ltd. to further expand noncore business activities and take advantage of rising opportunities in the pharmaceutical industry. Earlier, in 2010, BDMS first forayed into the market with its acquisition of ANB Laboratories (Ulloa, 2010; Tris Rating Credit News, 2014).

As Thailand's medical industry sustains its progress, the company also intends to further strengthen their market leadership by continuing to grow their network of hospitals on a nationwide scale. Chief Financial Officer Narumol Noi-am shares that BDMS is presently targeting to achieve a network of fifty hospitals all over Thailand by 2016. In addition to its thirty-nine hospitals in operation, four hospitals are now under construction, which brings the company's total network to forty-three hospitals. The management team is positive that the company will be able to reach its goal of having a fifty-hospital network by the end of 2016.

Aside from geographical reach, the company is also pushing to attain a wider market segment by targeting more middle-income and social security patients, as evidenced by its recent acquisitions of secondary care hospitals serving middle-income patients in Thailand's provinces. Noi-am also mentions that the company intends to have more primary and secondary care facilities as well as "telecare" clinics in the near future.

Although BDMS has not engaged with other health care companies in its current expansion pursuits, it has been actively seeking affiliations with different institutions such as the Oregon Health and Science University and the Mahidol University for the development of education, research, expertise, and resources for medical services. Most recently, BDMS has partnered with Japan's Nagoya University with the primary aim of developing the skills of its medical staff (The Nation, 2014, 2015).

Similar to BDMS, Mudajaya was founded as a construction firm by a network of professional engineers. Their first project as a construction firm was to build the Muda Irrigation Project. The World Bank-funded project jumped start Mudajaya's growth as a competitive construction firm, where the company gained more contacts due to the prominence of the Muda Irrigation Project. Mudajaya gained Japanese and other contractors that helped establish the brand name of the company (World Bank, 2014).

Because the construction sector in Malaysia was relatively young during the founding of Mudajaya, the company had the advantage of there being fewer competitors in the industry. Furthermore, competitors were limited due to a huge barrier of entry; deep expertise in engineering and construction was needed in order to compete in the said market. Mudajaya developed the reputation as one of the very few companies with expertise in constructing power plants. The company started to diversify when it pursued the development of its first township in Kuching Sarawak, East Malaysia. Mudajaya entered a joint venture with the city of Kuching Sarawak in which the city would continuously contribute land while the company would bring in capital to develop its township.

As Mudajaya foresees the on-streaming of major power plant projects in the near future, it also intends to capitalize on these initiatives, given its strong track record and technical capabilities in power plant construction. With this, it aims to acquire or develop strategic assets that satisfy the risk-return profile and provide future recurrent income streams.

In keeping with its focus on hiring professional engineers with deep industry expertise, Mudajaya believes in the importance of people development. Hence, it has organized several in-house trainings as well as external courses for its employees. The company's employees include engineers, who are part of its strong, professional, and skilled workforce.

Other ASEAN Champions: QAF Brunei Sdn. Bhd., Adinin Group of Companies, and Advanced Info Services PCL

For many Western observers, unrelated diversification is rare and daunting. In this part of Asia, however, large conglomerates with very broad interests tend to be a far more common phenomenon. From Myanmar to Singapore, many markets in ASEAN economies are dominated by businesses that are part of large business groups that harness synergies across both related and seemingly unrelated activities. In the smaller ASEAN markets like Brunei, conglomerates tend to hold favorable positions as market leaders and preferred business partners of foreign investors given their greater capacities to pool resources, develop expertise, and build synergies across their businesses. QAF Brunei Sendirian Berhad (Sdn. Bhd.), and the Adinin Group of Companies are prime examples.

QAF Brunei Sdn. Bhd. is a conglomerate in Brunei with interests in automobile dealership, media, fast food, supermarkets, livestock production, industrial machinery, and marketing & promotions. Most recently, the company has ventured also into the telecommunications and IT infrastructure business.

QAF originally started out as a foreign offshoot of a Singaporean company. The company began investing in multiple industries to take advantage of the rising Brunei economy, engaging in a deliberate strategy of horizontal diversification to cast as wide a net as possible over the emerging market. In the 1990s, Prince Abdul Qawi, a member of the Brunei Royal Family acquired QAF, and the company became a Bruneian firm thereafter.

QAF's main line of business has been in auto trading and importing luxury vehicles, which it later extended to auto leasing. To sustain growth amidst a very small but increasingly wealthy domestic market of a little over four hundred thousand people, the company aggressively sought a strategy of unrelated diversification. In 2003, it ventured into telecommunications and IT, constructing and managing telecom/IT infrastructure, and providing electronic business solutions and value-added data communication services. It also maintains smaller operations in the businesses mentioned earlier, including fast food, livestock, supermarkets, media, and industrial machinery.

Although QAF can trace its roots to a foreign venture into Brunei that had a deliberate strategy of diversification from the beginning, the Adinin Group of Companies was mainly homegrown and realized the benefits of synergistic diversification as it grew. Originally set up as family business by Haji Adnin bin Pehin Dato Haji Ibrahim and his son, Musa Adnin, the company that would later become the Adinin Group started out as a medium-sized company in the business of distributing paint products. An increase in construction activities following Brunei's independence from the United Kingdom in 1984 presented an opportunity to the company to enter the construction business.

"When we were selling paints, some of the customers asked: 'Since you know the product best, could you apply the paint for us as well?' So we replied: 'Okay!' And we went into that. Now, we sell and then we apply the paint." – Musa Adnin, Managing Director

Beginning with painting services, the company soon ventured into plumbing and other construction-related services. Its success in paint, trading and construction services encouraged the company to expand the business further, taking advantage of another opportunity arising from developments in the business environment. Many foreign companies had begun selling their assets as the country transitioned from British rule to independent government. The Adinin Group started acquiring some of these assets, including hardware shops and petroleum-based services. The company's interest in petroleum was piqued when Musa Adnin participated in a special program for local businessmen developed by the Brunei Government and the Brunei Shell Group. Adinin's acquisitions led to the creation of Deladi Petroleum Services in 1985, which subsequently won contracts with Brunei Shell Group and Total E&P Borneo. Adinin's petroleum services subsidiary specialized in servicing machines and equipment used in the petroleum and gas industries. The company later diversified even further, venturing into automation in 2006. Today, the company's broad portfolio of businesses includes civil engineering, machine fabrication, electrical and instrumentation services, manufacturing, interior design, information technology, travel agencies, and manpower supply.

Although unrelated diversification can hold center stage on account of a perceived higher level of risk, synergies can likewise be built and cultivated through related diversification. In our research, one company – Advanced Info Service PCL, or AIS – has been exemplary in this regard. Founded in 1986, it is a fully integrated telecommunications company based in Thailand catering to the Thai market, and it is the current market leader in the industry. From its modest beginnings as a computer rental company, the company was given an exclusive 20-year concession agreement by the Telephone Organization of Thailand (TOT) to run mobile telephone services on a 900-MHz frequency. It has since launched a number of products and services that have solidified its market power in telecommunications. Such offerings include GSM Advance and Global System Mobile Communications, MobileLIFE services in accordance with Wireless Application Protocol (WAP) technology, a customer service software called "C-Care Smart System," and the "Advanced in Building Network." In the future, the company plans to transition itself from a purely mobile service operator into a "digital life" service provider. The firm plans to integrate its mobile business and the fixed broadband business to create an integrated, all-digital business in its aim to serve market demands and achieve greater profitability.

Conclusions

Synergy can be defined in many ways, but perhaps the simplest depiction is "1 + 1 = 3." Our profiles of firms in this chapter reveal different paths taken to achieve synergy. From our narratives, size and synergy are closely related; large firms have the capacity to broaden their product and market offerings through diversification – a capability that smaller and less endowed firms cannot afford. A synthesis of our findings is presented in Exhibit 9.1.

Still, larger size matters less without leadership and corporate governance. In our cases, broader horizons were accompanied by astute, dedicated, and often visionary leadership. Serge Pun of Yoma Strategic Holdings and Haji Adnin and his son Musa Adnin of the Adinin Group believed in the roles that their companies played in the rising markets they served. They took on the challenges of underdevelopment, inadequate supporting services, and "institutional voids" and turned them into opportunities for creating synergistic umbrellas of like-minded and goal-oriented companies under the same visionary leadership.

Some firms, particularly those operating in small, emergent markets had to start up their own complementary businesses, as Yoma and QAF had to do. Other firms chose to enter into joint ventures with foreign or local companies to extend their reach or expand their capabilities. Many firms engaged in acquisition activities to diversify horizontally across related or seemingly unrelated businesses like what Global Mediacom

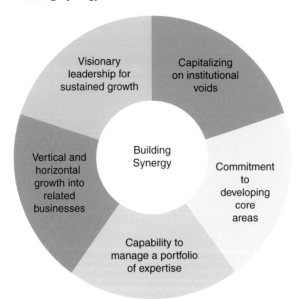

Exhibit 9.1 Building Synergy

did in media; vertically along the value chain like what Malindo Feedmill did in the poultry business; or both, as Indofood, the Indonesian food giant, successfully demonstrated.

ASEAN champions emerged through related vertical and/or horizontal diversification of businesses by capitalizing on institutional voids in the early developing economies. Scope economies were also possible by managing a network of expertise such as BDMS' health care management and Mudajaya's construction expertise. While unrelated diversification would be discounted in the West, some of the champions mobilized holding companies of unrelated businesses to supplement market inefficiencies with necessary competences.

These cases underscore an important distinction from that taken from largely developed economies. Criticisms of large portfolios tend to emphasize control and coordination costs that overwhelm strategic focus. This occurs when the portfolio is treated primarily in financial terms or when returns from the overall portfolio are expected to be larger than the simple aggregation of individual returns. In the cases presented in this chapter, the overarching consideration is not so much the financial return – although this is an important goal – but the advantage, if not necessity, of synergistic complementarity among a company's business activities. In this regard, our ASEAN champions have successfully harnessed the synergies of the related and seemingly unrelated activities they have diversified. To fully capitalize on synergy, these firms also have to excel in managing human capital – the subject of the next chapter.

10   Nurturing Human Capital

Introduction

Although human capital is widely acknowledged to be a requisite for managerial success, its precise impact on financial performance is not as tangible as other measures. Not at all surprisingly, it is given short shrift when considered in the total context of a firm's sustained success. In terms of a metric, it is typically lumped as an administrative cost. Yet, in a landmark book, *The Competitive Advantage through People*, management professor Jeffrey Pfeffer (1994) whittled away this belief with supportive empirical studies that indicate an opposite effect. Pfeffer compared various firms against the usual correlates – strategy, structure, technology, patents – using four common measures of stock valuation. His findings indicate that none of the factors above predicted sustained financial success more so than the firm's ability to manage its workplace. This finding was reaffirmed in ensuing documented studies by Pfeffer (1998) and his coauthored work with colleague Charles O'Reilly, *Hidden Value: How Great Companies Achieve Extraordinary Results with Ordinary People* (2000).

The importance of having good-to-great people in any organization has been a prominent staple in strategy and management (see Davenport, 1999). Accentuating this advocacy, Pfeffer cites an influential management consultancy firm, McKinsey & Company, which famously declared, "superior talent will be tomorrow's prime source of competitive advantage" (Charles Fishman, 1998, quoted in O'Reilly & Pfeffer, 2000: 1). However, Pfeffer and his associates remind readers that attracting talent alone is hardly sufficient; creating and nourishing talent over the long run is the added component of sustained success.

The efficacy of human capital for Asian firms has run the gauntlet from universalistic application to contingent refinement. The success of Japan, the acknowledged poster child of post–world war economic miracles, is largely attributed to the discipline and commitment of its well-trained workforce (Ouchi, 1982). Similarly, the rapid rise of South Korea has been explained by the attention placed on workforce skills and shop-floor management (Amsden, 1989), which enabled Koreans to move from sheer imitation to newfound innovation (Kim, 1990). At the euphoric height of Asia's resurgence, when Singapore, Taiwan, Hong Kong, and South Korea had evolved into powerful export economies, the new term "Asian Values," attributed largely to Malaysia's Mahatir Mohamad and Singapore's Lee Kuan Yew, was invoked to describe the unique personal style underpinned by valuable connections that forged the human capital of these Asian economies.

The aftermath of the 1999 Asian Crisis undermined these claims, fueling contrarian arguments that the purportedly cultural strengths such as personal connections were limited or even corrupt practices. Even so, with Asia – and specifically the potential of emerging economies – back on the rise, there has been a resurgent interest in human capital as a correlate of economic success. In a sweeping account of this renaissance, economic journalist Michael Schuman, in the tellingly titled book *The Miracle: The Epic Story of Asia's Quest for Wealth* (2009: xxxv), declares, "Theories on economic development tend to leave out the human element. Yet it is in the lives of people that the secret to Asian success is found."

In Schuman's account, human capital is deeply interwoven with political/economic/cultural origins. While it is derivative of these roots, human capital has its own integral quality. It is manifest in the types of management structures and processes that are developed to support the strategies of any given firm. It forms the basis of the dreams and vision of entrepreneurs who founded and led exemplary firms. The particular application that combines the "best practices" of successful firms in developed countries with the underlying cultural context of developing countries is what makes human capital organic in form and prepotent in its emphases.

Unlike the previous chapters that highlighted specific firms, here we present different characteristics of human capital that define ASEAN champions. Altogether, these firms embrace various facets of human capital ranging from visionary leadership to succession planning. It is evident that these firms have been able to employ various facets of human capital to align structures, processes, and systems in support of their corporate strategies.

Visionary Leadership and Execution

Lao Brewery Co. Ltd.

Lao Brewery considers leadership and vision to be integral core competencies that impact a company's success. Long-term sustainability cannot be achieved without competent leadership and a solid vision for the company's corporate goals and objectives. To ensure that the vision is translated to action, a high level of coordination is undertaken, involving the Lao Management Team, Top Level Management Team, and the rest of the team managers throughout the organization. These groups constantly interact with each other in driving the company's vision into practice. This combination of long-term and short-term orientation ensures that the company concentrates not on short-term profitability but rather on long-term sustainability to make Lao Brewery more competitive in the market.

The management can be described as a top-down system combined with essences of being democratic and participatory. Mr. Mads Brinks, Deputy Managing Director, mentions that there is close collaboration between management and employees, especially when it comes to making decisions integral to the goals of the company.

Moreover, the level of coordination also mediates possible conflicts in advance. A company spokesperson describes this coordination as a traditional way of reaching satisfaction across levels and hierarchies within the company's workforce. Human resource issues are also resolved through a party within the company, which is similar to the concept of a "union" in Western management philosophy. In all, the leadership style employed by Lao Brewery is considered to be democratic and participatory.

"I think this dual structure really is quite interesting for me as a Westerner because there's the daily interaction between the employee and the manager and all the way to the system, which is a very traditional way of making sure that we have satisfied employees." – Mads Brinks, Deputy Managing Director

Bangkok Cable Co. Ltd.

In the cable industry, an entrepreneur cannot simply enter into the industry by relying solely on access to capital and ability to purchase modern technology. Such expertise would be difficult to imitate since not all entrepreneurs have this capability. Even so, visionary leadership in itself is not enough. Execution has to follow for success to ensue.

The company sees a strong workforce and personnel supported with decentralization of administrative responsibilities as key areas of success. It achieves this by developing its workforce through training courses and programs. Bangkok Cable emphasizes workforce quality by providing training on different levels. New recruits go through an on-the-job training program that involves practices related to basic skills and knowledge needed for the production process. It is after this process that new recruits undergo an exam (Rogovsky & Tolentino 2010).

The continuous flow of talented employees is undertaken through systemic training. Those who pass are given a vocational education certificate. The company also provides an outside training course to those who have been working in the production line for a certain period of time. Those who have undergone outside training are encouraged to share best practices and expertise acquired from said training programs. Sharing such practices is also done through an in-house training course. For employees working in technical fields, a competency-based training system is in place (Rogovsky & Tolentino 2010).

These training courses provide a theoretical and practical approach that is tailored to the responsibilities and capabilities of workers. Furthermore, technical staff members take an annual competency test. The apprentice and training programs have resulted in a higher rate of employee retention since their establishment. They have also resulted in more positive behavior, discipline, and greater collaboration among workers (Rogovsky & Tolentino 2010). The company's business development manager Mr. Somsak Ngamprompong also underscores the importance of having experienced industry professionals in the company with regard to sustainability: *"In our company, we have a lot of good people that have a lot of experience in this industry. That's why we have been able to keep our company running for 50 years"* (Mr. Somsak Ngamprompong 2014).

Dao-Heuang Group

The consultative and participatory management style in Dao-Heuang Group is seen as one of its strengths. Managers and employees collaborate to share best practices and exchanging solutions for several challenges faced by the company. According to a company spokesperson, the leadership style of the firms is first to ensure that the management team understands the vision and strategic mission of the corporation. Furthermore, the leadership of the organization has to show sincerity and treat the organization's employees in the spirit of being both a family and a team.

Leaders need to extend their hand to the team in order to promote an environment of stability and helping one another achieve targets. The leaders should also sacrifice more for the team and be ready to actively help in solving problems of the organization. In this way the team will be able to understand the direction of the firm and happily work harder for the company. This type of environment helps the company achieve success in the long run.

At each level of employment, the company trains its employees to develop their leadership capacities. The second type of leadership training that CPF holds caters specifically to young leaders. If the company sees potential and talent in a young individual, it has a development plan that gives them the opportunity to exercise their talents and skills and offers them mentorship from senior leaders in the company.

About 70 percent of the company's total workforce consists of Laotians, while the remaining 30 percent are foreign workers. Most of the company's foreign workers come from neighboring countries such as Vietnam and Thailand. Dao-Heuang also hires experts from other countries through its strong international network. It is due to the diverse nature of the company's workforce that Dao-Heuang benefits from the sharing of best practices, which transpires whenever foreign and local employees collaborate with each other.

EDL-Generation Public Company

EDL-Generation keeps its staff competitive and highly trained through professional training, including both in-house and overseas training. Each training is also conducted differently, as each training program focuses on a certain skill or asset needed by EDL-Generation. This includes training courses in English to prepare its staff for ASEAN integration.

Moreover, the company coordinates with technical schools and universities to keep its training programs consistent with the needs of EDL-Generation. The company's training programs are also supported by EDL-Generation's emphasis in hiring domestic and foreign new graduates with highly technical backgrounds to strengthen the technical core of the company's staff.

The company was the first company to be listed in the Lao Stock Exchange. EDL Generation inherited its management system from its parent company, EDL, and uses a similar corporate structure that emphasizes professional management. This means that leadership is still top-down, but the top management remains responsive of the needs of its department. The Managing Director, Mr. Bounoum, mentions that these types of meetings happen at least once a month.

PT Lippo Karawaci Tbk.

The leadership style employed by the company's management team is top-down with regard to corporate policies and strategies. In terms of feedback, Lippo Karawaci employs a bottom-up approach. A company spokesperson mentions that the company receives market feedback through its consultants and uses the feedback to adjust its strategies.

Through its roadmap, "On A Transformational Journey," the company seeks to improve its infrastructures, management, and manpower skills. It plans to do this by nurturing its workforce inside the company and implementing a systemized form of succession plan for management teams. Furthermore, the company's talent management hires highly skilled graduates, subsequently profiling these individuals for the next 3 to 5 years in order to prepare them for key positions.

The company believes that its workforce is a key ingredient in terms of guaranteeing quality products. As such, it prioritizes a competency-based policy in managing its human resources and pursues human resource development to strengthen the skills and capabilities of its workforce. It conducts internal and outside updates and training programs for all employees. The company also incentivizes its people by determining rewards and promotions based on evaluation results.

PTT Exploration and Production PCL (PTTEP)

The management style of the company can be described as participative. The company also tries to pursue this participative-based management style laterally, partially top-down and partially bottom-up. Since PTTEP has subsidiaries outside of Thailand, the workforce composition of the PTTEP Group can be described as diverse and multicultural. There is a total of three thousand personnel in PTTEP. The number of employees is small relative to the company's size because PTTEP relies heavily on employee productivity and output.

PTTEP is publicly traded in the Thailand stock exchange and has been trading since 1989. As mentioned previously, the company has one of the largest capital shares in said stock exchange. Due to the company's meritocratic nature, PTTEP is professionally managed. Executives who are well experienced in the oil and gas exploration industry hold key positions within the company.

Human Resource Management Training

Hanoi Production Services Import-Export Joint Stock Company (Haprosimex)

Among the distinctive aspects of Haprosimex's training is the focus on the environment along with people development. The company is currently working with several training schools in Ho Chi Minh City. These training schools provide services to the company's employees to increase their capabilities. Haprosimex employees are trained in various practices, such as management, sales, administration, and software application.

These training programs help Haprosimex keep its employees well prepared to meet several challenges associated with the export and manufacturing industry. Moreover, the company also trains local farmers how to drain rainwater and recycle it for their crops. Technical practices are also taught to the local farmers, such as how to keep records of the number of crops they have planted and sold during the harvest season. Haprosimex has even established a school for the children of the local farmers to ensure their welfare.

PT Petrosea Tbk.

Petrosea takes great efforts to develop a highly skilled, highly trained workforce. It believes that human capital is a valuable element in its commitment to provide reliability of services and its creation of spare capacity in anticipation of future growth. To maintain its pool of competent and driven personnel, the company is continually launching initiatives to strengthen its human resource management. Especially in recent years, MAP has been ardently introducing a number of programs to augment the potential of its people, placing emphasis on training and development as well as organizational improvement. Examples include such initiatives as the key performance indicator (KPI)-based New Performance Management System, the MAP Fast Track Management Trainee Program, and English literacy programs.

The company's Petrosea Academy is its training and skills development facility for employees and workers. Additionally, the Human Capital and Organization Department of Petrosea conducts initiatives to increase employee training. In 2011, training programs such as the Supervisory Development Program, which targets potential leaders, were added to the roster of training conducted (PT Petrosea Tbk., 2012). Virendra Prakash, Vice President and Director, opines in a 2012 interview with The Jakarta Post, "The company's main driver of success is not technology or machinery, but its people. MAP is blessed to have dedicated people run the business and make sure that it is always ahead of the game."

EEI Corporation

EEI is a privately owned, professionally managed company under the Yuchengco Group of Companies. President and Chief Executive Officer, Roberto Jose L. Castillo describes his personal management style as being quite open; he walks the grounds and job sites and tries to relate to his employees. He tries to know what's happening on the ground, and this allows him to make informed managerial decisions. Furthermore, he treats his people with respect and does not try to expect the impossible from his employees.

On the ability of the company to maintain a skilled and well-trained workforce, EEI has a strong training program and has been able to utilize this in developing its people. In fact, according to Mr. Castillo, EEI's employees are often pirated by other companies due to an EEI employee's reputation for being well trained. The company identifies Human Resource Development as an integral component of the firm's overall strategy. It is through developing its people that EEI is able to ensure that the company's projects are supported by an effective manpower complement (EEI Corporation, 2013:18).

Today, EEI invests heavily in skills training and personnel development and offers further education and advanced training to its employees (EEI Corporation, 2013: 22). EEI has also been able to improve excellence in training by partnering with other institutions and organizations such as TESDA in providing classroom and practical training (EEI Corporation, 2013: 22). EEI also has its own facilities in the Philippines and abroad where workers can undergo training and refresher courses; among these are EEI's welding academy in Saudi Arabia.

Sembcorp Marine Limited

Sembcorp Marine believes that human capital is essential for the company's long-term growth and competitive edge. Thus it has embodied a human resource strategy that has several key elements. First, the company prioritizes manpower availability. This is defined as the ability of the company to secure the right people for the appropriate roles within the organization. The second element in the company's human resource strategy is manpower development, which entails training workers and enhancing their skills. Third, the company recognizes that manpower retention is the key to sustainable growth, and it rewards its people based on merit. Fourth, Sembcorp Marine believes that creating an environment that is healthful, safe, and secure is essential for its employees. By maintaining a positive work environment, the company ensures its workers that employee welfare and care is a continued commitment of Sembcorp Marine to its employees. Fifth, part of its Human Resource strategy is organizational development. This means that the way the company is structured should gear employees toward contributing to the vision of the company. Lastly, the company promotes a sense of belonging to Sembcorp Marine's corporate values among its workers. This is achieved through employee engagement events and activities. IT and the Internet are also used by the company as means of connecting with its employees.

Phnom Penh Water Supply Authority (PPWSA)

PPWSA's training department is quite active. Training sessions are organized and held in-house. Short training sessions are conducted in which experts are invited to give guest lectures. The company also sends staff members from relevant departments to external training sessions depending on the type of program. Furthermore, PPWSA employees have also attended training sessions conducted by other water utility entities. After trainings, it is common for all personnel who attended to undergo an exam so that this can contribute to employee performance ratings.

Performance-based incentives in PPWSA ensure that employees remain motivated and driven to perform at a high level. For instance, the company has what it calls a collection incentive scheme wherein employees are given monetary compensation based on their collection rate. Furthermore, if employees are able to attain a 100 percent collection rate, then they are given a bonus on top of their salaries.

Continuous Learning and Improvement

Holcim Philippines, Inc.

Attributing its initial strengths to its focus on people, Holcim Philippines, Inc. maintains the building of a culture that engages its employees and promotes continuous learning. With its various strategies on employee engagement, the company's people are expected to continue to be the force that thrusts the company forward. Its corporate strategy, called the Holcim Leadership Journey, puts people at its core as it encompasses "passion for safety, manufacturing excellence, people engagement, and customer value management" (Holcim Philippines, 2013).

Putting workplace safety at the top of its priorities, the company has plotted several courses of action to prevent accidents and encourage a healthy environment. Further, it seeks to encourage employee engagement by fostering a people-oriented corporate culture. The company also has its unique "trust" program, wherein employees identified as "hi-po" ("high potential") are given training locally or overseas (Holcim Philippines, 2013). "Hi-po" employees are treated by their managers as equals, even in management committee meetings, where they are not excluded from discussions of confidential matters. Besides taking care of its employees, the company also believes in taking care of the environment and its "host" communities, which makes its CSR practices also central to the company's philosophy.

Manila Electric Company (Meralco)

In terms of corporate culture, Meralco emphasizes both technical and professional excellence as well as a culture of teamwork and working as one toward corporate goals. The company's cultivation of a highly technical and professional culture is critical since the nature of the work is highly technical in itself.

While Meralco executives represent a combination of highly skilled technicians and well-experienced business professionals, this competence is not difficult to imitate, but Meralco does try to do its best to land the top professionals in the market. In fact, in the past 2 to 3 years, Meralco has been hiring executives from all over the globe in order to create the best talent pool for the organization. Another value the company believes in is "One Meralco," which places an emphasis on teamwork and transparency within the organization.

The prioritization of value creation has allowed the company as a whole to transform into a forward-looking, goal-oriented organization. Stakeholder value creation and customer value creation are important for Meralco because by keeping stakeholders and customers satisfied with the company, Meralco positions itself toward sustainable growth. This is accomplished through organizational leadership that allows exploration into new opportunities by innovating and investing in related and unrelated profitable industries locally and abroad.

People Development

Jollibee Foods Corporation

A prominent component of Jollibee's success is its people. The company takes pride in its strong corporate culture, which fosters the values of excellence, spirit of family and fun, humility to learn and listen, integrity, frugality, respect for the individual, and teamwork. Another key driver of Jollibee's corporate culture, especially in the Philippine market, is its strong branding and marketing strategies. From its early years, the company has been staunchly establishing its brand as a fun, family-oriented, proudly Filipino restaurant, which has made it endearing to Filipino customers. Moreover, Jollibee has always been keen and active in the formulation of its promotions and campaigns, from the company's logo to its television ads to its various projects for children.

PT Solusi Tunas Pratama Tbk.

A distinctive part of the company's success is its hiring strategies. According to a company spokesperson, most of its employees are under 40 years old as a result of the strategy employed by its human resource management. Hiring younger and less experienced people is better for the company since these types of individuals are more willing to consider constructive criticism. Furthermore, hiring people with potential will allow the company to mold each employee to see where he or she fits in the company.

Moreover, the company's corporate culture encourages productivity to assure that the office is not as uptight compared to other office environments. This type of productive thinking induced by its corporate culture has led to company innovations such as the creation of an application that would allow telecom-based media companies to share technologies. Relatedly, speed and flexibility are core competences for Solusi Tunas's services. In meeting demands and gaining an advantage over competitors, quick decision-making within the company is important. This is made possible due to the company being relatively smaller compared to other firms. This allows Solusi Tunas to be more flexible due to the minimal bureaucratic slowdowns that it experiences when it comes to its projects.

Thai Metal Trade Public Company Limited

People development and service quality are crucial for Thai Metal. In terms of people development, a company executive indicated that the company needs people who are familiar with the steel industry in Thailand. He said that customer trust can only be gained if the company makes minimal mistakes, which can only happen in Thai Metal's operations if its workforce has the competency and experience to meet industry standards. Thus, Thai Metal prepares its employees through its in-house knowledge center, where the company trains its people to share best practices and enhance employee capabilities.

Service quality is also important for the company, as it allows Thai Metal to compete against larger companies with huge financial capitals. Thai Metal relies on its excellent service quality as its comparative advantage in order to attract customers and ask for prices a bit higher than those of other competitors. It's due to its service quality that Thai Metal has invested heavily in quality-control operations and has even allowed its customers to provide the company their specifications to ensure that the best steel products are delivered.

Leadership Style and Management Systems

Lafarge Republic, Inc.

The company heads tend to use a collaborative leadership style that draws on the skills and experiences of coworkers and subordinates. However, leadership in the company is not as hands-on to prevent employees from being too dependent. A company executive finds this type of leadership sufficient in guiding employees toward the company's corporate goals.

The company uses Lafarge's Plant Operating Model (POM) as a training guide for people working in Lafarge Republic's plants. POM aims to train people to make efficient and quality products, but the model also aims to instill the mindset that the company's employees are cobusiness holders.

The company's emphasis on people development – such as through its exchange programs and training seminars – ensures that its workforce is able to contribute to the competitiveness of Lafarge Republic.

Mudajaya Corporation

Mudajaya believes in the importance of developing people through management systems. Hence, it has organized several in-house trainings as well as external courses for its employees. The company's workforce consists of engineers, which has been a long tradition for Mudajaya to emphasize in having a strong, professional, and skilled workforce. This is also important for the company since its clients tend to look for competent contractors with relevant experience.

Moreover, the company works with labor agents especially with regard to sourcing workers overseas. Right now, most of Mudajaya's professionals are from Malaysia, while several of its general workers are foreigners. The company has plans in the near future to hire engineers from neighboring countries. However, legal impediments have made it difficult for the company to hire foreign engineers. Nonetheless, the company's highly professionalized workforce ensures that Mudajaya's projects are usually finished on time and in an efficient manner.

In terms of operational excellence, the company adheres to health, safety, and environment (HSE) principles. It has launched campaigns and in-house regulations that aim to assure that all employees are instilled with a culture of safety and comply with company standards in this regard. Furthermore, the company has achieved operational efficiency through the implementation of automation initiatives such as the use of Flexspeed, a high-speed LPG cylinder filling system, in the Melaka LPG terminal. It is the first installation of this kind in Malaysia and the tenth in the world. SDD also carries out an Infrastructure Planning Study each year to improve tankage utilization and strategic expansion of storage facilities and develop better road tanker utilization. Lastly, the Organizational Effectiveness pillar is achieved through ensuring that PDB's workforce is highly skilled and technically capable. Toward this end, the company invests in the development of its people.

Siam Cement Group (SCG)

Dutch executives helped SCG grow from the company's founding in 1913 until 1974. During the company's first 60 years, SCG learned how to establish and operate a cement brand within Thailand. The company also learned how to keep and maintain a professional management system from its Dutch executives. Significant experience and knowledge transfers paved the way for the strong corporate culture of SCG.

Along with promoting innovation, the company has also focused on increasing human capabilities and improving human resources. Several programs have been implemented by SCG in order to improve the capabilities of its workforce. Harmonizing business and personal development within the workforce provides a shared understanding of organizational goals, which leads to establishing such goals efficiently. SCG's core competencies are concentrating on people development, management and leadership style, and its capabilities of CSR. The company strongly emphasizes the welfare of its workforce. Currently, the company has initiated several programs that ensure the loyalty of its employees through several financial and social benefits. The company also focuses on increasing the capabilities of its workforce through several educational programs, such as workshops initiated by SCG's training centers.

Professional Management

SM Prime Holdings, Inc.

The company is primarily family run but also includes aspects of being professionally managed. The children of Mr. Henry Sy Sr. are involved in the business in differing capacities and areas. However, the family decided to hire professionals to run the business alongside the family as the company grew. Although SM is a family corporation, they reasoned it was better to keep it in the hands of the children because whether or not disagreements arise, there is still a sense of having to settle them at the end of the day. If members of the extended family are involved, this increases risk, as it could divide the family.

The company has what it calls as a "Family Board" that evaluates decisions and proposals before they go to the formal corporate board. Professionals have slots in these meetings and present their ideas to the family members, who then give their input. Once the proposal is brought to the formal board, the family members take a step back and allow the independent directors to give their input. Currently, SM Prime Holdings is publicly traded in the Philippine Stock Exchange, where it has been listed since 1994.

Singapore Aero Engine Services Private Limited

SAESL corporate leadership is based on a professionally managed system in which meritocracy is greatly emphasized. Overall, management is headed by the CEO of the company. Under the CEO, various positions include the Human Resource Department, Engineering Department, Operations Department, Finance & Admin Department, Planning, Control & IT Department, Customer Business Department, and Programmes & Business Development Department (SAESL, 2013b).

The firm's approach to people development allows the company to provide internships and on-site training programs for future aviation engineers. Through this, SAESL has ties with local universities and polytechnic institutions (SAESL, 2013a).

Adinin Group of Companies

In this company, managers are empowered by giving them autonomy over their operations. This type of management system allows the company's managers to handle a subsidiary in a style with which they are comfortable. The autonomy-based management system has been successful, and no major complaints have occurred.

The company ensures that its subsidiaries are able to deliver its projects and other services on time. Adinin and its subsidiaries have in their mindset to identify and accept offers they deem as doable. This is to ensure that the company does not take offers or contracts that it knows it won't be able to deliver on time or outside of customer expectations.

Moreover, its services are amplified by the company's highly technical workforce; employees have years of experience and training under their belt, ensuring the highest quality of service and standard. Through the company's Adinin Training and Development Centre, employees remain in top shape to compete in local markets.

Boon Rawd Brewery System

The company is privately managed, and leadership of the company is top-down, but executives are open to collaboration with managers within the company. People development is also an important aspect of the company. Boon Rawd invests in several in-house training programs and scholarships for its employees. The company has partnered with local universities in Thailand so that its employees could get scholarships in MBA courses. Boon Rawd is also very open to graduating college students looking to complete their internships with the company.

Yoma Strategic Holdings Limited

Meritocracy is the fundamental principle running the management of Yoma. This means that not even family members are given special treatment within the company. This is due to the belief that inexperienced people running executive positions would be detrimental to the growth of the company.

Through its meritocratic system, Yoma is able to hire talented individuals fit for the different positions of the company. The company was also able to create a system to attract talented individuals. Moreover, Yoma also conducts training and knowledge transfers in order to constantly prepare its workforce for challenges within the market. Yoma also recognizes the importance of maintaining a trained pool of human resources and a strong management team to lead them. Furthermore, the company also believes in aligning career growth opportunities to employees' career prospects. Opportunities are offered to promising employees based on their personal performance. The company also has a policy of internal promotion and transfer, which means that higher positions are ideally filled with people from inside the company, and people are only hired from outside when there is no suitable candidate within the organization.

Conclusions

It is fitting that the requisite for attaining excellence is substantiated in large part by supportive management. It has become widely acknowledged that great implementation and execution through people and systems are critical to the successful implementation of any strategy. In fact, there are those who believe that effective execution might overcome any deficiencies in a corporate strategy. This belief redounds to a classical precept that one cannot succeed even with a sound strategy without the people to support the strategy.

Harnessing human talent is particularly daunting in emerging and developing economies where it is well acknowledged that levels of education attainment fare poorly relative to those of the most advanced countries. This argument prompts further questions on the extent to which mainstream business theories apply to emerging markets. Reflecting modernization arguments, one position is that it is just a matter of time before erstwhile managers in emerging countries adopt mainstream theories. Others argue that management training should be particularistic and reflect the local conditions of changing development. Still others, notably management scholars Ming-Jer Chen and Danny Miller (2011), posit a relativist conception that combines the "best" features of Eastern and Western intellectual traditions as a better theoretical anchor for understanding Asia, and by extension, (Asian) emerging economies. To some extent, this combination of universalistic and particularistic orientation is a part of our ASEAN champions approach to building human capital. A synthesis of our findings is presented in Exhibit 10.1.

Collectively, human capital and advanced management systems constitute the glue that holds different parts of an organization together. This glue is the difference that determines whether synergy materializes or not. It might just be that a fitting tribute to ASEAN champions – one that differentiates them from other firms – is their ability to nurture and harness their employees. In particular, we point out six human-resource-related elements that make companies better. They exhibit exceptional visionary leadership that finds the right balance between long-term goals and short-term operations, and between top-down control and bottom-up and horizontal collaboration. These local champions have well-developed and systemic training programs supported by corporate governance that values human resource training. Continuous learning is embedded in their corporate cultures, which is further enforced through external recruiting of senior leaders. Their recruiting and people

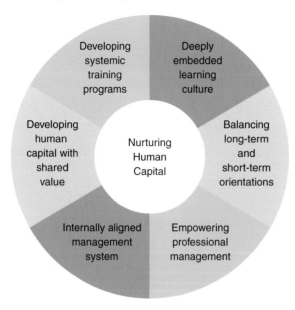

Exhibit 10.1 Nurturing Human Capital

development often turn to young and inexperienced people who can be easily nurtured into their own corporate values and norms. These companies put in place professional management systems that could enforce consistent stakeholder-oriented value systems. They generally remain family-owned companies, but they rely on professional management teams for strategic and operational decisions, while they exert their influence through shared board and leadership structures.

Part III

Strategic Imperatives and Policy Implications

Under what circumstances might the ASEAN champions get involved and participate in the AEC's integrative activities? Specifically, what are the facilitators and barriers to their participation? And what are implications for management and public policy?

In our concluding section, we present two chapters that address why and how ASEAN champions might become more involved in the AEC. We also present data from previous research as well as our own on the circumstances that will determine their propensity to become involved.

Chapter 11 details our assessment on these questions and issues. We argue for better clarity on the role of the private sector, inclusive of both local and international firms; the consideration of a wider geographical region to realize the full benefits of a single market and production base, and the potential of regional production platforms for integrating financial and human resources.

Chapter 12 is our epilogue that features various commentaries from business leaders, academicians, and policy makers on the future of the AEC.

11 Implications for Management and Policy

Introduction

Where is ASEAN headed? What is the future of the ASEAN Economic Community (AEC)? The jury is still out on what might happen to ASEAN, and based on current developments, it might take several years before any final verdict is reached. There are as many critics of ASEAN as there are supporters, with many other pundits simply acknowledging that this regional bloc faces a highly uncertain future.

Consider the two scenarios as outcomes of this question:

Scenario 1 – The Optimistic Narrative: Amid much fanfare the AEC was formally launched in December 2015. The formal declaration held in Malaysia was quietly mentioned in business news around the world. The implementation of the four pillars, duly recorded in the AEC Scorecard, was better than expected. Although progress was scored at 67.5 percent in 2010, it reached a high of 92 percent upon enactment. While the official AEC Scorecard was suspended, optimism was rekindled with new goals set for 2025. In the years leading to 2025, numerous firms from other countries had signed MOAs with various regional associations. Trade between ASEAN countries was expected to reach 60 percent, and the CLMV countries reported significant advances in infrastructural development, market openness, and institutional growth. A single production base, once a distant goal, came closer to reality as new regional agreements were reached on semiconductors, computers, peripherals, social media, and services to complement those already maintained in the automobile and electronic industries. China, Japan, South Korea, and India, once feared to have potential to overwhelm ASEAN, turned out to be significant partners in trade and investments. Already, a new blueprint for climate change and the reduction of poverty was being drawn.

Scenario 2 – The Pessimistic Narrative: Although the AEC was formally launched in December 2015, the reception throughout the world was much less enthusiastic than expected. In the years leading to 2025, however, there were ominous signals, such as sporadic demonstrators in various countries decrying adverse impacts on local industries and the corrupting entry of globetrotting multinationals. Despite heady efforts by the countries involved, progress in implementation barely reached 70 percent, due principally to the difficulties in dismantling nontariff barriers, prompting some ASEAN member countries to question whether intra-ASEAN trade could really be achieved. Moreover, the lack of a legal structure for compliance – long discarded in favor of the nebulous "Asian way" – impeded progress and triggered a gaping fissure between the more developed and less developed members of ASEAN. With growing doubts about the future of ASEAN, there were overtures for bilateral trade agreements with individual countries in the region and the looming specter of the Trans Pacific Partnership (TPP) further undermining the shared goals of a single ASEAN market and production base. Moreover, the dispute between China, Vietnam, and the Philippines over the Spratley Islands escalated to feverish heights, prompting a deep distrust of China's intentions. In an ominous signal to the world, global investors and multinationals began to pour resources into China and India, further undermining the ASEAN initiatives.

Which of the two scenarios is most likely will be a subject of deliberation and speculation, depending in large part on political, economic, cultural, and institutional developments. In this chapter, we present a perspective from the standpoint of ASEAN's most successful firms (ASEAN champions) and the role of foreign multinationals. The chapter is organized in three sections: (1) a reassessment of AEC's four pillars, (2) a discussion of facilitators and barriers taken largely from other sources, and (3) an extended perspective that builds on quotations from firms interviewed for this study. In conclusion, implications for the private sector, specifically the ASEAN champions, and for future research are presented for further consideration.

Reassessing AEC's Goals for Regional Integration

Single Market and Production Base

As indicated in Chapter 3, the objective of a single market and production base underpins a commitment to eliminating tariffs among participants, as well as to enhancing the mobility of investment and capital within ASEAN. In short, this commitment comports with the precepts of a free-market system. Correspondingly, five core elements comprise the goal of a single market and production base: (1) free flow of goods,

(2) free flow of services, (3) free flow of investment, (4) freer flow of capital, and (5) free flow of skilled labor.

The popular narrative has been to focus on reducing trade barriers between ASEAN countries. This is understandable given the objective of creating a single market. In this regard, the AEC Scorecard has been encouraging in reporting this reduction, as literally 100 percent of merchandise goods will be traded freely, with services not far behind. Among supporters, this is the area in which the AEC has demonstrated significant and compelling progress.

Nevertheless, this is also the area that has received much scrutiny and skepticism. While a single market exudes confidence, approximating an idyllic scenario, the impressive strides recorded in the AEC Scorecard have been met with concerns about the lack of political will and the concomitant absence of a strict implementation regimen to ensure control and compliance (Inama & Sim, 2015). Consistent with arguments from analysts (Inama & Sim, 2015), which we will discuss later in the chapter, there is more potential and tractability regarding the goal of achieving a single production base (along with the free movement of labor, goods, and capital). Arguably, this is within the control of the private sector, both within ASEAN (such as the ASEAN champions) and among established foreign multinationals. Finally, as some commentators have noted, the added difficulty of tracking progress in terms of the AEC Scorecard is that metrics are generally self-reports that require more validation, and the data are organized by AEC objectives rather than by national compliance (Rillo, 2011, 2013). Our analysis accentuates the need for an even more fine-grained measure, such as company reports on the factors that can facilitate or impede their participation. This issue is addressed later in this chapter.

Three areas demarcate the boundaries of this ongoing debate: (1) intra- and inter-ASEAN trade, (2) the type and pattern of exports that facilitate trade liberalization, and (3) the reliance on the "Asian way" to resolve conflicts and, in this case, to expedite trade transactions. We review each of these areas in turn.

Intra- and Inter-Regional Trade. This topic has previously been explored in Chapter 3, but we revisit the issues attendant to the topic as they relate to trade liberalization. To the extent that historical decisions foreshadow the intent and motivation of countries to trade, they represent a good gauge of what happens in the future, barring extraordinary events that change the trajectory of trade transactions. Taken in this context, ASEAN future trade signals a cautionary note: 26 percent of ASEAN exports are traded within the region, while 74 percent are traded outside the region. Similarly, intra-ASEAN imports represent

Country	Intra-ASEAN exports		Extra-ASEAN exports		Total exports in million US$	Intra-ASEAN imports		Extra-ASEAN imports		Total imports (in million US$)
	Value (in million US$)	Share to total exports (%)	Value (in million US$)	Share to total exports (%)		Value (in million US$)	Share to total imports (%)	Value (in million US$)	Share to total imports (%)	
Brunei	2,644.3	23.1	8,801.1	76.9	11,445.4	1,843.6	51.0	1,768.2	49.0	3,611.8
Cambodia	1,300.9	14.2	7,847.3	85.8	9,148.2	2,818.2	30.7	6,357.7	69.3	9,176.0
Indonesia	40,630.8	22.3	141,921.0	77.7	182,551.8	54,031.0	29.0	132,597.7	71.0	186,628.7
Laos	1,234.3	47.6	1,358.5	52.4	2,592.8	2,495.0	75.8	797.1	24.2	3,292.0
Malaysia	63,981.6	28.0	164,349.7	72.0	228,331.3	55,050.6	26.7	150,846.8	73.3	205,897.4
Myanmar	5,624.9	49.2	5,811.4	50.8	11,436.3	4,244.0	35.3	7,765.1	64.7	12,009.1
Philippines	8,614.9	16.0	45,363.4	84.0	53,978.3	14,171.4	21.8	50,959.3	78.2	65,130.6
Singapore	128,787.0	31.4	281,462.7	68.6	410,249.7	77,885.3	20.9	295,130.5	79.1	373,015.8
Thailand	59,320.5	25.9	169,409.7	74.1	228,730.2	44,348.1	17.8	205,169.0	82.2	249,517.1
Viet Nam	18,178.9	13.7	114,485.2	86.3	132,664.1	21,353.0	16.2	110,756.9	83.8	132,109.9
ASEAN	**330,318.1**	**26.0**	**940,810.1**	**74.0**	**1,271,128.1**	**278,240.2**	**22.4**	**962,148.2**	**77.6**	**1,240,388.4**

Source: ASEAN Statistics (ASEAN Secretariat, 2014)

Exhibit 11.1 ASEAN Intra- and Inter-Regional Trade (2013)

22 percent of its total trade, while 78 percent are inter-ASEAN exports (Exhibit 11.1). Even more ominous is that close to a significantly high proportion of intra-ASEAN exports are between two countries – Singapore and Malaysia.[1] To determine whether this pattern of trade lies burrowed in structural causes or is a matter of discretion, the nature of the types of exports and imports is examined in the next section.

Types of Intra- and Inter-Regional Exports and Imports. In Exhibit 11.2, we present the top three exports for each ASEAN country for 2013. To a large extent, it can be discerned that most of these countries produce similar or related commodities, stemming largely from their history as former colonies that were historically employed to produce raw materials for manufacturing by the advanced/developed countries. Note the prevalence of petroleum, gas, minerals, integrated circuits, and rubber/footwear. In this regard, without significant change, the outlook of trade will be more competitive rather than complementary. The pattern of trade belies the reality that the nations of ASEAN will continue to export to countries outside of the region and will have minimal incentives to engage in direct trade with each other. One significant change will be policies adopted by the larger ASEAN community to promote trade liberalization among

---

[1] With regard to Singapore–Malaysia trade, a lot of companies based or operating in Singapore (whether local or multinational) use Malaysia (especially as part of the Singapore–Johor Bahru–Batam triangle) as production/assembly sites, as part of their intra-regional value chains. Thus they would have imports/exports belonging to the same category but that are really the same products at different stages of production.

Country	Top Three Exports		
Brunei	Crude Petroleum	Petroleum Gas	Acyclic Alcohols
Cambodia	Postage Stamps	Knit Sweaters	Knit Women's Suits
Indonesia	Coal Briquettes	Petroleum Gas	Palm Oil
Laos	Refined Copper	Copper Ore	Rough Wood
Malaysia	Refined Petroleum	Petroleum Gas	Palm Oil
Myanmar	Petroleum Gas	Rough Wood	Dried Legumes
Philippines	Integrated Circuits	Computers	Semiconductor Devices
Singapore	Refined Petroleum	Integrated Circuits	Computers
Thailand	Computers	Rubber	Delivery Trucks
Viet Nam	Broadcasting Equipment	Crude Petroleum	Leather Footwear

Data Source: The Observatory of Economic Complexity

Exhibit 11.2 Three Main Export Commodities in ASEAN Countries (2012)

themselves. This will depend largely on noncoercive policies, notably the ASEAN Way, which is discussed in the next section.

The ASEAN Way. A topic that has captivated many analysts and pundits is whether ASEAN has a forceful way of enforcing desired goals, such as the formation of a single market. Comparisons with the EU have been drawn, and perhaps unfairly, the verdict is that ASEAN lacks the necessary institutions and legal framework for enforcement (Beeson, 2009; Inama & Sim, 2015). What emerges from these narratives is an informal method of cooperation that is referred to as the "ASEAN Way." To this end, we review accounts on the extent to which the ASEAN Way can be transformed from an informal modality to a formal/legal code for accomplishing AEC's goal of a single market.

Couched in its original formulation, the ASEAN Way is an informal agreement for extensive consultations without resorting to undue pressure or military means to resolve intramural conflicts (see Beeson, 2009; Acharya, 2012). It also reaffirms a belief that countries can progress on their pace of economic development without undue pressure from others (i.e., the principle of noninterference). It stands in contrast to the contractual and enforceable legal language that underlies most formal contracts in advanced Western societies (Acharya, 2012). In his rather extensive study, Jurgen Haacke synthesizes three distinctive elements of the ASEAN way: a method of resolving conflict through consultation, an inclusive decision-making process among designated participants, and a "process of identity-building" (Haacke, 2003, quoted by Beeson, 2009: 21).

The degree to which the ASEAN way has succeeded resembles the proverbial interpretation of a halfway-filled glass as being half empty or half full. For critics, the ASEAN way has been more a deterrent to regional integration that has prevented member countries from fully accomplishing goals because of the lack of enforceability (see Inama & Lim, 2015). Understandably, this argument is credible from the standpoint of having reached the goal of a security community that is the hallmark of genuine regional integration. Moreover, critics – again perhaps unfairly – envision the EU as the gold standard to be emulated, though there are some questions whether the EU has indeed reached this standard of perfection (Beeson, 2009).

Even so, Jones (2005) argues that claims about noninterference are grossly overstated, and that, in fact, the meaning and context of noninterference reflects changing social forces as interpreted by the region's dominant players. But, even as applied in the area of human rights where some degree of consensus is anticipated, the ASEAN Human Rights Declaration famously enacted in 2012 is subject to differing interpretations, depending on the progressiveness of member states (Davis, 2014). In total context, therefore, the extent to which the ASEAN way can advance the cause of regional integration is far too restrictive, questionable, and contestable given historical trends arising from the geopolitical dynamics, patterns of intra- and inter-ASEAN trade, and uneven economic development among ASEAN countries.

Among sympathizers of the ASEAN way, the comparisons to the EU raise concerns surrounding whether the application of modernization, which we discussed in Chapter 1, again raises its ugly head in touting sheer emulation of the experiences of the advanced economies instead of creative adaptation based on the historical and institutional characteristics of Southeast Asia. In fact, these supporters of the Asian Way have argued that the very absence of direct military conflict and interregional skirmishes between the countries since the inception of ASEAN is sufficient progress. Moreover, they argue that the Asian Way that is an informal and consensual approach to decision is more effective than formal rules, particularly in that such an approach is more aligned and embedded in the cultures and traditions of countries of the region. Although these supporters do not go as far in arguing that the ASEAN Way will significantly advance trade liberalization, it can be inferred that this approach to more informal consensus building will evolve through the years and could become an integral glue in the transformation of ASEAN.

Our focus on the private sector, and on the ASEAN champions in particular, suggests that *firms will only engage in trade liberalization to the extent that they have a competitive advantage or that they conceive of favorable opportunities in the future*. Hence, firms that are already involved in extensive intra-ASEAN trade will continue to do so, and any reductions in tariffs and nontariff barriers will enable their resolve to trade, provided that they continue to reap competitive advantages. Contrariwise, firms that do not see any advantages in intra-ASEAN trade will refrain from trade, regardless of government-mediated barrier reductions. Some of these sentiments are discussed in the later part of this chapter. However, an issue that might serve most firms within the AEC is the proposal of a single production base and a competitive economic region, which is covered in the next section.

Single Production Base. A single production base, while hardly original, is a provocative and soothing image of the AEC: a collectivity of supplier–manufacturer networks (components, procurement, testing, prototype manufacturing, services, human resource management, and training) from different ASEAN countries tied closely together through a central production platform and bounded by long-term shared objectives, with manufactured products and services that are priced competitively in the world market. Dieter Ernst, an expert in global networks, describes this shift from partial to systemic globalization: "In order to cope with the increasingly demanding requirements of globalization, companies are forced to integrate erstwhile stand-alone operations in individual host countries into increasingly complex international production networks. Companies break down the value chain into discrete functions, and locate them wherever they can be carried out most effectively and where they are needed to facilitate the penetration of important growth markets" (Ernst, 1997: 3).

This recent development in globalization accentuates not only the transition of worldwide production from single countries in advanced economies to multiple locations in emerging markets, but also a shift in mindset from its initial orientation toward centralized control to systemic coordination between nodes of expert knowledge (Ando & Kimura, 2003). This is prompted by a concern to develop capabilities at a quicker pace and presumably lower cost (Ernst, 1997: 3; Ando & Kimura, 2003), if not an intent to move closer to sources of supply at present to lucrative consumer markets in the future. Moreover, it is argued that technology in emerging markets, particularly Asia, has now become sophisticated to the point that "global innovation networks" will materialize soon with knowledge hubs centered in Asia (Ernst, 2006; 2009).

However attractive this idea might be, its implementation within ASEAN has historically been a challenging one. The Philippines, once designated as a production base, failed in its sole attempt to establish this platform, while efforts in other ASEAN countries have either fizzled or remained dormant (Lim, 2004). To be fair, the circumstances underlying these initiatives are different and less favorable in comparison to the resurgent goal and support for a single production base as a part of the AEC's four pillars.

The potential for a single production base might be gleaned from the success of the Japanese in developing systemic networks for electronics and automobiles across East Asia, with strong connections to several ASEAN countries. In an extensive study of international production featuring firms and networks from the United States, Europe, and Japan, Ernst (1997) identifies the following types of inter-firm production networks that can be broadly used as a guide for positioning interested firms within ASEAN:

> *supplier networks*: provide major manufacturing inputs;
> *producer networks*: integrate all production inputs into a common pool;
> *consumer networks*: act as intermediaries to buyers and retailers;
> *standard coalitions*: tasked with "locking in" firms with common product standards;
> *technology cooperation networks*: facilitate exchange, development, and strategic partnerships.

From these different types of production networks, one implication for ASEAN is the purposeful plan of creating "systemic" rather than "partial" forms of globalization (Ernst, 1997). For these to succeed, the participation of small-to-medium firms is critical, as is keenly illustrated in Japan's success. This relates to the third pillar of the AEC, which is discussed in the next section.

Competitive Economic Region

The main goal of a competitive economic region is "to foster a culture of fair competition." The productive growth of an economy depends on a balance between large corporations and small-to-medium enterprises. In this regard, ancillary goals include the "introduction of a common competition policy within ASEAN, the establishment of a network of authorities and agencies charged with implementation, the focus on capacity building programmes, and regional guidelines for competition policy" (see ASEAN 2008. *ASEAN Economic Community Blueprint.* Jakarta: ASEAN Secretariat).

Consistent with the goal of a single production base, small-to-medium firms have to participate as suppliers, procurers, component manufacturers, or volume producers in support of an overarching manufacturing/

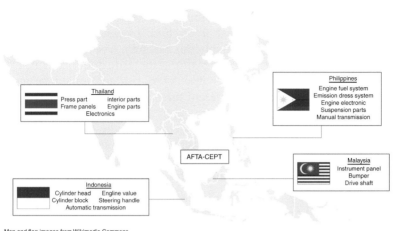

Map and flag images from Wikimedia Commons
Adapted from Hiratsuka (2006). "Characteristics and determinants of East Asia's trade patterns", in Hiratsuka, D. & Uchida, Y. (eds.). Input trade and product networks in East Asia.

Exhibit 11.3 Example of an ASEAN Production Network for Automotive Components

service platform. To ensure this success, there has to be a free flow of goods, materials, and to some extent labor across different ASEAN countries. The current barriers to such fuller integration have been discussed in Chapter 2 and elaborated further in this chapter. A sample representation of how different parts and components might be sourced from different ASEAN countries for automobile production to enhance the competitiveness of the region is provided in Exhibit 11.3.

Integration into the Global Economy

The ASEAN Charter states: *"ASEAN operates in an increasingly global environment, with interdependent markets and globalized industries. In order to enable ASEAN businesses to compete internationally, to make ASEAN a more dynamic and stronger segment of the global supply chain and to ensure that the internal market remains attractive to foreign investment, it is crucial for ASEAN to look beyond the borders of AEC. External rules and regulations must increasingly be taken into account when developing policies related to AEC."*

The charter attests to the reality that the world is becoming increasingly global. Isolation or autarky may become a dinosaur in historical trade archives. But what does integration into a global economy mean for the AEC? Two items are noteworthy: First, as stated in the charter, the AEC could be an attractive destination for foreign investment. Our earlier discussion of international production, a single production base, and a competitive region fall well into this category. A second item would be the AEC functioning as a strong platform for trade under the auspices of a single market. Per our earlier discussion, this goal might be more rhetorical than realizable at the present time.

We have alluded to several barriers – both structural and procedural – to a single market. The type of exports comprises the first barrier, and the lack of an enforceable protocol represents the second barrier. We intimated that firms will engage in intra-ASEAN trade to the extent that they retain or develop a competitive advantage. Further, we follow the lead of others in suggesting that a single production base holds more potential for short-term implementation than a flushed-out single market. Taken in the context of the AEC alone, these concerns are both palpable and compelling.

However, when the boundaries outside of ASEAN are extended, then there are more promising opportunities. One brewing platform is the ASEAN Plus Three (APT), with China, Japan, and South Korea comprising the other three in question (Beeson, 2007). Membership in this context is paramount in that the inclusion now comprises the most competitive region in Asia, with all three regarded as economic powerhouses. It can be arguably maintained, however, that the success of APT will also depend on ongoing relationships between Japan, China, and South Korea that have not been as complementary or as cooperative in recent years owing to historical disputes over Japan's role in World War II as one specific example (Beeson, 2007, 2010). Nevertheless, the expanded objective of APT that goes beyond inter-ASEAN trade to monetary policy is regarded to be not only desirable but an imperative for genuine regional integration to occur (Thomas, 2002, quoted by Besson, 2007: 234). In this context, APT holds considerably more potential for extending trade significantly across a broader region (East Asia) than simply depending on, if not hoping, that lowered trade barriers will intensify intra-ASEAN trade. For an illustration of how a broader regional area could accommodate international partnerships and cooperation, see Exhibit 11.4.

Perceived Barriers and Facilitators to ASEAN Integration

In the next section, we address private sector perceptions regarding the AEC. In an informative study consisting of field interviews, Sanchita Basu Das (2012) compiles a list based on a brainstorming session that

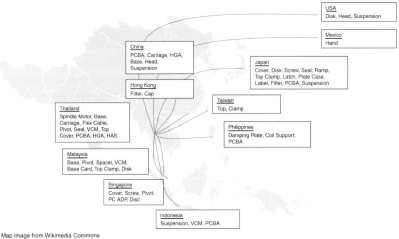

Map image from Wikimedia Commons
Adapted from Hiratsuka (2005). Vertical intra-regional production networks in East Asia: A case study of hard disk drive industry.

Exhibit 11.4 Different Sources of Raw Materials for a Hard Disk Drive Assembly in Thailand

was held at the ASEAN Studies Center at the Institute for Southeast Asian Studies in Singapore.

According to Das (2012), optimism for integration is also accompanied by "caution and disappointment" owing to the slow pace of implementation. Das (2012) provides several reasons why caution is needed. The AEC Scorecard is confined to official measures by way of self-reports. The scorecard lacks a comprehensive analysis of the full costs and benefits of integration. There is a lack of awareness and understanding of ASEAN agreements, particularly among the small-to-medium firms. The utilization rate of tariff preferences – or the current measure of ASEAN participation – is quite low. Those in the private sector attribute this to similar products that are imported from one another. The elimination of nontariff barriers remains an important goal and lingering concern. Some actors see government domestic policies that are oriented toward protecting local businesses as a problem.

Size matters. Larger firms are generally more informed about ASEAN developments and are also more favorably disposed to integration. ASEAN is considered an opportunity by firms (local and multinational) to diversify their portfolios and investments. There are language limitations, often reflected in the lack of proper translation of ASEAN documents, in the less developed countries of ASEAN (Das, 2012).

In addition, Das and her associates argue that under the "ASEAN Way," agreements have preceded important operational details, and this has limited the full participation of the private sector. In all, there is a lack of awareness of ASEAN economic integration, and structural barriers – domestic policies and institutions – remain formidable roadblocks to changing the mindsets of those firms interviewed. We now turn to our own research on the ASEAN champions to assess their thoughts regarding ASEAN integration and initiatives.

Implications

In this book, we advocate the role of the private sector in ASEAN regional integration. By way of summary, our ASEAN champions are characterized as weathering dire institutional obstacles and capitalizing on opportunities that were either bequeathed to them by legacy and fortuitous circumstances, or forged through their own abilities to pioneer marketing strategies, build synergistic collaborations, leverage market power, deepen localization, develop appropriate management structures and processes, and internalize human assets and capabilities. Collectively, we have termed these their ability to "harness institutional grassroots," which emphasizes the frontier-like settings that they were surrounded with and their enduring desire to nurture competitive advantages ahead of foreign competition.

In this section, we synthesize some generic implications for firms – ASEAN champions or foreign multinationals – becoming stronger players within ASEAN. In the case of our ASEAN champions, we paraphrase one observer who sees a trajectory in terms of "moving from national to regional champions."

1.   Expand on Opportunities for Broader Trade and Investment.

The underlying logic for a single market is the benefit derived from the free flow of goods and services (unimpeded trade) within the region. This logic comports with an enduring belief by mainstream orthodox economists that trade confers benefits to participating parties and that additional rents can accrue from the expansion of trade markets. As such, firms that are already engaged in intraregional trade can reap additional advantages, but those firms that have planned expansion in trade and investment are likely to benefit as well. Any ease in restrictions will also motivate foreign multinationals to intensify their activities in the region. Although there are shortcomings to trade liberalization, which we cover in this section, the elimination of formal and informal trade barriers should yield positive outcomes, particularly for the ASEAN champions that have already invested in this area. Some observations were put forth by ASEAN champions interviewed for this study.

In regard to air travel, the AEC will afford more opportunities for expansion. Specifically, Cebu Air sees opportunities to open up new routes in Southeast Asia, involving more cities and at a higher frequency. Furthermore, AEC will also spur tourism in the region. Nevertheless, according to an industry spokesperson, it is also believed that competition will intensify but companies could compete to the extent that they have resources and slack.

Similar opportunities abound for other industries. For example, CPF Trading, a subsidiary of CPF, sees Vietnam and Malaysia as excellent outlets. In addition, the company has increased investments in Laos (a new feed mill plant), Cambodia (a new silo for maize), and the Philippines (agro-industrial businesses). Investing in these local markets is seen to be more effective than sheer exports. In the case of Jollibee, the AEC could result in easier importation of goods that will lower the company's raw material sourcing and provide more affordable meals to its consumers. In addition, regional expansion will benefit the company in improving training and labor mobilization in overseas operations. In the case of Thai Union Frozen Products (TUF), it expects the United States to remain the company's largest overseas market for its seafood products, but it also expects heightened demand from ASEAN countries once the AEC is formally launched. TUF has a positive outlook on the ASEAN integration and expects the AEC to support the growth of the Thai seafood industry as it pushes for trading expansion and product pricing.

In the case of power generation, prospects for the AEC look promising. Philippines' Meralco sees a possible advantage from ASEAN integration in terms of a freer flow of goods and services that are part of the company's cost of operation (Remo, 2013). In the hospitality industry, prospects for growth are bullish. The Philippine BPO sector may even begin catering to other ASEAN companies who have yet to enter the Philippines. According to a company official, there is optimism in the hospitality sector in terms of labor. Furthermore, he believes that the Philippines has a lot of potential in medical tourism as well.

More intraregional trade will open new vistas for penetrating local markets and fashioning cooperative strategies. For the Dao-Heuang Group, the removal of import duties will only improve relations with neighboring countries, as well as encourage joint ventures and facilitate the ease of knowledge transfers. For EEI, in addition to a single market, additional advantages will accrue from the influx of workers from the region, especially from Burma and Cambodia, which could offer competitive wages, provided that there is significant reduction in investment barriers and labor restrictions. For Far Eastern University, there are opportunities for joint training programs and partnerships. Similarly, QAF Brunei seeks better ways of hiring skilled and technical resources from others in the region. For the Holcim Group, more trade will facilitate the transfer of key resources. Summing up, a spokesperson for this cement company opined that integration will likewise promote a more integrative and less insular mind-set. SM sees that it can gain more tenants from ASEAN countries.

Investment opportunities abound. In the case of Thai Brewery, a company official noted that it plans to target growth economies through different levels of investments, presumably with liberalized investments in the region. The company plans to use Myanmar and Vietnam as a starting point for Thai Beverage to increase its market share and become the leading beverage firm in Southeast Asia. These countries would be the focus for the company since they are emerging markets. Even so, adjusting to different cultures is imperative, and the task is not taken lightly.

2.   *Strengthen Competitiveness by Enhancing Core and Distinctive Competencies.*

In sports, a widely held belief is that the best offense is an excellent defense. This is applied to a variety of sports, including basketball, tennis or football, but the idea is the same: that excellent defenses lead to botches, errors, and penalties that can be converted to productive offensive plays. Taken in our context, firms that are in the best position to engage in trade and investment across their borders are also strong and competitive in their own right in their respective national markets.

Competitive strength can be assessed by the ability of a firm to acquire, develop, enhance, and leverage competencies – a school of thought in strategic management called the resource-based theory of the firm (Barney & Clarke, 2007). Such competencies, in turn, can be provisionally classified as *core*, which is central to achieving a firm's corporate strategy, and *distinctive*, which is an area in which a firm excels relative to competitors. While it is ideal to have both types, most firms are only able to maintain core competencies because distinctive competencies can be eroded by falling entry barriers or by sheer imitation. As applied to our ASEAN champions, we observe the following:

For the Aboitiz Power Corporation, the cost and reliability of power supply (its core competencies) will play a key role and affect the competitiveness of Philippine products. In the past, the energy industry has become more competitive by capitalizing on efficiencies from the volume of available power supply.

Ayala Land, on the other hand, sees strengths from enhancing its abundant human resource pool. Similarly, TOA (Thailand) Paint intends to use the competencies of its brand – continuous improvement of products and services, maintenance of strength of cooperation with business alliances, and most importantly, and development of potential of human resources – as leverage in AEC expansion.

Innovation is necessary to sustain competitive advantages. Vietnam's Vinamilk recognizes the need to raise its standards and further uplift the quality of its products. It hopes to do so by upgrading both production and management systems. Furthermore, the company is keen on adopting new agricultural and manufacturing practices in farming to improve the quality of the raw milk it uses in producing its products. Masan Consumer plans to address AEC integration by investing in research and development and maintaining its strengths in sales and marketing.

Tapping new resource pools is essential to maintaining an advantage. Building on its expertise in construction, Mudajaya sees opportunities for integration when it comes to new market access and skilled labor. Mudajaya foresees the on-streaming of major power plant projects in the near future, and it also intends to capitalize on these initiatives given its strong track record and technical capabilities in power plant construction. With the largest ICT workforce of 6,500 experts and roughly 17,500 people overall, FPT considers its corporate culture to be the "power" that binds the company and leads it to sustainable development. As FPT prepares to become a global leader, it recognizes the need to first establish its leadership in the regional market.

ASEAN integration would encourage more investments, allowing greater demand as a country continues to grow. Phnom Penh Water Supply Authority (PPWSA) expects that with more investments there will be an increase of demand for water in Cambodia, hence the need for the company to also increase production and supply. According to a company official, 15 percent of PPWSA's revenue is sourced from commercial industries. Revenues from commercial industries can be increased beyond 15 percent when private companies in Cambodia start benefiting from ASEAN integration.

The ASEAN Economic Integration in 2015 is seen as a "game changer" by a leading executive of SM Prime. She opines that the company needs to think globally in its current and future endeavors. The move to consolidate SM Prime's property interests was made in response to regional integration. Due to the consolidation, an industry expert notes that SM

Prime is one of the largest property players in the region and has an economy of scale upon entering integration.

3.   *Adopt a Purposeful Plan to Develop Human Talent and Resources.*

The formalization of the AEC will indubitably reorder strategic priorities, initiatives, strategies, and resources. Firms will need to assess current assumptions and re-examine the far-reaching consequences of extant and projected strategies. Among the pivotal areas of consideration borne out of our interviews is the positioning of human resources. Without question, respondents think that this is a specific area that will be most affected by regional integration, whether in terms of accrued benefits or anticipated risks.

If corporate strategies are the cognate of purposeful action, it is the human aspect that can either lubricate or impede their effective implementation. Currently, some firms are better positioned than others simply because of the abundance or dearth of skilled and unskilled labor in their local markets. Of interest to many in terms of regional integration is the planned free flow of skilled labor. In this regard, several areas are illuminated by respondents in this study.

One immediate benefit is the free movement of skilled labor. Specifically, an industry spokesperson from PTT Exploration and Production PCL (PTTEP) notes that the company is open to worldwide human resource procurement, especially in terms of engineers and geologists. In fact, this spokesperson argues that, given that Thailand only produces twenty petroleum engineers per year and that the company has quite aggressive growth targets, there is a need to employ non-Thai professionals in order to continue to meet growth targets.

Similarly, integration would provide several opportunities for Adinin. One of these opportunities is the ability to tap resources – especially oil and gas – outside of Brunei. Human resources through free flow of labor are also seen as beneficial for the company when integration begins. For Musa Adnin, ASEAN integration would allow Adinin to easily access highly skilled labor such as engineers and other technical specialists that it needs to promote the growth of the company, provided that harmonization of standards takes place.

Even so, challenges remain, such as the need to develop people who understand the business, its targets, and its strategies. It is also a challenge for people of different cultures and languages to work cohesively as a team. Thus, people preparation and development needs to cope with these future realities of an integrated ASEAN. In the case of EDL, human resources may become a concern. The company is worried that it may not be able to reach the 2015 deadline for ensuring that its workforce is competitive, specifically in the ability to speak English. The company is considering taking advantage of integration by hiring specialists to train its workforce, which would be easily done within an area that allows free movement of labor. The company plans to use such specialists as tools for knowledge transfer, in hopes of making the EDL Generation's workforce competitive in the long run.

Pruksa Real Estate sees this labor movement as problematic because the Thai construction industry has experienced labor shortages since 2010. According to a company official, the shortages are said to be fueled by an increasing demand for infrastructure and residential projects. Free movement of labor may encourage Pruksa's foreign workers to move back to their home countries, as most of them are from Thailand's neighboring countries such as Laos and Cambodia. This would result from ASEAN integration providing greater job opportunities to Thailand's neighboring countries, where Pruksa's foreign workers would choose to work in their home countries instead of in a foreign state such as Thailand.

Although SCG has already established plants in several ASEAN countries, the company feels that there is a further need to study the different market cultures in each ASEAN country. Besides localization challenges, it was noted by a company official that SCG sees people development as a continuing challenge in ASEAN. Specifically, the company's investments in constantly training new employees from different ASEAN countries is seen as a logistical and investment challenge that SCG has to face once ASEAN integration starts in 2015. Regardless, the company views these challenges as short-term road blocks vis-à-vis the long-term benefits of ASEAN integration.

Human capital is key to preparing for competition. A company official noted that Yoma's human capital serves as its comparative advantage when ASEAN begins integrating in 2015. This is due to Yoma's depth of management, which is difficult to imitate. Within Myanmar, greater competition promoted by ASEAN integration would be more advantageous for less developed economies. This is because countries such as Myanmar will become targets for companies from developed countries that would try to invest and exploit untapped opportunities. For Yoma, an increase in investments would lead to productive growth, such as the establishment of factories that would provide Myanmar's people with increased job opportunities.

Summarecon stands to gain from the free movement of labor once the AEC is created. During the interviews, it was noted that the company currently suffers from a lack of skilled human resources. For instance, the company sees a huge gap in the number of skilled contractors. Thus, it has even taken it upon itself to train its contractors to properly build houses to the company's standards. It is also embarking on setting up a low-level institute to train contractors because of this. Thus, if the free flow of labor and business comes to fruition, in the short to medium term, this could help fill the gap in the level of skilled workers needed by the company.

4.   *Formulate a Defensive Posture against Better Financed Competitors.*

Despite the enthusiasm surrounding the AEC, respondents realize that regional integration is a mixed blessing and that the impact would be felt differently across nations and industry sectors. While trade liberalization opens up vistas for more intensive intraregional trade, it also brings about the entry of better financed multinationals into the region. After all, a single market and production base act as incentives for foreign investment.

Unless regional firms are competitive, they can fall prey to such multinationals. An industry expert noted: "We have to adjust ourselves, and we have to. I mean, can we foresee what other competitors do? If they do better than us, we have to do better than them. I mean it goes hand in hand like this is a competition. It's a free [competitive] market." Furthermore, the economic differences between the advanced and less developed countries in ASEAN become more prominent when considering the entry of foreign multinationals. Some concerns are echoed in the responses detailed below. Suffice to say, it is prudent for firms to develop defensive strategies and contingency plans under varying economics and assumptions about competition. The tenor of the responses is presented as follows.

There is a fair amount of skepticism about regional integration. From interviews, it was suggested that one reason is the difficulty of harmonizing laws and regulations among ASEAN member states. This is important in that integration without harmonization would be difficult, especially in areas where there are conflicting laws and regulations. Another reason is the difficulty of removing nontariff barriers. Moreover, it will take time before the full benefits emanating from the free flow of labor and capital can be realized. In this regard, some respondents suggest looking at the model of the EU for ways to accelerate the integration process.

Other experts believe that medium- and smaller-sized business will be more affected by the AEC than big businesses. Retaining employees given the freer movement of labor when ASEAN integrates is likewise another challenge.

Competitive strength matters. Although some companies within ASEAN have stronger branding strategies than others, success is not guaranteed. As one spokesperson opined, "... Despite the fact that we have a very strong brand, despite the fact that we're very strong and despite the fact that our management is very strong in technology and that the product is very strong, we actually do not, as I said before, [have] the capability or the capacity to go out and conquer the rest of ASEAN." In terms of foreign competition, battles are expected to rage in matters of price and production capacity, but other experts also think that government assistance could make the difference in spelling out a firm's advantage over others. In the cement industry, for example, cost competition is both a detriment and an advantage when foreign cement companies start competing in the Philippine market.

Creating a new mind-set is important. ASEAN integration would encourage the flooding of cheap goods into local markets. One analyst noted, "among the losers is agriculture. If sugar and rice from Indonesia is cheaper and sold in the Philippines, local farmers would suffer. This is something that should be addressed seriously because these are the sources of social unrest." An observer indicated that even in a growing market like Indonesia, companies can no longer afford to remain completely inward and must look for opportunities abroad by strengthening existing structures and investing in areas that the company has yet to enter.

ASEAN could be stabilizing or destabilizing, depending on actions that firms take. With freer trade, unintended consequences may include leakages to destabilization. For instance, if a country within ASEAN were to be adversely affected economically by integration, it may pass between countries, resulting in an increase in inflation. One respondent suggested, "At first, [ASEAN integration] is more of a caution for us to be honest. What else I think is the wrong step forward and because it's just the nature we do, [it] is not an immediate obvious opportunity where we're going..." This point particularly resonated in the airline industry.

Localization may prove to be an advantage against foreign competition. PT Sumber Alfaria sees ASEAN integration as minimally affecting its business. According to a company spokesperson, this is due to the fact that the retail industry in Indonesia is very local as opposed to other lines of business. The local understanding of the market is of high importance within the retail industry, which the company can use as an advantage. One other company stated that it will continue to focus on the development of product quality, which it believes will be brought about by a stronger human resource pool and more investments in technology.

5.   *Create Opportunities for Extensive Networking.*

Networking and connectivity provide the hallmark of purposeful interaction and collaboration. When fully realized, a collaborative union validates the statutes and intents of any given regional integration. Even so, this is not as easily realized and oftentimes remains a "work in progress." Much like any union, such as a joint venture or strategic partnership, a high-performing network evolves through a process of familiarity, shared goals, planned cooperation, and mutual trust. The potential for failure, specifically the nonrealization of the goals of the partnership, could also be high, reflecting the difficulty of sustaining prolonged cooperation, such as an equity joint venture, over time (see Park & Ungson, 1997).

The gains in any successful partnership can be enormous and significant. As indicated earlier, benefits accrue from sheer agreements on common goals to a more sophisticated network such as a regional manufacturing platform. In the latter, small and medium-sized firms are able to participate in meaningful ways as suppliers, prototype manufacturers, retailers, or volume producers, depending on the nature of the strategic partnership. In this study, a number of respondents alluded to anticipated partnerships, the challenges attendant on these collaborative agreements, and even more grandiose schemes to develop a regional platform.

Despite many benefits, networks face the challenge of harmonizing different market cultures and language barriers and overcoming logistical obstacles and the lack of institutional facilitators. To reduce cultural distance, firms – such as Boon Rawd Brewery, for example – favor partnerships with firms in Thailand's neighboring countries, particularly in Myanmar, Laos, Cambodia, and to a certain extent Vietnam. It was noted during the interviews that this is due to the fact that areas near the borders of Thailand and its neighboring countries tend to have a similar market culture. Moreover, geographical constraints within Indochina are not as prominent compared to those in other areas of Southeast Asia, making it easier for the company to establish distribution networks with minimal costs.

To minimize any adverse impact from direct competition, the Energy Development Corporation (EDC) has been preparing itself for ASEAN integration mostly by increasing cooperative and joint venture projects abroad. For EDC, the opportunity to diversify its services beyond renewable energy construction and management is a major plus. While there are possible opportunities to provide technical services, drilling services, and consultancy services to other companies within ASEAN also involved in geothermal and renewable energy, it was also noted that competition could intensify for participants and could be disruptive to corporate strategies.

In the case of PetroVietnam Gas Joint Stock Corporation (PV Gas), the company intends to gradually reach out to become "one of the top gas corporations in the region." From company reports, it is stated that its parent company is currently active in the trans-ASEAN pipeline project, a project aimed to link existing and prospective pipeline networks in the ASEAN countries and build a regional gas grid by the year 2020. As such, company spokespersons surmised that with this active participation, the company will be looking forward to establishing networks and building its presence across ASEAN.

For Pruksa Real Estate, it was disclosed by a company representative that the bordering area includes Udon Thani province of Thailand, which could act as a gateway to Vientiane, Laos. It was likewise noted that Udon Thani contains all the facilities to support people's lifestyles, which includes infrastructure linking Udon to Vientiane, Laos's capital city. This province is said to be suitable as a hub for investment in Laos when the ASEAN Economic Community is formed in 2015, due to the complete facilities and accessibility between Vientiane and Thailand. Even so, the company also notes that labor mobility is a double-edged sword and could create risks for the company.

For the telecommunications industry, potential benefits of a network could be realized through an ongoing alliance with five other broadcasting companies in the ASEAN region, recognizing the economies of scale that could benefit media companies in the long run as the ASEAN integration takes place. Company records disclose that the alliance, named SMART, consists of Media Nusantara Citra (Indonesia), the Philippines' ABS-CBN, Thailand's BBTV, Vietnam's International Media Corporation, Malaysia's Media Prima, and Singapore's MediaCorp.

The impediments to successful networking arise from the lack of information. One respondent opined that his company is not aware of what ASEAN policy makers are doing that would benefit his company or industry. "I think the lack of knowledge [is a challenge] you know. I mean, I don't know what's going on in ASEAN. To tell you the truth, I have no idea what's going on, what kind of policy they tend to make. There's only so little people who knows the advantage of being in ASEAN."

Similarly, other experts reported that the lack of information about ASEAN integration – especially in the private sector – continues to be a challenge. To address this gap, governments of ASEAN members should cooperate more with the private sector, and that integration should be done step by step to ensure that several roadblocks are mitigated. Issues such as immigration and visa restrictions should be tackled incrementally in order for integration to be successful. One industry expert notes: "... I actually think that the overexpectation is also based on ignorance of not understanding what the integration really means: the lack of some very evident, easy-to-understand small steps."

Despite the challenges and problems facing the AEC, respondents are generally optimistic and see benefits trumping the costs of regional integration in the long run. Although they did not explicitly address this issue, the respondents expect the lack of infrastructure to remain a major obstacle to overcome, particularly because it is outside their control. Even so, the respondents are bullish about the prospects of enhancing the human resource base that is anticipated with the AEC. One such pundit proclaimed: "The key is education in each country. Give them the right skills, the education there. From that the people then start to move around, they have the qualification and the skills to move around, wherever it's good to provide them with the best. Generally, we're hoping we'll grow."

Conclusions

With any book that extols the virtues of exemplary firms, there is the persistent concern that today's champions might soon be tomorrow's failures. In fact, with each publication of the best firms came searing criticisms of this "select the winners' approach. Although methodological deficiencies have been readily addressed, the most serious criticism is that success tends to be ephemeral, and every too often, firms listed as high performing in a period of time are not able to sustain their performance systematically over time. Most of these narratives draw on economist Joseph Schumpeter's much acclaimed proposition that the dynamism of capitalism lies in the continuous disruption of evolving technologies that gives rise to upstarts displacing incumbents (Schumpeter, 1934/ 1994). In his empirical case-work, Harvard marketing and strategy guru Clayton Christensen (*Innovators' Dilemma*, 1997) illustrated how new upstarts dislodge incumbents and blindsided by consumers' preferences for less radical technological innovations.

In this context, how might one assess the future of the ASEAN champions? Drawing from management professor Rita McGrath's work, *The End of Competitive Advantage* (2013), we agree that success cannot indeed be sustained over time. In Chapter 1, we acknowledge that late bloomers can play a key role in the AEC as well. In all, we adopt McGrath's perspective that the overarching issue is not as much longevity, but how exemplary firms, such as the ASEAN champions, capitalize and exploit advantages during the period, however temporary, in which they are successful. Hence the extent to which they participate in the AEC will have enduring influences in the future of ASEAN.

ASEAN integration will constitute a challenge, even a daunting one. Its success will depend on the ability of the regional members to address and overcome a number of barriers, as well as capitalize on factors that facilitate integration. Among the beacons of optimism is the enthusiasm for the region's munificence in human resources, from the standpoint of both maintaining national prominence and enabling more integration. While there are formidable barriers to greater intraregional trade, there are also promising venues for a broader platform, such as the Asian Plus 3 (APT). Our final chapter presents snapshots from different commentators on their prognostications for ASEAN in the immediate future.

12   Epilogue

Living in interesting times – the well-weathered Chinese adage – evokes various interpretations – anticipation, restlessness, and eventfulness. The evolution of ASEAN from its fledging origins in 1967 to its formal enactment as the AEC in December 2015 has been closely watched by pundits and critics in the world's economic stage with a tepid sense of excitement and precariousness. While we have no crystal ball to forecast what will happen, we have a good idea of the issues and concepts that have preceded the anticipated launch of the AEC. In this final chapter, we present a potpourri of ideas, statements, beliefs, arguments, and speculations of an assortment of thought leaders from government and industry about the AEC.

Jaime Augusto Zobel de Ayala, Chairman and CEO, Ayala Corporation

from the article "What Does ASEAN Mean to You?" published October 28, 2011, by the ASEAN Business Club (http://www.aseanbusinessclub .org/what-does-asean-mean-to-you):

"A fully implemented and operating AEC will open greater opportunities for our business in terms of broadening the market for our products and services, enhancing our materials sourcing and procurement, expanding pool of capital and human resources and expanding manufacturing platforms. It will also expand partnerships across the region. A fully implemented AEC also improves overall competitiveness of nations and business and therefore further raises standards altogether to ensure we remain relevant in a One ASEAN market."

"I think the ASEAN has sufficiently defined itself as an entity in terms of what it wants to achieve – that is to create a stable, competitive, and prosperous economic region. The challenge is in the implementation of the big ideas that already exist. A commitment to the region also has a way of raising standards which by itself can define ASEAN. This ultimately creates strong nations individually and therefore a strong ASEAN."

Teresita Sy-Coson, Vice Chairperson, SM Investments Corporation

from the article "Tessie Sy on ASEAN Integration: Awareness Up, IT to Lead," published October 30, 2014 by Rappler (http://www.rappler.com/business/73540-asean-integration-tessie-sy-forbes):

"The world is moving from competition to more collaboration. There are always challenges in whatever mode you take, whether competition or collaboration, but at least we know we are part of a bigger world."

U Thura Ko Ko, Chairman, ASEAN Business Club Forum 2015

from the article "Structured Channels for Private Sector's Industry-Based Input and Participation Critically Missing in ASEAN – Impeding Real Partnership for Meaningful Integration," published May 19,2015 by the ASEAN Business Club (https://aseanbusinessclub.squarespace.com/press-release/2015/5/19/structured-channels-for-private-sectors-industry-based-input-and-participation-critically-missing-in-asean-impeding-real-partnership-for-meaningful-integration):

"The ASEAN economic region is increasingly recognised as a major global economic and trading powerhouse but more needs to be done to bring the benefits of economic integration to the region's SMEs and micro enterprises who are so critical to creating opportunities, employment and inclusive prosperity across all our citizens."

Serge Pun, Chairman, Serge Pun & Associates (SPA) Group

from the article "ASEAN States 'Too Disparate' to Come Together for Common Market," published May 19, 2015, by the ASEAN Business Club (http://www.aseanbusinessclub.org/latest-news/2015/5/19/asean-states-too-disparate-to-come-together-for-common-market):

"Talking pragmatically, the convergence of the AEC is really not easy. It goes against the entire ASEAN culture of noninterference, of maintaining sovereignty and independence. But then again, we all realise we have to do it. So even though the future is very unclear, we just have to leap with it, take a leap of faith – and hope we land somewhere."

Piyush Gupta, Chief Executive Officer, Development Bank of Singapore

from the article "Bankers Lament Slow Pace of ASEAN Integration," published May 19, 2015, by the ASEAN Business Club (http:// www.aseanbusinessclub.org/latest-news/2015/5/19/bankers-lament-slow-pace-of-asean-integration):

"There is tremendous opportunity and need for ASEAN to integrate the financial and capital markets. If we collectively put our minds to it and given today's technology, there are big opportunities waiting to be seized."

Nestor Rañeses, Director, University of the Philippines Institute for Small-Scale Industries

from the article "ASEAN Integration: An Opportunity, Not a Threat to PH SMEs," published May 12, 2014, by Rappler (http://www.rappler .com/business/57824-asean-integration-smes):

"The ASEAN integration will happen, whether we like it or not. We will never be ready unless we do something about it. There will be winners and losers. To win, we must systematically improve our abilities and capabilities to compete now."

Ambassador Delia Albert, Former Philippine Secretary of Foreign Affairs

from her speech "Building the ASEAN Community through Integration," delivered April 29, 2014, at The Peninsula Manila, for the Management Association of the Philippines (http://map.org.ph/attachments/ article/279/ALBERT,%20DELIA%20-%20%20Building%20the%20 ASEAN%20Community%20Through%20Integration.pdf):

"At this point however the building of the ASEAN Community architecture should not only be the function of diplomats but more importantly it is the responsibility of the wider community of stakeholders – including of course the private sector who stand to gain with the success of ASEAN. For the past 47 years diplomats and other technical people have contributed to bringing about where ASEAN is today, one of the most successful regional organizations in the world."

Cesar Purisima, Finance Secretary of the Philippines

from the article "Integration Just the Start for ASEAN," published February 16, 2014, by Business World (http://www.bworldonline.com/content.php?section=TopStory&title=Integration-just-the-start-for-ASEAN&id=83514):

"The ASEAN is in the right place of the world for the next 30 to 50 years. If looked at as a single country, ASEAN will be among the top ten economies in terms of population, and probably among the youngest with an average age of twenty-seven years old … the young and the middle class are the drivers of growth. However, we cannot capitalize on these opportunities if we do not do the right things. … We have to accept that although we can reap countless benefits from integration in the future, we have to strive much harder to achieve them. We have to ensure first that our institutions, our standards, and our people grow to be harmonized."

"Businesses will boom if ASEAN integrates successfully but this is not possible without their participation. … That is the challenge for the private sector, to become a catalyst for integration itself. It will be a more daunting challenge for smaller sections of the private sector but this is where the government can step in to facilitate the sharing of information."

Moe Thuzar, Lead Researcher for Socio-Cultural Affairs for the ASEAN Studies Centre of the Institute of Southeast Asian Studies (ISEAS)

from the article "ASEAN's Missing Links Need to be Bridged," published March 5, 2015, by The Straits Times (http://www.straitstimes.com/opinion/aseans-missing-links-need-to-be-bridged):

"A successful regional effort, however, has to be given effect by implementation and commitment at sub-regional and national levels. In fact, implementation is most crucial at the national level. Public servants in the relevant national agencies need to be prepared for the changes that will take place with better regional connectivity, greater use of the knowledge economy and new procedures under a more seamless regulatory framework. Businesses also need to play their part and be ready to adapt to regional changes rather than claim protection for fear of external competition. It is all about changing mindsets and cultivating an outlook that sees the benefit of working regionally."

from the article "ASEAN at 45," published August 8, 2012, by the ASEAN Studies Centre (http://asc.iseas.edu.sg/images/stories/pdf/ASEAN_at_45.pdf):

"ASEAN is progressing. Much of it is happening at the national level. At the regional level, ASEAN facilitates the sharing and exchanging of ideas, challenges and concerns. ASEAN member states can build on this foundation as they continue their journey toward regional integration."

Simon Tay, Chairman, Singapore Institute of International Affairs

from the article "ASEAN Economic Integration Faces Tough Road Ahead," published December 30, 2014, by Today Online (http://www.todayonline.com/world/asia/asean-economic-integration-faces-tough-road-ahead?singlepage=true):

"The analogy is that we are waiting for a train of complete integration. The train will probably be a bit late and it's running slower than we had hoped, but it has not been knocked off of the rails. But if we try driving it too fast, we will also have a derailment. So I think a steady, step-by-step process is needed."

Rodolfo Severino, Head of the ASEAN Studies Centre of the Institute of Southeast Asian Studies and Former ASEAN Secretary General

from the article "Look Beyond 2015," published January 5, 2014, by The Straits Times (http://news.asiaone.com/news/asia/look-beyond-2015):

"AEC 2015 should be seen as a re-affirmation of the aspiration for and commitment to efficiency in trading, market openness and linkages with the international community. It should not be regarded as a target year, in which ASEAN, its objectives and the way it does things are suddenly transformed. Rather, it should be regarded as a benchmark or milestone for the measurement of progress toward regional economic integration."

Sanchita Basu Das, Lead Researcher for Economic Affairs at the ASEAN Studies Centre of the Institute of Southeast Asian Studies (ISEAS)

from the article "Increased Transparency, Streamlining of the Processes and Inter-Agency Coordination within ASEAN Is Key," published April 26, 2013, by The Business Times (http://asc.iseas.edu.sg/images/stories/pdf/BT260413.pdf):

"The time is ripe for ASEAN to continue with its attractiveness to the international community. While internally the incremental liberalisation as well as improved facilitation is attracting FDI, the external conditions are also offering opportunities. Thus, by implementing the key AEC measures in the run-up to

Dec 31, 2015, ASEAN will establish the foundation for an integrated and globally connected economic community. The implementation of the rest of the AEC
initiatives can be carried out beyond 2015."

from the article "AEC Should Be Seen as a Work in Progress," published
May 20, 2015, by The Business Times (http://asc.iseas.edu.sg/images/
Sanchita-AEC-BT-20May2015.pdf):

"The AEC should be seen as a work in progress, where some promises have
been met, but significant challenges remain. Nevertheless, now, more than
ever, is the time when the countries should come together to strengthen the
economic community. The AEC-2015 may not be able to deliver on a fully
integrated single market and production base for ASEAN stakeholders, but it
will help ASEAN members to withstand the next global crisis with confidence,
whenever it arrives."

from the article "AEC Not Just about the Economics," published January
31, 2015, by East Asia Forum (http://www.eastasiaforum.org/2015/01/
31/aec-not-just-about-the-economics):

"The success of the AEC can be observed in ASEAN's assertive manner in dealing with the international community. Going forward, the AEC – as a strategic
project – will continue to be developed to attract more FDI into the region, help
member countries participate in global supply chains, and strengthen member
countries' bargaining power in international economic, financial and strategic
matters. And that has to be a good thing for ASEAN."

Niceto Poblador, former Management professor at the University of the Philippines Mindanao and member of the Management Association of the Philippines

from the article "Bracing for the ASEAN Economic Integration,"
published September 23, 2013, by Business World (http://www
.bworldonline.com/content.php?section=Opinion&title=Bracing-for-
the-ASEAN-economic-integration&id=76873):

"On balance, we believe that the potential benefits from AEC far outweigh the
perceived problems and difficulties associated with it. In responding to the situ-
ation, business organizations should therefore focus their attention and devote
their energies on the advantages that integration offers, rather than sulk over
the problems and uncertainties that lie ahead. It is our belief that thriving in the
emerging regional economic community requires business strategies intended
to develop the firm's human capital, which includes not only knowledge and
human skills, but also an organizational culture that nourishes mutual trust and
collaboration – intangible assets that are the main drivers of business success in
the global economy."

David Abrenilla, Founder and Managing Director, Philippine SME Business Exposition

from the article "ASEAN Integration Cuts Both Ways as Opportunity, Challenge – SMEs," published November 18, 2014, by Business World (http://www.bworldonline.com/content.php?section=Economy &title=asean-integration-cuts-both-ways-as-opportunity-challenge——smes&id=98133):

"It's a two-sided knife. ASEAN integration is both an opportunity and a challenge. There is still a lot of room for improvements and there is still a lot of work ahead of us. I think as a regional community, to be able to compete on a global level, we have to innovate and do things. Companies need to invest in infrastructure. If they won't be able to do it, they won't be able to compete, and if you're not able to compete, you'll be forced to close shop."

H.E. U Thein Sein, President of the Republic of the Union of Myanmar

from his opening statement at the 25th ASEAN Summit, November 12, 2014, in Nay Pyi Taw, Myanmar (published by the ASEAN website at http://www .asean.org/images/pdf/2014_upload/OpeningStatementeng201525summit .pdf):

"There is no room to be complacent with our achievements and we should not rest on our laurels made so far. Our Community building is a work in progress. The evolvement of ASEAN Community in 2015 will be a new beginning for a new ASEAN calling for greater unity and integration, enhanced operational efficiency, better coordination, stronger resilience and greater competitiveness of the Community."

Yab Dato' Sri Mohd Najib Tun Abdul Razak, Prime Minister of Malaysia

from his opening statement at the 26th ASEAN Summit, April 27, 2015, in Kuala Lumpur, Malaysia (published by the ASEAN website at http://www.asean.org/images/2015/april/26th_asean_summit/PM%20-%20Opening%20Ceremony%20-%20PMO%20-%20A4%202.pdf):

"Our potential, after all, is huge. We already have the third largest workforce in the world. We have a largely youthful, talented and increasingly skilled population of over 600 million people. Our burgeoning middle class makes us one of the most potent and dynamic regions – leading one publication to ask last week if ASEAN was Asia's 'hottest investment'.

"This is ASEAN's time. And that is why it is essential that we continue with the measures to establish the ASEAN Economic Community. We must accelerate programmes to harmonise standards, increasing capital market and financial integration, and promoting the freer movement of goods, services, investments and talents between our countries. The results of such reforms would be transformative. It would result in a further 7 trillion dollars spending on infrastructure. This potential growth would mean astonishing improvements both to our economies and to the standards of living of our citizens. And those prizes are within our grasp."

H.E. Dr. Susilo Bambang Yudhoyono, Former President of the Republic of Indonesia

from his speech at the 2011 ASEAN Business and Investment Summit, November 17, 2011, in Bali, Indonesia (published by the ASEAN website at http://www.asean.org/news/item/speech-he-dr-susilo-bambang-yudhoyono-president-of-the-republic-of-indonesia-at-the-asean-business-and-investment-summit):

"ASEAN is a region fast being transformed. We are becoming an ASEAN Community. One defining feature of that ASEAN Community – we hope – is the spread of opportunity. Our citizens have acquired constitutionally guaranteed equality – but providing equal opportunity for all remains a challenge. The business community – from ASEAN and beyond – is indispensable in this effort. You have the power to change, to build, to empower, and to prosper. We believe that the best investments are those that are for the long haul, beneficial to the people, environmentally sustainable, and contribute to progress."

H.E. Nguyen Tan Dung, Prime Minister of the Socialist Republic of Vietnam

from his opening statement at the 16th ASEAN Summit, April 8, 2010, in Hanoi, Vietnam (published by the ASEAN website at http://www.asean.org/news/item/statement-by-he-prime-minister-nguyen-tan-dung-at-the-opening-ceremony-of-the-16th-asean-summit):

"The goal of an ASEAN Community manifests in itself the Member States' shared vision, earnest desire and strong determination. This goal is firmly premised upon the significant achievements in ASEAN cooperation over more than four decades. The problems that ASEAN is to address are neither new nor confined to the year 2010 alone. What is important now is our resolute and strong actions, harmoniously combining national interests with the common ones of the entire region, thus improving the quality of our 'unity in diversity.' Reality shows that ASEAN is truly a regional organisation with vitality and adaptability to the changes of the time. Undoubtedly, ASEAN's vision, determination, resilience, success and time-honoured values all serve as the foundation of our conviction that ASEAN shall make further accomplishments in the process of community building."

Federico Macaranas, Economics professor and AIM ASEAN 2015 Project Co-Director, Asian Institute of Management

from his concluding remarks at the 5th ASEAN Leaderspeak Forum, November 25, 2014, at the Asian Institute of Management:

"In December 2015, ASEAN is supposed to announce to the world that it is finally being integrated. But it is a mistake to believe that the integration means we have solved all the problems so that we can live as one happy family. We believe that ASEAN is a process rather than an outcome. We believe ASEAN is a journey, rather than an end."

References

Abidin, M. Z., and Rosli, F. 2013. "Infrastructure development in ASEAN," in Das, S. B. (ed.), *ASEAN Economic Community Scorecard: Performance and Perception*, pp. 136–162. Hong Kong: ISEAS Publishing.

Acemoglu, D., Johnson, S., and Robinson, J. 2005. "Institutions as a fundamental cause of long-run growth," in Aghion, P. and Durlauf, S. N. (eds.), *Handbook of Economic Growth*, pp. 385–472. Amsterdam: Elsevier.

Acharya, A. 2012. *The making of Southeast Asia: International relations of a region.* Singapore: Oxford University Press.

Acharya, A., and Rajah, A. 1999. "Introduction: Reconceptualizing Southeast Asia," *Southeast Asian Journal of Social Science* 27: 1–6.

Adelman, J. 2015. "What Caused Capitalism?: Assessing the Roles of the West and the Rest," *Foreign Affairs* 94(3): 136–144.

Afriani, E., Dewi, F. R., and Mulyati, A. 2012. "On Reconceptualizing Southeast Asia, use of long-run growth," *International Journal of Science and Research* 3: 608–611.

Albarracin, M. B. 1969. "The Philippine cement industry," *Philippine Review of Economics* 6: 47–81.

Alfonso, F. B., and Neelankavil, J. P. 2012. *Jollibee Foods Corporation: The next challenge* (Case study). Makati: Asian Institute of Management.

Allio, R. J. 1990. "Flaws in Porter's competitive diamond?," *Planning Review* 18: 28–32.

Amsden, A. 1989. *Asia's next giant: South Korea and late industrialization.* Oxford: Oxford University Press.

 1992. *Asia's next giant: South Korea and late industrialization.* Oxford: Oxford University Press.

Ando, M., and Kimura, F. 2003. "The formation of international production and distribution networks in East Asia," Working Paper No. 10167 in *NBER papers in international trade and investment.* Cambridge, MA: The National Bureau of Economic Research.

Ando, M., and Obashi, A. 2010. "The pervasiveness of non-tariff measures in ASEAN – evidences from the inventory approach," in Mikic, M. and Wermelinger, M. (eds.), *Rising non-tariff protectionism and crisis recovery: A study of Asia-Pacific Research and Training Network on Trade.* Bangkok: United Nations Economic and Social Commission for Asia and the Pacific.

Ansoff, I. 1957. "Strategies for diversification," *Harvard Business Review* 35, 113–124.

222   References

Araral, E. 2008. "Public provision for urban water: Getting prices and governance right," in *Governance: An International Journal of Policy, Administration, and Institutions* 21: 527–549.

ASEAN 2008. *ASEAN Economic Community Blueprint*. Jakarta: ASEAN Secretariat.

2012. *ASEAN Economic Community Scorecard*. Jakarta: ASEAN Secretariat.

2014. *Thinking globally, prospering regionally: ASEAN Economic Community 2015*. Jakarta: ASEAN Secretariat.

2015a. *AEC 2015 progress and key achievements*. Jakarta: ASEAN Secretariat.

2015b. *Chairman's statement of the 26th ASEAN Summit, Kuala Lumpur and Langkawi, 27 April 2015, "Our people, our community, our vision"*. Jakarta: ASEAN Secretariat.

ASEAN Secretariat 2008. ASEAN Economic Community Blueprint, online http://asean.org/storage/images/archive/21083.pdf.

Ayala Land 2014. "Ayala Land named Best Real Estate Developer in South East Asia," online http://www.atayala.com/news/2014-10-24/ayala-land-named-best-real-estate-developer-in-south-east-asia.

Bagwell, K., and Staiger, R. W. 2002. *The economics of the world trading system*. Cambridge, MA: Massachusetts Institute of Technology Press.

Bain, J. S. 1956. *Barriers to new competition*. Cambridge, MA: Harvard University Press.

Balangue-Tarriela, M.I.R., and Mendoza, J.P. 2015. "Updates on geothermal energy development in the Philippines," in *World Geothermal Congress 2015 Proceedings*, online https://pangea.stanford.edu/ERE/db/WGC/papers/WGC/2015/16092.pdf.

Balassa, B. 1961. *The theory of economic integration*. New York: Routledge.

Bangkok Cable Co. Ltd. 2014. "Marketing," online http://www.bangkokcable.com/about/marketing.php.

Bangkok Dusit Medical Services PCL 2014. "Annual report 2013," online http://bgh.listedcompany.com/misc/ar/20140320-BGH-AR2013-EN-04.pdf.

Bangkok Hospital 2015. "Our history," online https://www.bangkokhospital.com/en/about-us/our-history.

Bangkok Post 2014. "TUF wraps up deals for producers," online http://www.bangkokpost.com/business/news/441270/tuf-wraps-up-deals-for-producers.

Barney, J.B. and Clarke, D.N. 2007. *Resource-based theory: Creating and sustaining competitive advantage*. New York: Oxford University Press.

Bartlett, C.A. and Ghoshal, S. 1987. "Managing across borders: New strategic requirements," *Sloan Management Review* 28: 7–17.

Bangkok Post 1990. online http://www.bangkokp *McKinsey Quarterly*: 31–41.

Bartlett, C.A. and O'Connell, J. 1998. "Jollibee Foods Corporation (A): International expansion" (Harvard Business School case study), online http://imm-gsm.s3.amazonaws.com/docs/Assignment_Q_2013_1/EIT_Case_Study_1_2013_Jollibee_Foods_Harvard.pdf.

Beckert, S. 2014. *Empire of Cotton: A Global History*. New York: Alfred A. Knopf.

Beeson, M. 2007. *Regionalism and globalization in East Asia: Politics, security and economic development*. New York and London: Palgrave MacMillan.

2009. *Institutions of the Asia-Pacific: ASEAN, APEC and beyond*. New York: Routledge.

2010. "Asymmetrical regionalism: China, Southeast Asia and uneven development," in *East Asia: An international quarterly* 27: 329–343.

Bellah, R., Madsen, R., Tipton, S., Sullivan, W. and Swidler, A. 1992. *The good society*. New York: Vintage Books.

Bhasin, B. 2010. *Doing business in the ASEAN countries*. New York: Business Expert Press.

Bhaskaran, M. 2013. "The investment dimension of ASEAN," in Das, S.B. (ed.), *ASEAN Economic Community Scorecard: Performance and perception*, pp. 79–106. Hong Kong: ISEAS Publishing.

Biswas, A. K. and Tortajada, C. 2010. "Water supply of Phnom Penh: An example of good governance," in *International Journal of Water Resources Development* 26: 157–172.

Bloomberg Businessweek 2014. "Keppel FELS Limited: Private company information," online http://investing.businessweek.com/research/stocks/private/snapshot.asp?privcapId=5632965, accessed 9 June 2014].

Boericke, W. F. 1945. Rehabilitation of mines in the Philippines, *Far Eastern Survey* 14: 300–303.

Booth, J. 2014. *Emerging markets in an upside down world*. New York: Wiley & Sons.

Borroughs, T. 2012. "Carlyle completes first Southeast Asia deal," in *Asia Venture Capital Journal*. Hong Kong: AVCJ Group Limited.

Bown, S. 2010. *Merchant kings: When companies ruled the world, 1600–1900*. New York: Thomas Dunne Books.

Buckley, P.J. 1983. "New theories of international business: Some unresolved issues," in M.C. Casson (ed.), *The Growth of International Business* (London: Allen & Unwin.)

Business Standard 2010. "TOA Group to set up paint facility near Chennai," online http://www.business-standard.com/article/companies/toa-group-to-set-up-paint-facility-near-chennai-110092500068_1.html, accessed 11 November 2014].

Businessweek n.d. "Boon Rawd Brewery," online http://investing.businessweek.com/research/stocks/private/snapshot.asp?privcapId=250657402, accessed 13 December 2014].

n.d. Ketut Budi Wijaya, online http://investing.businessweek.com/research/stocks/people/person.asp?personid=13620526&ticker=LPKR:IJ&previousCapId=5540945&previousTitle=LIPPO%20LTD, October 2014.

Casson, M. and Lee, J.S. 2011. "The origin and development of markets: A business history perspective," in *Business History Review* 85: 9–37.

Cattaneo, O., Gereffi, G. and Staritz, C. 2010. *Global value chains in a postcrisis world: A development perspective*. Washington, DC: The World Bank.

Cavusgil, T., Knight, G. and Riesenberger, J.R. 2014. *International business strategy, management and the new realities*. Upper Saddle River: Prentice Hall.

Cebu Air 2014. "About Cebu Pacific," online https://www.cebupacificair.com/about-us/Pages/company-info.aspx.

Chachavalpongpun, P. 2006. "In search of an ASEAN identity," in *The Nation*, online http://www.nationmultimedia.com/2006/05/04/opinion/opinion_30003161.php.

Chanda, Nayan, 2007. *Bound Together: How Traders, Preachers, Adventurers and Warriors Shaped Globalization*. New Haven: Yale University Press.

Chandler, A.D. 1962. *Strategy and structure: Chapters in the history of the American industrial enterprise*. Boston: MIT Press.

Chang, H.J. 2002. *Kicking away the ladder: Development strategy in historical perspective*. London: Anthem Press.

Chattopadhyay, A. and Batra, R. (with Ozsomer, A.). 2012. *The new emerging market multinationals*. New York: McGraw-Hill.

Chen, M.J. and Miller, D. 2011. "The relational perspective as a business mindset: Managerial implications for East and West," in *The Academy of Management Perspectives* 25: 6–18.

Christensen, C. 1997. *The innovator's dilemma*. Boston: Harvard University Business Press.

Chungsiriwat, P. and Panapol, V. 2009. "Thailand: An industry shaped by government support," in *Smallholder dairy development: Lessons learned in Asia*. Bangkok: Food and Agriculture Organization of the United Nations.

Cohen, M. 2006. "Thai Union Frozen Products PCL," in *The International Directory of Company Histories*, online http://www.encyclopedia.com/doc/1G2-3445200104.html.

Collins, J. 2001. *Good to great: Why some companies make the leap... and others don't*. New York: John Wiley & Sons.

Collins, J. and Porras, J. 1994. *Built to last: Successful habits of visionary companies*. New York: Harper & Row.

Commission on Higher Education (CHED) 2012. "Higher education institutions," online http://www.ched.gov.ph/index.php/higher-education-in-numbers/higher-education-institutions

Country Studies n.d. 'Thailand – Energy," online http://countrystudies.us/thailand/74.htm, accessed 25 August 2015.

Cuervo-Cazurra, A. and Ramamurti, R. 2014. *Understanding multinationals from emerging markets*. Cambridge: Cambridge University Press.

Das, B., Ek, S.C., Visoth, C., Pangare, G. and Simpson, R. 2010. "Sharing the reform process: Learning from the Phnom Penh Water Supply Authority," online https://cmsdata.iucn.org/downloads/phnom_penh_waterfinal.pdf.

Das, S.B. (ed.) 2012. *Achieving the ASEAN Economic Community: Challenges for member countries & businesses*. Hong Kong: ISEAS Publishing.

(ed). 2013. *ASEAN Economic Community Scorecard: Performance and perception*. Hong Kong: ISEAS Publishing.

D'Aveni, R. 1994. *Hypercompetition*. New York: The Free Press.

Davenport, T. 1999. *Human Capital: What it is and why people invest in it*. San Francisco: Jossey Bass.

Davis, M. 2014. "An agreement to disagree: The ASEAN Human Rights Declaration and the absence of regional identity in Southeast Asia," in *Journal of Current Southeast Asian Affairs* 3: 107–129.

De Soto, H. 2000. *The mystery of capital: Why capitalism triumphs in the West and fails everywhere else*. New York: Basic Books.

Delhaise, P. 1998. *Asia in crisis: The implosion of banking and finance systems*. New York: Wiley.

Deutch, K.W., Burrell, S. and Kann, R. 1957. *Political community and the North Atlantic Area: International organization in the light of historical experience*. New York: Greenwood Press.

Dieleman, M. 2007. *The rhythm of strategy: A corporate biography of the Salim Group of Indonesia*. Amsterdam: Amsterdam University Press.

DKSH 2014. "DKSH brings Thailand's most popular sport drink to Vietnam," online http://www.dksh.com.vn/htm/388/en_VN/DKSH-brings-Thailand%E2%80%99s-most-popular-sport-drink-to-Vietnam.htm?Id=609358.

Dunning, J.H. 1990. "Dunning's Eclectic Paradigm," online http://www.researchomatic.com/Dunnings-Eclectic-Paradigm-21815.html.

The Economist 2008. "Emerging market multinationals: The challengers," online http://www.economist.com/node/10496684.

2013. *The Economist explains: Why does Kenya lead the world in mobile money?*. London: The Economist Newspaper Limited.

EDL-Generation Public Company 2015. "Power plants," online http://www.edlgen.com.la/en/page.php?post_id=33#.

EEI Corporation 2013. "Annual report 2012," online http://www.eei.com.ph/content/corporate%20governance/pdf/annualreport2012.pdf.

2014. "Annual report 2012," online http://www.eeei.com.ph/content/corhistory.php#/2.

El-Agraa, A.M. 2011. *The European Union: Economics and politics*. Cambridge, UK: Cambridge University Press.

Ellisa, E. 2014. "The entrepreneurial city of Kelapa Gading, Jakarta," *Journal of Urbanism: International Research on Placemaking and Urban Sustainability* 7: 130–151.

Ernst, D. 1997. "From partial to systemic globalization: International production networks in the electronics industry' (report to Sloan Foundation), published as *The Data Storage Industry Globalization Project Report 97–02*. San Diego: Graduate School of International Relations and Pacific Studies, University of California at San Diego.

2006. *Innovation offshoring: Asia's emerging role in global innovation networks*. Honolulu: East West Center.

2009. *A new geography of knowledge in electronics industry? Asia's role in global innovation networks*. Singapore: Institute of Southeast Asian Studies.

Euromonitor International 2013. "Passport: Red Bull GmbH in soft drinks (World)," online http://www.euromonitor.com/medialibrary/PDF/RedBull-Company-Profile-SWOT-Analysis.pdf.

Evers, H. 1999. "Review of 'Reconceptualizing Southeast Asia'," in *International Quarterly for Asian Studies* 30: 414.

Fernquest, J. 2012. "Thai billionaire & Red Bull founder dies," in *Bangkok Post*, online http://www.bangkokpost.com/learning/learning-from-news/285049/thai-billionaire-red-bull-founder-dies.

Fishman, C. 1998. "The war for talent," in *Fast Company*, online http://www.fastcompany.com/34512/war-talent, accessed 26 August 2015.

Flightglobal n.d. "The interview – Lance Gokongwei, Cebu Pacific," online http://www.flightglobal.com/interviews/year/12/lance-gokongwei/the-interview.

Forbes n.d. "Henry Sy and family," online http://www.forbes.com/profile/henry-sy.

Gerlach, M. 1982. *Alliance capitalism: The social organization of Japanese business*. Berkeley: University of California Berkeley Press.

1990. "Trust is not enough: Cooperation and conflict in Kikkoman's American development," *Journal of Japanese Studies* 16: 389–425.

GMA News 2013. "Ayala Land finds joint ventures the way to expand nationwide," online http://www.gmanetwork.com/news/story/330978/economy/companies/ayala-land-finds-joint-ventures-the-way-to-expand-nationwide.

Goldstein, M. 1998. *The Asian Financial Crisis: Causes, Cures, and Systemic Implications.* Washington D.C.: Institute for International Economics.

Grazella, M. 2012. "MAPI to spend Rp 600B, open 300 new stores," in *The Jakarta Post*, online http://www.thejakartapost.com/news/2012/02/17/mapi-spend-rp-600b-open-300-new-stores.html.

2013a. "MAPI hits new highs amid middle-class growth," in *The Jakarta Post*, online http://www.thejakartapost.com/news/2013/03/28/mapi-hits-new-highs-amid-middle-class-growth.html.

2013b. "Tower sector to grow by 15%: Analysts," in *The Jakarta Post*, online http://www.thejakartapost.com/news/2013/02/12/tower-sector-grow-15-analysts.html.

Guillen, M. and Garcia-Canal, E. 2013. *Emerging markets rule.* New York: McGraw Hill.

Gujarat Money 2010. "Thai paint major TOA Group eyes Gujarat to set up $70-million plant," online http://gujaratmoney.com/2010/09/26/thai-paint-major-toa-group-eyes-gujarat-to-set-up-70-million-plant.

Haacke, J. 2003. *ASEAN diplomatic and security culture: Origins, developments and prospects.* London: Routledge Curzon.

The Hindu Business Line 2011. "Thailand's TOA Group launches Kerala operations," online http://www.thehindubusinessline.com/companies/thailands-toa-group-launches-kerala-operations/article2302846.ece.

Hiratsuka, D. 2006. Vertical Intra-Regional Production Networks in East Asia: A Case Study of the Hard Disk Drive Industry. In *East Asia's De Facto Economic Integration*, edited by D. Hiratsuka. Basingstoke: Palgrave Macmillan.

Holcim Philippines, Inc. 2010. "Consortium Conference (ASCC)," online http://www.holcim.com.ph/productadvisor/products/concrete.html.

Holcim Philippines 2013. *Holcim Philippines annual report 2012.* Taguig: Holcim Philippines.

Horn, R. 2012. "Duck farmer to billionaire: Red Bull co-founder dies," in *Time*, online http:// content.time.com/time/world/article/0,8599,2109386,00 .html.

Inama, S. and Sim, E.W. 2015. *The foundation of the ASEAN Economic Community: An institutional and legal profile.* Cambridge: Cambridge University Press.

Isbister, J. 2006. *Promises not kept: Poverty and the betrayal of Third World development.* Bloomfield, CT: Kunarian Press.

ISN Hotnews 2011. "TOA close to putting a new coat on three more countries," online http://en.isnhotnews.com/?p=10584.

Jittapong, K. 2014. "Canned tuna giant Thai Union Frozen plans to buy Norway's seafood firm King Oscar," in Reuters, online http://www.dailymail.co.uk/wires/reuters/article-2755973/Canned-tuna-giant-Thai-Union-Frozen-plans-buy-Norways-seafood-firm-King-Oscar.html.

Johnson, C. 1982. *MITI and the Japanese miracle: The growth of industrial policy, 1925–1975*. Stanford, CA: Stanford University Press.

Jollibee Foods Corporation 2013. "Annual report 2012," online http://www.jollibee.com.ph/wp-content/themes/jollibee/pdf/annualreport_2012.pdf, accessed 18 December 2014.

    2014a. "About us," online http://www.jollibee.com.ph/about-us.

    2014b. "Milestones / History," online http://www.jollibee.com.ph/about-us/#milestones-history.

Jones, L. 2005. "ASEAN's unchanged melody? The theory and practice of 'non-interference' in Southeast Asia," in *The Pacific Review* 23: 479–502.

Jovanovic, M. 2006. *The economics of international integration*. Northampton, MA: Edward Elgar Publishing, Inc.

Kartika, P. and Atje, R. 2013. "Towards AEC 2015: Free flow of goods within ASEAN," in Das, S.B. (ed.), *ASEAN Economic Community Scorecard: Performance and perception*, pp. 28–46. Hong Kong: ISEAS Publishing.

Katzenstein, P.J. 2005. *A world of regions: Asia and Europe in America imperium*. Ithaca, NY: Cornell University Press.

Keppel Offshore and Marine 2014. "Corporate structure," online http://www.keppelom.com/en/content.aspx?sid=2686.

Khanna, T. and Palepu, K.G. 1997. "Why focused strategies may be wrong for emerging markets,' in *Harvard Business Review*, July-August: 41–51.

    2010. *Winning in emerging markets: A road map for strategy and execution*. Boston: Harvard Business Publishing.

Kim, L. 1990. *Imitation to innovation: The dynamics of Korea's technological learning*. Boston: Harvard Business School Press.

Klein, N. 2007. *The Shock Doctrine: The Rise of Disaster Capitalism*. Knopf Canada.

Klein, P.G. and Saidenberg, M. 1997. "Diversification, Organization and Efficiency: Evidence from Bank Holding Companies," online http://fic.wharton.upenn.edu/fic/papers/97/klein.pdf.

Koh, J. 2012. "Thai beverage to pay s$2.78 billion for OCBC's F&N stake," in *BloombergBusiness*, online http://www.bloomberg.com/news/2012-07-18/thai-beverage-to-pay-s-2-78-billion-for-ocbc-s-f-n-stake.html.

Kohlberg Kravis Roberts & Co. LP 2011. "Masan Group raises US$159 million with 10% sale of Masan Consumer to KKR," online http://media.kkr.com/media/media_releasedetail.cfm?ReleaseID=568586.

Kotler, P., Kartajaya, H. and Hooi, D.H. 2015. *Think new ASEAN! Rethinking marketing towards ASEAN Economic Community*. New York: McGraw-Hill Education.

Kritayanavaj, B. n.d. "Affordable housing in Thailand," online http://www.ghbhomecenter.com/journal/download.php?file=1525Dec12sVuWaXb.32-43_Affordable+housing+in+Thailand.pdf.

Lee, L. 2013. "How Choo Chiau Beng shaped Keppel for the future," online http://bambooinnovator.com/2013/12/26/how-choo-chiau-beng-shaped-keppel-for-the-future.

Levitt, T. 1975. "Marketing myopia," in *Harvard Business Review* 53: 26–183.

Lieberman, M.B. and Montgomery, D.B. 1998. "First-mover (dis)advantages: Retrospective and link with the resource-based view," in *Strategic Management Journal* 19: 1111–1125.

Lieberman, V. 1995. "An age of commerce in Southeast Asia? Problems of regional coherence," in *Journal of Asian Studies* 54: 796–807.

Lim C.Y. 2004. *Southeast Asia: The long road ahead.* Singapore: World Scientific Publishing Company Pte. Ltd.

Lutz, Richard and Barton Wietz. 2005. "Strategic Marketing – Delivering Customer Value," in *What the Best MBAs Know*, ed. Peter Navarro. New York: McGraw-Hill.

Machlup, F. 1977. *A history of thought on economic integration.* Basingstoke: Macmillan.

Manila Bulletin 2014. "PLDT expands global market with strategic Samsung, SM tieup," online http://www.mb.com.ph/pldt-expands-global-market-with-strategic-samsung-sm-tieup

2016. "ASEAN Economic Community seen as a trading powerhouse," online http://www.mb.com.ph/asean-economic-community-seen-as-a-trading-powerhouse.

Martin, S. 1988. *Industrial Economics: Economic Analysis and Public Policy.* New York: Macmillan Publishing Company.

Masan Group 2014a. "About us: Overview," online http://www.masangroup.com/masanconsumer/en/about-us/overview

2014b. "About us: Strategy," online http://www.masangroup.com/masanconsumer/en/about-us/strategy

Mayagita, M. and Eslita, U. 2014. "Best of the best," online http://forbesindonesia.com/berita-694-no-1.-malindo-feedmill.html.

McGrath, R.G. 2013. *The end of competitive advantage: How to keep your strategy moving as fast as your business.* Boston, MA: Harvard Business Publishing.

Mendoza, R. and Siriban, C. 2014. "Winners and losers in ASEAN 2015," in *Rappler*, online http://www.rappler.com/thought-leaders/54766-winners-losers-asean-2015

Mills, P. 1986. *Managing service industries: Organizational practices in a postindustrial economy.* Cambridge, MA: Ballinger Publishing Company.

Mokyr, J. 2010. "Entrepreneurship and the industrial revolution in Britain," in Landes, D., Mokyr, J. and Baumol, W.J. (eds.), *The invention of enterprise*, pp. 183–210. Princeton, NJ: Princeton University Press.

Morales, N.J.C. 2013. "Jollibee going to Indonesia, Canada," in *The Philippine Star*, online http://www.philstar.com/business/2013/10/07/1242231/jollibee-going-indonesia-canada

The Nation 2014. "Businessman of the year," online http://www.nationmultimedia.com/business/Businessman-of-the-year-30250360.html.

2015. "Bangkok Dusit Medical Services partners Nagoya University to boost staff Standards," online http://www.nationmultimedia.com/business/Bangkok-Dusit-Medical-Services-partners-Nagoya-uni-30253433.html.

Nikomborirak, D. and Jitdumrong, S. 2013. "An assessment of services sector liberalization in ASEAN," in Das, S.B. (ed.), *ASEAN Economic Community Scorecard: Performance and perception*, pp. 47–78. Hong Kong: ISEAS Publishing.

North, D.C. 1990. *Institutions, institutional change and economic performance (Political economy of institutions and decisions).* Cambridge: Cambridge University Press.

1991. "Institutions," *The Journal of Economic Perspectives* 5: 97–112.

North, D.C. and Thomas, R.P. 1973. *The rise of the Western world: A new economic history*. Cambridge: Cambridge University Press.

Onkvisit, S. and Shaw, J. 2009. *International marketing: Strategy and theory* (5th edition). New York: Routledge.

O'Reilly, C.A. and Pfeffer, J. 2000. *Hidden value: How great companies achieve extraordinary results with ordinary people*. Boston: Harvard Business School Press.

Organisation for Economic Cooperation and Development (OECD) 2014. "Economic outlook for Southeast Asia, China, and India," online http://www.oecd.org/site/seao/Pocket%20Edition%20SAEO2014.pdf.

Osborne, M. 2013. *Southeast Asia: An introductory history*. New South Wales: Allen & Unwin.

Ouchi, W. 1982. *Theory Z: How American business can meet the Japanese challenge*. New York: Avon Books.

Oxford Business Group n.d. "The big three: A battle for subscribers and profit," online http://www.oxfordbusinessgroup.com/analysis/big-three-battle-subscribers-and-profit.

Park, S.H. and Ungson, G.R. 1997. "The effect of national culture, organizational complementarity, and economic motivation on joint venture dissolution," in *Academy of Management Journal* 40: 279–307.

Park, S.H., Ungson, G.R. and Cosgrove A. 2015. *Scaling the tail: Managing profitable growth in emerging countries*. New York: Palgrave MacMillan.

Park, S.H., Zhou, N. and Ungson, G.R. 2013. *Rough diamonds: The four traits of successful breakout firms in BRIC countries*. San Francisco: Jossey-Bass.

Paterno, R. M. 2010. "History," online http://www.meralco.com.ph/company/page-about-corporateinfo-history.html.

PetroVietnam 2012. "Annual report 2011," online http://english.pvn.vn/cms/data/files/file/03_2013/03_2013_12.pdf.

PetroVietnam Gas Joint Stock Corporation 2013. "Development goals of PV Gas until 2015," online http://www.pvgas.com.vn/introduction/overview/objectives-and-goals.

Pfeffer, J. 1994. *Competitive advantage through people: Unleashing the power of the work force*. Boston: Harvard Business School Press.

1998. *The human equation: Building profits by putting people first*. Boston: Harvard Business School Press.

Porter, M. 1987. "From Competitive Advantage to Corporate Strategy." *Harvard Business Review* 65: 43–43:

1990. *The competitive advantage of nations*. New York: The Free Press.

Prahalad, C.K. and Ramaswamy, V. 2004a. *The future of competition: Co-creating unique value with customers*. Boston: Harvard Business School Press.

2004b. "Co-creation experiences: The next practice in value creation," in *Journal of Interactive Marketing* 18: 5–14.

Pruksa Real Estate PCL 2014a. "Company history," online http://www.pruksa.com/en/about-us/company-history, accessed 30 September 2014.

2014b. "Pruksa Real Estate unveils 2014 business plan which targets revenue worth 40,000–42,000 million baht," online http://www.pruksa.com/en/about-us/press-release/3531/pruksa-real-estate-unveils-2014-business-plan-which-targets-revenue-worth-4#.U3XPUdKSwbs.

PT FKS Multiagro Tbk. 2014. *Annual report 2013*. Jakarta, Indonesia: PT FKS Multiagro Tbk.

PT Mitra Adiperkasa Tbk. 2014. "Annual report 2013" (Part 1 of 8), online http://www.map-indonesia.com/annual/2013/mitra-adiperkasa-annual-2013-1.pdf.

PT Petrosea Tbk. 2012. "Annual report 2011," online http://www.petrosea.com/petrofiles/PETROSEA_AR%202011.pdf.

PT Solusi Tunas Pratama Tbk. 2014. "Annual report 2013," online http://www.stptower.com/files/Annual%20Report%202012%20STP_FINAL.pdf.

PT Ultrajaya Milk Industry and Trading Company Tbk. 2012. "About us: Technology," online http://www.ultrajaya.co.id/aboutus/technology/?ver=eng.
    2014. "Annual report 2013," online http://www.ultrajaya.co.id/uploads/AR2013Ultrajaya.pdf.

Ramamurti, R. and Singh, J. (eds.) 2009. *Emerging multinationals in emerging markets*. Cambridge, UK: Cambridge University Press.

Ramon Magsaysay Award Foundation 2012. "Ek Sonn Chan," online http://www.rmaf.org.ph/newrmaf/main/awardees/awardee/profile/140.

The Red Bull Beverage Co. Ltd. n.d.a. "History of Kratingdaeng," online http://www.kratingdaeng.com/en/vdo.php.
    n.d.b. "Kratingdaeng: Activity," online http://www.kratingdaeng.com/en/activities.php.

Reinhart, C.M. and Rogoff, K.S. 2009. *This time is different: Eight centuries of financial folly*. Princeton, NJ: Princeton University Press.

Remo, A. R. 2013. "Meralco eyes power plants in ASEAN countries," in *The Philippine Daily Inquirer*, online http://business.inquirer.net/109639/meralco-eyes-power-plants-in-asean-countries.

Reuters 2013. "KKR signs Vietnam's top private equity deal with $200 million Masan Consumer buy," online http://www.reuters.com/article/2013/01/09/us-kkr-masan-idUSBRE90802920130109.

Rillo, A.D. 2011. "AEC Scorecard: The road to ASEAN single market" (Presentation), in *Conference on Network of Reformers*, Mombasa, Kenya.
    2013. "Monitoring the ASEAN Economic Community: Issues and challenges," in Das, S.B. (ed.), *ASEAN Economic Community Scorecard: Performance and perception*, pp. 20–27. Hong Kong: ISEAS Publishing.

Rivera, D. 2014a. "Jollibee to open, operate own restaurants in UAE," in *GMA News*, online http://www.gmanetwork.com/news/story/350065/economy/companies/jollibee-to-open-operate-own-restaurants-in-uae.
    2014b. "Jollibee to export homegrown brands to Malaysia, Indonesia," in *GMA News*, online http://www.gmanetwork.com/news/story/373637/economy/companies/jollibee-to-export-homegrown-brands-to-malaysia-indonesia.

Roberts, C.B. 2012. *ASEAN regionalism: Cooperation, values and institutionalization*. New York: Routledge.

Rogovsky, N. and Tolentino, A. 2010. *Sustainable enterprise promotion through good workplace practices and human resource management (3rd edition)*. Turin: International Training Centre of the International Labour Organization.

Rostow, W.W. 1960. *The stages of economic growth: A non-communist manifesto* Cambridge, UK: Cambridge University Press.

Roxas, S.K. 1970. "An ideology for Asian management." Speech delivered at the Asian Institute of Management on occasion of the First Graduation, April 26, Paseo de Roxas, Makati, Rizal, Philippines.

2000. *Jueteng gate: The parable of a nation in crisis.* Manila: Bancom Corporation.

Rugman, A.M. 1980. "Internalization as a general theory of foreign direct investment, a reappraisal of the literature," *Weltwirtschaftliches Archive*, 116(2): 365–79.

Santiso, J. 2013. *The decade of Multilatinas.* Cambridge, UK: Cambridge University Press.

Sauvant, K. (ed.). 2008. *The rise of transnational corporations from emerging markets – threat or opportunity?*. Gloucester, UK: Edward Edgar Publishing Limited.

Scherer, F.M. 1980. *Industrial Market Structure and Economic Performance.* Boston: Houghton Mifflin Company.

Schuman, M. 2009. *The miracle: The epic story of Asia's quest for wealth.* New York: HarperCollins Publishers.

Schumpeter, J.A. 1934/1994. *Capitalism, socialism and democracy* (reprint). London: Routledge.

Seatrade 2012. *Growing into the future: A special report on Keppel Offshore & Marine.* Singapore: Chris Hayman.

Singapore Aero Engine Services Private Limited 2013a. "Industrial attachment programme," online http://www.saesl.com.sg/industrial.asp.

2013b. "Our management team," online http://www.saesl.com.sg/ourmanagementTeam.asp.

SM Shoemart n.d. "History," online http://www.sm-shoemart.com/history.htm.

Soravji n.d. "Praya Bhirom Bhakdi," online http://www.soravij.com/aristocracy/PrayaBhirom/bhirombhakdi.html.

Sotharith, C. 2013. "SME development in ASEAN: A Cambodian case study," in Das, S.B. (ed.), *ASEAN Economic Community Scorecard: Performance and perception*, pp. 163–181. Hong Kong: ISEAS Publishing.

Soukamneuth, B. 2006. "The political economy of transition in Laos: From peripheral socialism to the margins of global capital," online http://dspace.library.cornell.edu/bitstream/1813/3430/1/ The%20Political%20Economy%20of%20Transition%20in%20Laos.pdf.

Steinmetz, T. 2011. "Cebu Pacific celebrates its 50th million passenger," online http://www.eturbonews.com/20411/cebu-pacific-celebrates-its-50th-million-passenger.

Stopford, J.M. and Wells, L.T. 1972. *Managing the multinational enterprise: Organization of the firm and ownership of the subsidiaries* (vol. 2). New York: Basic Books.

Summit Auto Body Industry Co. Ltd. 2005a. "Auto Body Indu & assembly," online http://www.summitautogroup.com/metal.htm.

2005b. Summit Auto Body Industry Co. Ltd. 2005b. http://www.summitautogroup.com/metal.htm, accessed 5 November

TC Pharmaceutical Industries Co. Ltd. 2011. "Company profile," online http://export.redbullthailand.com/index.php/corporate/data.

Techakanont, K. 2011. "Thailand automotive parts industry," in Kagami, M. (ed.), *Intermediate goods trade in East Asia: Economic deepening through FTAs/EPAs*. Bangkok: IDE-JETRO Bangkok Research Center.

Thai Beverage PCL 2008. "IR newsletter: Volume 6," online http://thaibev.listedcompany.com/newsroom/IR_Newsletter_Vol6_2008.pdf.

Thai Metal Trade PCL 2010. "About us," online http://www.thaimetaltrade.com/2010/index.php/aboutus/company/en.

2014. *Annual report 2013*. Bangkok: Thai Metal Trade Public Company Limited.

Thai Union Frozen Products PCL 2012. "Corporate history," online http://www.thaiuniongroup.com/en/profile/corporate-history.ashx.

2014. "Annual report 2013," online http://tuf.listedcompany.com/misc/ar/20140326-tuf-ar-2013-en.pdf.

Thomas, N. 2002. "From ASEAN to an East Asian community? The role of functional cooperation," in *Working Paper Series* 28. Hong Kong: Southeast Asia Research Center.

TOA Group 2010. "History of TOA Group (Thailand)," online http://www.toagroup.com.vn/en/company_g.asp.

2013. "About TOA: the adoption of a global and international level" (translated from Thai), online http://goo.gl/lYyJ3k.

2014. "Group management," online http://toagroup.co.id/EN/GroupManagement.aspx, accessed 11 November 2014.

Toffler, A. 1980. *The third wave*. New York: Bantam Books.

Tran, M.A. 2005. "Jollibee international expansion" (University of California in Berkeley case study), online https://www.ocf.berkeley.edu/~matran/Files/proJollibee.doc.

Tris Rating Credit News 2014. "Bangkok Dusit Medical Services PLC," online http://bgh.listedcompany.com/misc/CR/20141203-bgh-trisno88-2014-en.pdf.

Tushman, M.L., Newman, W.H. and Romanelli, E. 1986. Convergence and upheaval: managing unsteady pace of organizational evolution. *California Management Review* 29: 29–44.

Ulloa, S. 2010. "Merger Increases Bangkok Dusit Medical Services (BGH) Hospital Network in Thailand. 2010 *GlobalSurance News*, online http://www.globalsurance.com/news/2010/12/16/merger-increases-bangkok-dusit-medical-services-bgh-hospital-network-in-thailand.

Ungson, G., Steers, R.M. and Park, S.H. 1997. *Korean enterprise: The quest for globalization*. Boston, MA: Harvard Business School Press.

Urata, S. and Ando, M. 2011. "Investment climate study of ASEAN member countries," in Urata, S. and Okabe, M. (eds.), *Toward a competitive ASEAN single market: Sectoral analysis*, pp. 137–204. Jakarta: Economic Research Institute for ASEAN and East Asia.

Vietnam Trade Promotion Agency 2011. "Strengths of Vietnam's plastic sector," online http://www.vietrade.gov.vn/en/index.php?option=com_content&view=article&id=966:strengths-of-vietnams-plastic-sector&catid=270:vietnam-industry-news&Itemid=232.

Vinamilk 2014. "Annual report 2013," online https://www.vinamilk.com.vn/home/reviewPdf/static/uploads/bc_thuong_nien/1412564299-c48e4d8fcfae78aa5c64b53c71a60b1197e34f65e52269b47dc7801b30f006d4.pdf.

Vinayak, H.V.,Thompson, F. and Tonby, O. 2014. "Understanding ASEAN: Seven things you need to know," in *McKinsey & Company*, online http://www.mckinsey.com/Insights/Public_Sector/Understanding_ASEAN_Seven_things_you_need_to_know?cid=other-eml-alt-mip-mck-oth-1405.

Viner, J. 1937. *Studies in the Theory of International Trade*. New York: Harper and Brothers Publishers.

1950. *The customs union issue*. New York: Carnegie Endowment for International Peace.

Wallerstein, I. 1974. *The modern world system I: Capitalist agriculture and the origins of the European world-economy in the sixteenth century*. New York: Academic Press.

1980. *The modern world system II: Mercantilism and the consolidation of the European world-economy, 1600–1750*. New York: Academic Press.

2004. "World-systems analysis," in Modelski, G. (ed.), *World system history: Encyclopedia of life support systems*. Oxford, UK: Eolss Publishers.

Wikipedia 2011. "Coevolution," online https://en.wikipedia.org/wiki/Coevolution, accessed 4 May 2015.

2015. "Mekong," online http://en.wikipedia.org/wiki/Mekong, accessed 27 August 2015.

Williamson, O. 1985. *The economic institutions of capitalism*. New York: McMillan Free Press.

World Bank 2014. "Muda irrigation project," online http://www.worldbank.org/projects/P004217/muda-irrigation-project?lang=en.

World Poultry 2013. "Malindo to produce processed chicken products," online http://www.worldpoultry.net/Broilers/Processing/2013/1/Malindo-to-produce-processed-chicken-products-1140054W.

Yip, G. 1992, 1995. *Total global strategy: Managing for worldwide competitive advantage*. Upper Saddle River: Prentice Hall.

Yue, C.S. 2013. "Free flow of skilled labour in ASEAN," in Das, S.B. (ed.), *ASEAN Economic Community Scorecard: Performance and perception*, pp. 107–135. Hong Kong: ISEAS Publishing.

Index

Abidin, M. Z., 57–58
Aboitiz Land, 80–81
Aboitiz Power Corp., 84–85, 202–204
Abrenilla, David, 218
ADB, 90–92
Adelman, 10
administrative heritage, institutional legacy and, 69–71
Adnin, Haji, 84–85, 164–168
Adnin, Musa, 84–85, 164–168, 204–206
Adnin Group of Companies, 84–85, 164–168, 182–183, 204–206
Advanced Info Services PCL, 164–166
AEC Scorecard, 49, 51, 189–190, 198–200
Age of Exploration, 22–23
air transport
    ASEAN initiatives in, 62–63
    market entry strategies in, 121–122
Albert, Delia, 214
Alcantara family, 80–81
Alsons Group, 80–81
AMFELS, 146–148
Amsden, Alice, 13–14
Ando, M., 62–63
Archaya, A., 26–27
ASEAN+1, 49–51
    global economic integration and, 60–62
ASEAN 6 (Singapore, Malaysia, Thailand, Philippines, Indonesia, Vietnam)
    economic success of, 30–33
    tariff elimination for, 52–56
ASEAN/Asian Way, 30–33, 189–190
    intra- and inter-regional trade and, 191–195
    single market and production base and, 190
"ASEAN Centrality" ideology, global economic integration, 60–62
ASEAN Champions
    core competency development by, 202–204

grassroots institutions and success of, 16–19
human capital development by, 169–170
industrialization in Southeast Asia and, 72–73, 74–76
institutional legacy of, 69–71, 85–86
institutional voids and, 39–41
internationalization strategies of, 142
list of, 89t. 1.1.
localization strategies of, 127–140
market entry strategies of, 89–122
market power of, 89–90, 102–104
regional integration and role of, 4–6
selection criteria for, 6–10
single market and production base and, 190
ASEAN Comprehensive Investment Agreement, 56
ASEAN Economic Community (AEC)
    competitive economic region development by, 57–58
    competitive economic regions and, 196–197
    core elements of, 52–53f. EXHIBIT 3.2
    equitable economic development pillar of, 59–60
    evolution of, 3–4
    expanded trade and investment opportunities and, 200–202
    future issues for, 189–190
    global economic integration pillar of, 60–62
    goals of, 4–6
    optimistic narrative for, 189–190
    pessimistic narrative concerning, 189–190
    pillars of progress in, 51
    regional integration goals for, 190–199
    selection criteria for firms in, 6–10

Printed in the United States
By Bookmasters